Old Manse Edition

THE COMPLETE WRITINGS OF
NATHANIEL HAWTHORNE

WITH PORTRAITS, ILLUSTRATIONS, AND FACSIMILES

IN TWENTY–TWO VOLUMES

VOLUME XXI

9

Bookstalls along the Seine, Paris

THE WRITINGS OF

Nathaniel Hawthorne

HOUGHTON, MIFFLIN AND COMPANY

NOTES OF TRAVEL

BY

NATHANIEL HAWTHORNE

IN FOUR VOLUMES

VOLUME III

BOSTON AND NEW YORK

HOUGHTON, MIFFLIN AND COMPANY

The Riverside Press, Cambridge

LIST OF ILLUSTRATIONS

NOTES OF TRAVEL

III

MELROSE, *July* 11, 1857. — We left
Edinburgh, where we had found Ad-
dison's, 87 Prince's Street, the most
comfortable hotel in Great Britain, and went to
Melrose, where we put up at the George. This
is all travelled ground with me, so that I need
not much perplex myself with further description, especially as it is impossible, by any repe-
tition of attempts, to describe Melrose Abbey.
We went thither immediately after tea, and
were shown over the ruins by a very delectable
old Scotchman, incomparably the best guide I
ever met with. I think he must take pains to
speak the Scotch dialect, he does it with such
pungent felicity and effect, and it gives a flavor
to everything he says like the mustard and vin-
egar in a salad. This is not the man I saw
when here before. The Scotch dialect is still,
in a greater or less degree, universally preva-
lent in Scotland, insomuch that we generally
find it difficult to comprehend the answers to
our questions, though more, I think, from the
unusual intonation than either from strange

words or pronunciation. But this old man, though he spoke the most unmitigated Scotch, was perfectly intelligible, — perhaps because his speech so well accorded with the classic standard of the Waverley Novels. Moreover, he is thoroughly acquainted with the Abbey, stone by stone; and it was curious to see him, as we walked among its aisles, and over the grass beneath its roofless portions, pick up the withered leaves that had fallen there, and do other such little things, as a good housewife might do to a parlor. I have met with two or three instances where the guardian of an old edifice seemed really to love it, and this was one, although the old man evidently had a Scotch Covenanter's contempt and dislike of the faith that founded the Abbey. He repeated King David's dictum that King David the First was " a sair saint for the crown," as bestowing so much wealth on religious edifices; but really, unless it be Walter Scott, I know not any Scotchman who has done so much for his country as this same St. David. As the founder of Melrose and many other beautiful churches and abbeys, he left magnificent specimens of the only kind of poetry which the age knew how to produce; and the world is the better for him to this day, — which is more, I believe, than can be said of any hero or statesman in Scottish annals.

We went all over the ruins, of course, and

saw the marble stone of King Alexander, and the spot where Bruce's heart is said to be buried, and the slab of Michael Scott, with the cross engraved upon it; also the exquisitely sculptured kail leaves, and other foliage and flowers, with which the Gothic artists enwreathed this edifice, bestowing more minute and faithful labor than an artist of these days would do on the most delicate piece of cabinet-work. We came away sooner than we wished, but we hoped to return thither this morning; and, for my part, I cherish a presentiment that this will not be our last visit to Scotland and Melrose. . . . Julian and I then walked to the Tweed, where we saw two or three people angling, with naked legs, or trousers turned up, and wading among the rude stones that make something like a dam over the wide and brawling stream. I did not observe that they caught any fish, but Julian was so fascinated with the spectacle that he pulled out his poor little fishing-line, and wished to try his chance forthwith. I never saw the angler's instinct stronger in anybody. We walked across the footbridge that here spans the Tweed; and Julian observed that he did not see how William of Deloraine could have found so much difficulty in swimming his horse across so shallow a river. Neither do I. It now began to sprinkle, and we hastened back to the hotel.

It was not a pleasant morning; but we started immediately after breakfast for Abbotsford, which is but about three miles distant. The country between Melrose and that place is not in the least beautiful, nor very noteworthy, — one or two old irregular villages; one tower that looks principally domestic, yet partly warlike, and seems to be of some antiquity; and an undulation, or rounded hilly surface of the landscape, sometimes affording wide vistas between the slopes. These hills, which, I suppose, are some of them on the Abbotsford estate, are partly covered with woods, but of Scotch fir, or some tree of that species, which creates no softened undulation, but overspreads the hill like a tightly fitting wig. It is a cold, dreary, disheartening neighborhood, that of Abbotsford, — at least, it has appeared so to me at both of my visits, one of which was on a bleak and windy May morning, and this one on a chill, showery morning of midsummer.

The entrance-way to the house is somewhat altered since my last visit; and we now, following the direction of a painted finger on the wall, went round to a side door in the basement story, where we found an elderly man waiting as if in expectation of visitors. He asked us to write our names in a book, and told us that the desk on the leaf of which it lay was the one in which Sir Walter found the forgotten manuscript of

Waverley, while looking for some fishing-tackle. There was another desk in the room, which had belonged to the Colonel Gardiner who appears in Waverley. The first apartment into which our guide showed us was Sir Walter's study, where I again saw his clothes, and remarked how the sleeve of his old green coat was worn at the cuff, — a minute circumstance that seemed to bring Sir Walter very near me. Thence into the library ; thence into the drawing-room, whence, methinks, we should have entered the dining-room, the most interesting of all, as being the room where he died. But this room seems not to be shown now. We saw the armory, with the gun of Rob Roy, into the muzzle of which I put my finger, and found the bore very large ; the beautifully wrought pistol of Claverhouse, and a pair of pistols that belonged to Napoleon ; the sword of Montrose, which I grasped, and drew half out of the scabbard ; and Queen Mary's iron jewel box, six or eight inches long, and two or three high, with a lid rounded like that of a trunk, and much corroded with rust. There is no use in making a catalogue of these curiosities. The feeling in visiting Abbotsford is not that of awe ; it is little more than going to a museum. I do abhor this mode of making pilgrimages to the shrines of departed great men. There is certainly something wrong in it, for it seldom or never produces (in me, at least) the right feeling. It is an odd truth, too, that a house is forever after spoiled and ruined as a home, by having been the abode of a great man. His spirit haunts it, as it were, with a malevolent effect, and takes hearth and hall away from the nominal possessors, giving all the world the right to enter there because he had such intimate relations with all the world.

We had intended to go to Dryburgh Abbey; but as the weather more than threatened rain, . . . we gave up the idea, and so took the rail for Berwick, after one o'clock. On our road we passed several ruins in Scotland, and some in England, — one old castle in particular, beautifully situated beside a deep-banked stream. The road lies for many miles along the coast, affording a fine view of the German Ocean, which was now blue, sunny, and breezy, the day having risen out of its morning sulks. We waited an hour or more at Berwick, and Julian and I took a hasty walk into the town. It is a rough and rude assemblage of rather mean houses, some of which are thatched. There seems to have been a wall about the town at a former period, and we passed through one of the gates. The view of the river Tweed here is very fine, both above and below the railway bridge, and especially where it flows, a broad tide, and between high banks, into the sea. Thence we went onward along the coast, as I have said, pausing a

6

few moments in smoky Newcastle, and reaching Durham about eight o'clock.

I wandered out in the dusk of the evening, —for the dusk comes on comparatively early as we draw southward,—and found a beautiful and shadowy path along the river-side, skirting its high banks, up and adown which grow noble elms. I could not well see, in that obscurity of twilight boughs, whither I was going, or what was around me; but I judged that the castle or cathedral, or both, crowned the highest line of the shore, and that I was walking at the base of their walls. There was a pair of lovers in front of me, and I passed two or three other tender couples. The walk appeared to go on interminably by the river-side, through the same sweet shadow; but I turned and found my way into the cathedral close, beneath an ancient archway, whence, issuing again, I inquired my way to the Waterloo Hotel, where we had put up.

ITEMS. — We saw the Norham Castle of Marmion, at a short distance from the station of the same name. Viewed from the railway, it has not a very picturesque appearance, — a high, square ruin of what I suppose was the keep. — At Abbotsford, treasured up in a glass case in the drawing-room, were memorials of Sir Walter Scott's servants and humble friends, — for instance, a brass snuff-box of Tom Purdy, —

there, too, among precious relics of illustrious persons. — In the armory, I grasped with some interest the sword of Sir Adam Ferguson, which he had worn in the Peninsular War. Our guide said, of his own knowledge, that " he was a very funny old gentleman." He died only a year or two since.

July 11. — The morning after our arrival in Durham being Sunday, we attended service in the cathedral. . . . We found a tolerable audience, seated on benches, within and in front of the choir ; and people continually strayed in and out of the sunny churchyard, and sat down, or walked softly and quietly up and down the side aisle. Sometimes, too, one of the vergers would come in with a handful of little boys, whom he had caught playing among the tombstones.

Durham Cathedral has one advantage over the others which I have seen, there being no organ screen, nor any sort of partition between the choir and nave; so that we saw its entire length, nearly five hundred feet, in one vista. The pillars of the nave are immensely thick, but hardly of proportionate height, and they support the round Norman arch; nor is there, as far as I remember, a single pointed arch in the cathedral. The effect is to give the edifice an air of heavy grandeur. It seems to have

been built before the best style of church architecture had established itself; so that it weighs
upon the soul, instead of helping it to aspire.
First, there are these round arches, supported
by gigantic columns; then, immediately above,
another row of round arches, behind which is
the usual gallery that runs, as it were, in the
thickness of the wall, around the nave of the
cathedral; then, above all, another row of round
arches, enclosing the windows of the clere-story.
The great pillars are ornamented in various
ways, — some with a great spiral groove running
from bottom to top; others with two spirals,
ascending in different directions, so as to cross
over one another; some are fluted or channelled
straight up and down; some are wrought with
chevrons, like those on the sleeve of a police
inspector.   There are zigzag cuttings and carvings, which I do not know how to name sci-
entifically, round the arches of the doors and
windows; but nothing that seems to have flow-
ered out spontaneously, as natural incidents of
a grand and beautiful design.   In the nave, between the columns of the side aisles, I saw one
or two monuments. . . .

The cathedral service is very long; and though
the choral part of it is pleasant enough, I thought
it not best to wait for the sermon, especially as
it would have been quite unintelligible, so remotely as I sat in the great space. So I left my

seat, and, after strolling up and down the aisle a few times, sallied forth into the churchyard. On the cathedral door there is a curious old knocker, in the form of a monstrous face, which was placed there, centuries ago, for the benefit of fugitives from justice, who used to be entitled to sanctuary here. The exterior of the cathedral, being huge, is therefore grand ; it has a great central tower, and two at the western end ; and reposes in vast and heavy length, without the multitude of niches, and crumbling statues, and richness of detail, that make the towers and fronts of some cathedrals so endlessly interesting. One piece of sculpture I remember, — a carving of a cow, a milkmaid, and a monk, in reference to the legend that the site of the cathedral was, in some way, determined by a woman bidding her cow go home to Dunholme. Cadmus was guided to the site of his destined city in some such way as this.

It was a very beautiful day, and though the shadow of the cathedral fell on this side, yet, it being about noontide, it did not cover the churchyard entirely, but left many of the graves in sunshine. There were not a great many monuments, and these were chiefly horizontal slabs, some of which looked aged, but on closer inspection proved to be mostly of the present century. I observed an old stone figure, however, half worn away, which seemed to have

something like a bishop's mitre on its head, and
may perhaps have lain in the proudest chapel of
the cathedral before occupying its present bed
among the grass. About fifteen paces from the
central tower, and within its shadow, I found a
weather-worn slab of marble, seven or eight feet
long, the inscription on which interested me
somewhat. It was to the memory of Robert
Dodsley, the bookseller, Johnson's acquaintance, who, as his tombstone rather superciliously
avers, had made a much better figure as an author than "could have been expected in his rank
of life." But, after all, it is inevitable that a
man's tombstone should look down on him, or,
at all events, comport itself towards him "de
haut en bas." I love to find the graves of men
connected with literature. They interest me
more, even though of no great eminence, than
those of persons far more illustrious in other
walks of life. I know not whether this is because I happen to be one of the literary kindred, or because all men feel themselves akin,
and on terms of intimacy, with those whom they
know, or might have known, in books. I rather
believe that the latter is the case.

My wife had stayed in the cathedral, but she
came out at the end of the sermon, and told me
of two little birds, who had got into the vast interior, and were in great trouble at not being
able to find their way out again. Thus, two

winged souls may often have been imprisoned within a faith of heavy ceremonials.

We went round the edifice, and, passing into the close, penetrated through an arched passage into the crypt, which, methought, was in a better style of architecture than the nave and choir. At one end stood a crowd of venerable figures leaning against the wall, being stone images of bearded saints, apostles, patriarchs, kings, — personages of great dignity, at all events, who had doubtless occupied conspicuous niches in and about the cathedral till finally imprisoned in this cellar. I looked at every one, and found not an entire nose among them, nor quite so many heads as they once had.

Thence we went into the cloisters, which are entire, but not particularly interesting. Indeed, this cathedral has not taken hold of my affections, except in one aspect, when it was exceedingly grand and beautiful.

After looking at the crypt and the cloisters, we returned through the close and the churchyard, and went back to the hotel through a path by the river-side. This is the same dim and dusky path through which I wandered the night before, and in the sunshine it looked quite as beautiful as I knew it must, — a shadow of elm-trees clothing the high bank, and overarching the paths above and below; some of the elms growing close to the water-side, and flinging up

their topmost boughs not nearly so high as where
we stood, and others climbing upward and upward, till our way wound among their roots;
while through the foliage the quiet river loitered
along, with this lovely shade on both its banks,
to pass through the centre of the town. The
stately cathedral rose high above us, and farther
onward, in a line with it, the battlemented walls
of the old Norman castle, gray and warlike,
though now it has become a University. This
delightful walk terminates at an old bridge in
the heart of the town; and the castle hangs immediately over its busiest street. On this bridge,
last night, in the embrasure, or just over the
pier, where there is a stone seat, I saw some old
men seated, smoking their pipes and chatting.
In my judgment, a river flowing through the
centre of a town, and not too broad to make
itself familiar, nor too swift, but idling along,
as if it loved better to stay there than to go, is
the pleasantest imaginable piece of scenery; so
transient as it is, and yet enduring, — just the
same from life's end to life's end; and this river
Wear, with its sylvan wildness, and yet so sweet
and placable, is the best of all little rivers, —
not that it is so very small, but with a bosom
broad enough to be crossed by a three-arched
bridge. Just above the cathedral there is a mill
upon its shore, as ancient as the times of the
Abbey.

We went homeward through the market-place and one or two narrow streets; for the town has the irregularity of all ancient settlements, and, moreover, undulates upward and downward, and is also made more unintelligible to a stranger, in its points and bearings, by the tortuous course of the river.

After dinner, Julian and I walked along the bank opposite to that on which the cathedral stands, and found the paths there equally delightful with those which I have attempted to describe. We went onward, while the river gleamed through the foliage beneath us, and passed so far beyond the cathedral that we began to think we were getting into the country, and that it was time to return; when all at once we saw a bridge before us, and beyond that, on the opposite bank of the Wear, the cathedral itself! The stream had made a circuit without our knowing it. We paused upon the bridge, and admired and wondered at the beauty and glory of the scene, with those vast, ancient towers rising out of the green shade, and looking as if they were based upon it. The situation of Durham Cathedral is certainly a noble one, finer even than that of Lincoln, though the latter stands even at a more lordly height above the town. But as I saw it then, it was grand, venerable, and sweet, all at once; and I never saw so lovely and magnificent a scene, nor, being content with

this, do I care to see a better. The castle beyond came also into the view, and the whole
picture was mirrored in the tranquil stream below.   And so, crossing the bridge, the path led
us back through many a bower of hollow shade;
and we then quitted the hotel, and took the rail
for York, where we arrived at about half past
nine.

We put up at the Black Swan, with which we
had already made acquaintance at our previous
visit to York.   It is a very·ancient hotel; for in
the coffee-room I saw on the wall an old printed
advertisement, announcing that a stage-coach
would leave the Black Swan in London and
arrive at the Black Swan in York, with God's
permission, in four days.   The date was 1706;
and still, after a hundred and fifty years, the
Black Swan receives travellers in Coney Street.
It is a very good hotel, and was much thronged
with guests when we arrived, as the Sessions
come on this week.   We found a very smart
waiter, whose English faculties have been brightened by a residence of several years in America.

In the morning, before breakfast, I strolled
out and walked round the cathedral, passing on
my way the sheriff's javelin-men, in long gowns
of faded purple embroidered with gold, carrying
halberds in their hands; also a gentleman in
a cocked hat, gold lace, and breeches, who no
doubt had something to do with the ceremonial

of the Sessions. I saw, too, a procession of a
good many old cabs and other carriages, filled
with people, and a banner flaunting above each
vehicle. These were the pianoforte-makers of
York, who were going out of town to have a
jollification together.

After breakfast we all went to the cathedral,
and no sooner were we within it than we found
how much our eyes had recently been educated,
by our greater power of appreciating this magnificent interior; for it impressed us both with
a joy that we never felt before. Julian felt it
too, and insisted that the cathedral must have
been altered and improved since we were last
here. But it is only that we have seen much
splendid architecture since then, and so have
grown in some degree fitted to enjoy it. York
Cathedral (I say it now, for it is my present feeling) is the most wonderful work that ever came
from the hands of man. Indeed, it seems like
" a house not made with hands," but rather to
have come down from above, bringing an awful
majesty and sweetness with it; and it is so light
and aspiring, with all its vast columns and pointed
arches, that one would hardly wonder if it should
ascend back to heaven again by its mere spiritu-
ality. Positively the pillars and arches of the
choir are so very beautiful that they give the
impression of being exquisitely polished, though

such is not the fact ; but their beauty throws a gleam around them. I thank God that I saw this cathedral again, and I thank him that he inspired the builder to make it, and that mankind has so long enjoyed it, and will continue to enjoy it.

July 14. — We left York at twelve o'clock, and were delayed an hour or two at Leeds, waiting for a train. I strolled up into the town, and saw a fair, with puppet-shows, booths of penny actors, merry-go-rounds, clowns, boxers, and other such things as I saw, above a year ago, at Greenwich fair, and likewise at Tranmere, during the Whitsuntide holidays.

We resumed our journey, and reached Southport in pretty good trim at about nine o'clock. It has been a very interesting tour. We find Southport just as we left it, with its regular streets of little and big lodging-houses, where the visitors perambulate to and fro without any imaginable object. The tide, too, seems not to have been up over the waste of sands since we went away ; and far seaward stands the same row of bathing-machines, and just on the verge of the horizon a gleam of water, — even this being not the sea, but the mouth of the river Ribble, seeking the sea amid the sandy desert. But we shall soon say good-by to Southport.

OLD TRAFFORD, MANCHESTER, *July* 22.— We left Southport for good on the 20th, and have established ourselves in this place, in lodgings that had been provided for us by Mr. Swain; our principal object being to spend a few weeks in the proximity of the Arts' Exhibition. We are here, about three miles from the Victoria Railway station in Manchester on one side, and nearly a mile from the Exhibition on the other. This is a suburb of Manchester, and consists of a long street, called the Stratford Road, bordered with brick houses two stories high, such as are usually the dwellings of tradesmen or respectable mechanics, but which are now in demand for lodgings, at high prices, on account of the Exhibition. It seems to be rather a new precinct of the city, and the houses, though ranged along a continuous street, are but a brick border of the green fields in the rear. Occasionally you get a glimpse of this country aspect between two houses; but the street itself, even with its little grass-plots and bits of shrubbery under the front windows, is as ugly as it can be made. Some of the houses are better than I have described; but the brick used here in building is very unsightly in hue and surface.

Betimes in the morning the Exhibition omnibuses begin to trundle along, and pass at intervals of two and a half minutes through the day, —immense vehicles constructed to carry thirty-

nine passengers, and generally with a good part
of that number inside and out.   The omnibuses
are painted scarlet, bordered with white, have
three horses abreast, and a conductor in a red
coat.   They perform the journey from this point
into town in about half an hour ; and yesterday
morning, being in a hurry to get to the railway
station, I found that I could outwalk them, taking into account their frequent stoppages.

We have taken the whole house (except some
inscrutable holes, into which the family creeps),
of respectable people, who never took lodgers
until this juncture.   Their furniture, however,
is of the true lodging-house pattern, — sofas
and chairs which have no possibility of repose in
them; rickety tables; an old piano and old music, with "Lady Helen Elizabeth" somebody's
name written on it.   It is very strange how nothing but a genuine home can ever look home-
like.   They appear to be good people ; a little
girl of twelve, a daughter, waits on table : and
there is an elder daughter, who yesterday answered the door-bell, looking very like a young
lady, besides five or six smaller children, who
make less uproar of grief or merriment than
could possibly be expected.   The husband is
not apparent, though I see his hat in the hall.
The house is new, and has a trim, light-colored
interior of half-gentility.   I suppose the rent,
in ordinary times, might be £25 per annum;

but we pay at the rate of £338 for the part which we occupy. This, like all the other houses in the neighborhood, was evidently built to be sold or let; the builder never thought of living in it himself, and so that subtile element, which would have enabled him to create a home, was entirely left out.

This morning, Julian and I set forth on a walk, first towards the palace of the Arts' Exhibition, which looked small compared with my idea of it, and seems to be of the Crystal Palace order of architecture, only with more iron to its glass. Its front is composed of three round arches in a row. We did not go in. . . . Turning to the right, we walked onward two or three miles, passing the Botanic Garden, and thence along by suburban villas, Belgrave terraces, and other such prettinesses in the modern Gothic or Elizabethan style, with fancifully ornamented flower-pots before them; thence by hedgerows and fields, and through two or three villages, with here and there an old plaster and timber-built thatched house, among a street full of modern brick-fronts, — the alehouse, or rural inn, being generally the most ancient house in the village. It was a sultry, heavy day, and I walked without much enjoyment of the air and exercise. We crossed a narrow and swift river, flowing between deep banks. It must have been either the Mersey, still an infant stream, and little

dreaming of the thousand mighty ships that float
on its farther tide, or else the Irwell, which emp-
ties into the Mersey. We passed through the
village beyond this stream, and went to the railway station, and then were brought back to Old
Trafford, and deposited close by the Exhibition.

It has showered this afternoon ; and I be-
guiled my time for half an hour by setting down
the vehicles that went past ; not that they were
particularly numerous, but for the sake of knowing the character of the travel along the road.

．　　．　　．　　．　　．　　．　　．　　．　　．

July 26. — Day before yesterday we went
to the Arts' Exhibition, of which I do not think
that I have a great deal to say. The edifice, being
built more for convenience than show, appears
better in the interior than from without, — long
vaulted vistas, lighted from above, extending far
away, all hung with pictures ; and, on the floor
below, statues, knights in armor, cabinets, vases,
and all manner of curious and beautiful things,
in a regular arrangement. Scatter five thousand
people through the scene, and I do not know
how to make a better outline sketch. I was un-
quiet, from a hopelessness of being able to enjoy
it fully. Nothing is more depressing to me than
the sight of a great many pictures together ; it
is like having innumerable books open before

21

you at once, and being able to read only a sentence or two in each. They bedazzle one another with cross lights. There never should be more than one picture in a room, nor more than one picture to be studied in one day. Galleries of pictures are surely the greatest absurdities that ever were contrived, there being no excuse for them, except that it is the only way in which pictures can be made generally available and accessible.

We went first into the Gallery of British Painters, where there were hundreds of pictures, every one of which would have interested me by itself; but I could not fix my mind on one more than another, so I wandered about, to get a general idea of the Exhibition. Truly it is very fine; truly, also, every great show is a kind of humbug. I doubt whether there were half a dozen people there who got the kind of enjoyment that it was intended to create, — very respectable people they seemed to be, and very well behaved, but all skimming the surface, as I did, and none of them so feeding on what was beautiful as to digest it, and make it a part of themselves. Such a quantity of objects must be utterly rejected before you can get any real profit from one! It seemed like throwing away time to look twice even at whatever was most precious; and it was dreary to think of not fully enjoying this collection, the very flower of Time, which never bloomed before, and never, by any possibility, can bloom again. Viewed hastily, moreover, it is somewhat sad to think that mankind, after centuries of cultivation of the beautiful arts, can produce no more splendid spectacle than this. It is not so very grand, although, poor as it is, I lack capacity to take in even the whole of it.

What gave me most pleasure (because it required no trouble nor study to come at the heart of it) were the individual relics of antiquity, of which there are some very curious ones in the cases ranged along the principal saloon or nave of the building. For example, the dagger with which Felton killed the Duke of Buckingham, — a knife with a bone handle and a curved blade, not more than three inches long ; sharp-pointed, murderous-looking, but of very coarse manufacture. Also, the Duke of Alva's leading staff of iron ; and the target of the Emperor Charles V., which seemed to be made of hard-ened leather, with designs artistically engraved upon it, and gilt. I saw Wolsey's portrait, and, in close proximity to it, his veritable cardinal's hat in a richly ornamented glass case, on which was an inscription to the effect that it had been bought by Charles Kean at the sale of Horace Walpole's collection. It is a felt hat with a brim about six inches wide all round, and a rather high crown ; the color was, doubtless, a bright red

originally, but now it is mottled with a grayish
hue, and there are cracks in the brim, as if the
hat had seen a good deal of wear.   I suppose
a far greater curiosity than this is the signet-
ring of one of the Pharaohs, who reigned over
Egypt during Joseph's prime ministry, — a large
ring to be worn on the thumb, if at all, — of
massive gold, seal part and all, and inscribed
with some characters that looked like Hebrew.
I had seen this before in Mr. Mayer's collection in Liverpool.   The mediæval and English
relics, however, interested me more, — such as
the golden and enamelled George worn by Sir
Thomas More ; or the embroidered shirt of
Charles I., — the very one, I presume, which
he wore at his execution.   There are no blood-
marks on it, it being very nicely washed and
folded.   The texture of the linen cloth — if
linen it be — is coarser than any peasant would
wear at this day, but the needlework is exceedingly fine and elaborate.   Another relic of the
same period, — the Cavalier General Sir Jacob
Astley's buff-coat, with his belt and sword ; the
leather of the buff-coat, for I took it between
my fingers, is about a quarter of an inch thick,
of the same material as a wash-leather glove,
and by no means smoothly dressed, though the
sleeves are covered with silver-lace.   Of old
armor, there are admirable specimens ; and it
makes one's head ache to look at the iron pots

which men used to thrust their heads into. Indeed, at one period they seem to have worn an
inner iron cap underneath the helmet. I doubt
whether there ever was any age of chivalry. . . .
It certainly was no chivalric sentiment that made
men case themselves in impenetrable iron, and
ride about in iron prisons, fearfully peeping at
their enemies through little slits and gimlet-
holes. The unprotected breast of a private
soldier must have shamed his leaders in those
days. The point of honor is very different
now.

I mean to go again and again, many times
more, and will take each day some one department, and so endeavor to get some real use and
improvement out of what I see. Much that
is most valuable must be immitigably rejected ;
but something, according to the measure of my
poor capacity, will really be taken into my mind.
After all, it was an agreeable day, and I think
the next one will be more so.

July 28. — Day before yesterday I paid a
second visit to the Exhibition, and devoted the
day mainly to seeing the works of British painters, which fill a very large space, — two or three
great saloons at the right side of the nave.
Among the earliest are Hogarth's pictures, including the Sigismunda, which I remember to
have seen before, with her lover's heart in her
hand, looking like a monstrous strawberry ; and

the March to Finchley, than which nothing
truer to English life and character was ever
painted, nor ever can be; and a large stately
portrait of Captain Coram, and others, all excellent in proportion as they come near to ordinary life, and are wrought out through its forms.
All English painters resemble Hogarth in this
respect. They cannot paint anything high, heroic, and ideal, and their attempts in that direction are wearisome to look at; but they sometimes produce good effects by means of awkward figures in ill-made coats and small-clothes,
and hard, coarse-complexioned faces, such as
they might see anywhere in the street. They
are strong in homeliness and ugliness, weak in
their efforts at the beautiful. Sir Thomas Law-
rence attains a sort of grace, which you feel to
be a trick, and therefore get disgusted with it.
Reynolds is not quite genuine, though certainly
he has produced some noble and beautiful heads.
But Hogarth is the only English painter, except in the landscape department; there are no
others who interpret life to me at all, unless it be
some of the modern Pre-Raphaelites. Pretty village scenes of common life, — pleasant domestic
passages, with a touch of easy humor in them,
— little pathoses and fancinesses, are abundant
enough; and Wilkie, to be sure, has done more
than this, though not a great deal more. His
merit lies, not in a high aim, but in accom-

plishing his aim so perfectly. It is unaccountable that the English painters' achievements should be so much inferior to those of the English poets, who have really elevated the human mind ; but, to be sure, painting has only become an English art subsequently to the epochs of the greatest poets, and since the beginning of the last century, during which England had no poets. I respect Haydon more than I once did, not for his pictures, they being detestable to see, but for his heroic rejection of whatever his countrymen and he himself could really do, and his bitter resolve to achieve something higher, — failing in which, he died.

No doubt I am doing vast injustice to a great many gifted men in what I have here written, — as, for instance, Copley, who certainly has painted a slain man to the life ; and to a crowd of landscape-painters, who have made wonderful reproductions of little English streams and shrubbery, and cottage doors and country lanes. And there is a picture called The Evening Gun, by Danby, — a ship of war on a calm, glassy tide, at sunset, with the cannon-smoke puffing from her port-hole ; it is very beautiful, and so effective that you can even hear the report breaking upon the stillness, with so grand a roar that it is almost like stillness too. As for Turner, I care no more for his light-colored pictures than for so much lacquered ware or

painted gingerbread. Doubtless this is my fault,
my own deficiency ; but I cannot help it,— not,
at least, without sophisticating myself by the
effort. The only modern pictures that accomplish a higher end than that of pleasing the eye
— the only ones that really take hold of my
mind, and with a kind of acerbity, like unripe
fruit — are the works of Hunt, and one or two
other painters of the Pre-Raphaelite school.
They seem wilfully to abjure all beauty, and to
make their pictures disagreeable out of mere
malice ; but at any rate, for the thought and
feeling which are ground up with the paint, they
will bear looking at, and disclose a deeper value
the longer you look. Never was anything so
stiff and unnatural as they appear ; although
every single thing represented seems to be taken
directly out of life and reality, and, as it were,
pasted down upon the canvas. They almost
paint even separate hairs. Accomplishing so
much, and so perfectly, it seems unaccountable
that the picture does not live ; but Nature has
an art beyond these painters, and they leave out
some medium,— some enchantment that should
intervene, and keep the object from pressing so
baldly and harshly upon the spectator's eyeballs.
With the most lifelike reproduction, there is no
illusion. I think if a semi-obscurity were thrown
over the picture after finishing it to this nicety,
it might bring it nearer to nature. I remember

a heap of autumn leaves, every one of which seems to have been stiffened with gum and varnish, and then put carefully down into the stiffly disordered heap. Perhaps these artists may hereafter succeed in combining the truth of detail with a broader and higher truth. Coming from such a depth as their pictures do, and having really an idea as the seed of them, it is strange that they should look like the most made-up things imaginable. One picture by Hunt that greatly interested me was of some sheep that had gone astray among heights and precipices, and I could have looked all day at these poor lost creatures, — so true was their meek alarm and hopeless bewilderment, their huddling together, without the slightest confidence of mutual help; all that the courage and wisdom of the bravest and wisest of them could do being to bleat, and only a few having spirits enough even for this.

After going through these modern masters, among whom were some French painters who do not interest me at all, I did a miscellaneous business, chiefly among the water-colors and photographs, and afterwards among the antiquities and works of ornamental art. I have forgotten what I saw, except the breastplate and helmet of Henry of Navarre, of steel, engraved with designs that have been half obliterated by scrubbing. I remember, too, a breastplate of

an Elector of Saxony, with a bullet-hole through
it. He received his mortal wound through that
hole, and died of it two days afterwards, three
hundred years ago.

There was a crowd of visitors, insomuch that
it was difficult to get a satisfactory view of the
most interesting objects. They were nearly all
middling-class people; the Exhibition, I think,
does not reach the lower classes at all; in fact,
it could not reach them, nor their betters either,
without a good deal of study to help it out. I
shall go to-day, and do my best to get profit
out of it.

July 30. — We all, with R—— and Fanny,
went to the Exhibition, yesterday, and spent the
day there; not Julian, however, for he went to
the Botanical Gardens. After some little skir-
mishing with other things, I devoted myself to
the historical portraits, which hang on both sides
of the great nave, and went through them pretty
faithfully. The oldest are pictures of Richard
II. and Henry IV. and Edward IV. and Jane
Shore, and seem to have little or no merit as
works of art, being cold and stiff, the life having,
perhaps, faded out of them; but these older
painters were trustworthy, inasmuch as they had
no idea of making a picture, but only of getting
the face before them on canvas as accurately as
they could. All English history scarcely sup-

plies half a dozen portraits before the time of
Henry VIII.; after that period, and through
the reigns of Elizabeth and James, there are
many ugly pictures by Dutchmen and Italians;
and the collection is wonderfully rich in portraits of the time of Charles I. and the Com-
monwealth. Vandyke seems to have brought
portrait-painting into fashion; and very likely
the king's love of art diffused a taste for it
throughout the nation, and remotely suggested,
even to his enemies, to get their pictures painted.
Elizabeth has perpetuated her cold, thin visage
on many canvases, and generally with some fantasy of costume that makes her ridiculous to
all time. There are several of Mary of Scotland, none of which have a gleam of beauty; but
the stiff old brushes of these painters could not
catch the beautiful. Of all the older pictures,
the only one that I took pleasure in looking
at was a portrait of Lord Deputy Falkland, by
Vansomer, in James I.'s time, — a very stately,
full-length figure in white, looking out of the
picture as if he saw you. The catalogue says
that this portrait suggested an incident in Horace Walpole's " Castle of Otranto; " but I do
not remember it.

I have a haunting doubt of the value of portrait-painting; that is to say, whether it gives
you a genuine idea of the person purporting to
be represented. I do not remember ever to have

recognized a man by having previously seen his portrait. Vandyke's pictures are full of grace and nobleness, but they do not look like Englishmen, — the burly, rough, wine-flushed and weather-reddened faces, and sturdy flesh and blood, which we see even at the present day, when they must naturally have become a good deal refined from either the country gentleman or the courtier of the Stuarts' age. There is an old, fat portrait of Gervoyse Holles, in a buff-coat, — a coarse, hoggish, yet manly man. The painter is unknown; but I honor him, and Gervoyse Holles too, — for one was willing to be truly rendered, and the other dared to do it. It seems to be the aim of portrait-painters generally, especially of those who have been most famous, to make their pictures as beautiful and noble as can anywise consist with retaining the very slightest resemblance to the person sitting to them. They seldom attain even the grace and beauty which they aim at, but only hit some temporary or individual taste. Vandyke, however, achieved graces that rise above time and fashion, and so did Sir Peter Lely, in his female portraits; but the doubt is, whether the works of either are genuine history. Not more so, I suspect, than the narrative of a historian who should seek to make poetry out of the events which he relates, rejecting those which could not possibly be thus idealized.

I observe, furthermore, that a full-length portrait has seldom face enough ; not that it lacks
its fair proportion by measurement, but the artist does not often find it possible to make the
face so intellectually prominent as to subordi-
nate the figure and drapery. Vandyke does
this, however.   In his pictures of Charles I.,
for instance, it is the melancholy grace of the
visage that attracts the eye, and it passes to
the rest of the composition only by an effort.
Earlier and later pictures are but a few inches
of face to several feet of figure and costume,
and more insignificant than the latter, because
seldom so well done; and I suspect the same
would generally be the case now, only that the
present simplicity of costume gives the face a
chance to be seen.

I was interrupted here, and cannot resume
the thread; but considering how much of his
own conceit the artist puts into a portrait, how
much affectation the sitter puts on, and then
again that no face is the same to any two spectators ; also, that these portraits are darkened
and faded with age, and can seldom be more
than half seen, being hung too high, or some-
how or other inconvenient, — on the whole, I
question whether there is much use in looking
at them.   The truest test would be, for a man
well read in English history and biography, and
himself an observer of insight, to go through

the series without knowing what personages they represented, and write beneath each the name which the portrait vindicated for itself.

After getting through the portrait-gallery, I went among the engravings and photographs, and then glanced along the old masters, but without seriously looking at anything. While I was among the Dutch painters, a gentleman accosted me. It was Mr. J——, whom I once met at dinner with Bennoch. He told me that " the Poet Laureate " (as he called him) was in the Exhibition rooms; and as I expressed great interest, Mr. J—— was kind enough to go in quest of him. Not for the purpose of intro-duction, however, for he was not acquainted with Tennyson. Soon Mr. J—— returned, and said that he had found the Poet Laureate, —and, going into the saloon of the old masters, we saw him there, in company with Mr. Wool-ner, whose bust of him is now in the Exhi-bition.

.   .   .   .

Gazing at him with all my eyes, I liked him well, and rejoiced more in him than in all the other wonders of the Exhibition.

.   .   .   .

How strange that in these two or three pages I cannot get one single touch that may call him up hereafter !

I would most gladly have seen more of this

one poet of our day, but forbore to follow him; for I must own that it seemed mean to be dogging him through the saloons, or even to look at him, since it was to be done stealthily, if at all.

.   .   .   .

He is as un-English as possible; indeed, an Englishman of genius usually lacks the national characteristics, and is great abnormally.   Even the great sailor, Nelson, was unlike his countrymen in the qualities that constituted him a hero; he was not the perfection of an Englishman, but a creature of another kind, — sensitive, nervous, excitable, and really more like a Frenchman.

Un-English as he was, Tennyson had not, however, an American look.   I cannot well describe the difference; but there was something more mellow in him, — softer, sweeter, broader, more simple than we are apt to be.   Living apart from men as he does would hurt any one of us more than it does him.   I may as well leave him here, for I cannot touch the central point.

August 2. — Day before yesterday I went again to the Exhibition, and began the day with looking at the old masters.   Positively, I do begin to receive some pleasure from looking at pictures; but as yet it has nothing to do with any technical merit, nor do I think I shall ever get so far as that. Some landscapes by Ruysdael, and some portraits by Murillo, Velasquez, and Titian, were those which I was most able to appreciate; and I see reason for allowing, contrary to my opinion, as expressed a few pages back, that a portrait may preserve some valuable characteristics of the person represented. The pictures in the English portrait-gallery are mostly very bad, and that may be the reason why I saw so little in them. I saw too, at this last visit, a Virgin and Child, which appeared to me to have an expression more adequate to the subject than most of the innumerable virgins and children, in which we see only repetitions of simple maternity; indeed, any mother, with her first child, would serve an artist for one of them. But in this picture the Virgin had a look as if she were loving the infant as her own child, and at the same time rendering him an awful worship as to her Creator.

While I was sitting in the central saloon, listening to the music, a young man accosted me, presuming that I was so-and-so, the American author. He himself was a traveller for a publishing firm; and he introduced conversation by talking of Uttoxeter, and my description of it in an annual. He said that the account had caused a good deal of pique among the good people of Uttoxeter, because of the ignorance which I attribute to them as to the circumstance which connects Johnson with their town. The spot where Johnson stood can, it appears, still be pointed out. It is on one side of the market - place, and not in the neighborhood of the church. I forget whether I recorded, at the time, that an Uttoxeter newspaper was sent me, containing a proposal that a statue or memorial should be erected on the spot. It would gratify me exceedingly if such a result should come from my pious pilgrimage thither.

My new acquaintance, who was cockneyish, but very intelligent and agreeable, went on to talk about many literary matters and characters; among others, about Miss Brontë, whom he had seen at the Chapter Coffee-House, when she and her sister Anne first went to London. He was at that time connected with the house of —— and ——, and he described the surprise and incredulity of Mr. ——, when this little, commonplace-looking woman presented herself as the author of Jane Eyre. His story brought out the insignificance of Charlotte Brontë's aspect, and the bluff rejection of her by Mr. ——, much more strongly than Mrs. Gaskell's narrative.

Chorlton Road, August 9. — We have changed our lodgings since my last date, those

at Old Trafford being inconvenient, and the
landlady a sharp, peremptory housewife, better
fitted to deal with her own family than to be
complaisant to guests. We are now a little
farther from the Exhibition, and not much better off as regards accommodation, but the house-
keeper is a pleasant, civil sort of a woman,
auspiciously named Mrs. Honey. The house is
a specimen of the poorer middle-class dwellings
as built nowadays, — narrow staircase, thin walls,
and, being constructed for sale, very ill put together indeed, — the floors with wide cracks
between the boards, and wide crevices admitting
both air and light over the doors, so that the
house is full of draughts. The outer walls, it
seems to me, are but of one brick in thickness,
and the partition walls certainly no thicker; and
the movements, and sometimes the voices, of
people in the contiguous house are audible to
us. The Exhibition has temporarily so raised
the value of lodgings here that we have to pay
a high price for even such a house as this.

Mr. Wilding having gone on a tour to Scotland, I had to be at the Consulate every day
last week till yesterday; when I absented myself from duty, and went to the Exhibition.
Una and I spent an hour together, looking
principally at the old Dutch masters, who seem
to me the most wonderful set of men that ever
handled a brush. Such lifelike representations

of cabbages, onions, brass kettles, and kitchen crockery; such blankets, with the woollen fuzz upon them ; such everything I never thought that the skill of man could produce ! Even the photograph cannot equal their miracles. The closer you look, the more minutely true the picture is found to be, and I doubt if even the microscope could see beyond the painter's touch. Gerard Dow seems to be the master among these queer magicians. A straw mat, in one of his pictures, is the most miraculous thing that human art has yet accomplished ; and there is a metal vase, with a dent in it, that is absolutely more real than reality. These painters accomplish all they aim at, — a praise, methinks, which can be given to no other men since the world began. They must have laid down their brushes with perfect satisfaction, knowing that each one of their million touches had been necessary to the effect, and that there was not one too few nor too many. And it is strange how spiritual and suggestive the commonest household article — an earthen pitcher, for example — becomes, when represented with entire accuracy. These Dutchmen got at the soul of common things, and so made them types and interpreters of the spiritual world.

Afterwards I looked at many of the pictures of the old masters, and found myself gradually getting a taste for them ; at least they give me

more and more pleasure the oftener I come to
see them.   Doubtless, I shall be able to pass
for a man of taste by the time I return to America. It is an acquired taste, like that for wines;
and I question whether a man is really any
truer, wiser, or better for possessing it.   From
the old masters, I went among the English
painters, and found myself more favorably inclined towards some of them than at my previous visits; seeing something wonderful even
in Turner's lights and mists and yeasty waves,
although I should like him still better if his
pictures looked in the least like what they typify.
The most disagreeable of English painters is
Etty, who had a diseased appetite for woman's
flesh, and spent his whole life, apparently, in
painting them with enormously developed busts.
I do not mind nudity in a modest and natural
way; but Etty's women really thrust their nudity upon you with malice aforethought, . . .
and the worst of it is they are not beautiful.

Among the last pictures that I looked at was
Hogarth's March to Finchley; and surely nothing can be covered more thick and deep with
English nature than that piece of canvas. The
face of the tall grenadier in the centre, between
two women, both of whom have claims on him,
wonderfully expresses trouble and perplexity;
and every touch in the picture meant something
and expresses what it meant.

The price of admission, after two o'clock, being sixpence, the Exhibition was thronged with a class of people who do not usually come in such large numbers. It was both pleasant and touching to see how earnestly some of them sought to get instruction from what they beheld. The English are a good and simple people, and take life in earnest.

August 14. — Passing by the gateway of the Manchester Cathedral the other morning, on my way to the station, I found a crowd collected, and, high overhead, the bells were chiming for a wedding. These chimes of bells are exceedingly impressive, so broadly gladsome as they are, filling the whole air, and every nook of one's heart, with sympathy. They are good for a people to rejoice with, and good also for a marriage, because through all their joy there is something solemn, — a tone of that voice which we have heard so often at funerals. It is good to see how everybody, up to this old age of the world, takes an interest in weddings, and seems to have a faith that now, at last, a couple have come together to make each other happy. The high, black, rough old cathedral tower sent out its chime of bells as earnestly as for any bridegroom and bride that came to be married five hundred years ago. I went into the church-yard, but there was such a throng of people on

41

its pavement of flat tombstones, and especially such a cluster along the pathway by which the bride was to depart, that I could only see a white dress waving along, and really do not know whether she was a beauty or a fright. The happy pair got into a post-chaise that was waiting at the gate, and immediately drew some crimson curtains, and so vanished into their Paradise. There were two other post-chaises and pairs, and all three had postilions in scarlet. This is the same cathedral where, last May, I saw a dozen couples married in the lump.

In a railway carriage, two or three days ago, an old merchant made rather a good point of one of the uncomfortable results of the electric telegraph. He said that formerly a man was safe from bad news, such as intelligence of failure of debtors, except at the hour of opening his letters in the morning; and then he was in some degree prepared for it, since among (say) fifteen letters, he would be pretty certain to find some " queer " one. But since the telegraph has come into play, he is never safe, and may be hit with news of failure, shipwreck, fall of stocks, or whatever disaster, at all hours of the day.

I went to the Exhibition on Wednesday with Una, and looked at the pencil sketches of the old masters; also at the pictures generally, old and new. I particularly remember a spring landscape, by John Linnell the younger. It is wonderfully good ; so tender and fresh that the artist seems really to have caught the evanescent April and made her permanent. Here at last is eternal spring.

I saw a little man, behind an immense beard, whom I take to be the Duke of Newcastle ; at least, there was a photograph of him in the gallery, with just such a beard. He was at the Palace on that day.

August 16. — I went again to the Exhibition day before yesterday, and looked much at both the modern and ancient pictures, as also at the water-colors. I am making some progress as a connoisseur, and have got so far as to be able to distinguish the broader differences of style, — as, for example, between Rubens and Rembrandt. I should hesitate to claim any more for myself thus far. In fact, however, I do begin to have a liking for good things, and to be sure that they are good. Murillo seems to me about the noblest and purest painter that ever lived, and his Good Shepherd the loveliest picture I have seen. It is a hopeful symptom, moreover, of improving taste, that I see more merit in the crowd of painters than I was at first competent to acknowledge. I could see some of their defects from the very first ; but that is the earliest stage of connoisseurship — after a formal and ignorant admiration. Mounting a few steps higher, one sees beauties. But how much study, how many opportunities, are requisite to form and cultivate a taste! The Exhibition must be quite thrown away on the mass of spectators.

Both they and I are better able to appreciate the specimens of ornamental art contained in the Oriental Room, and in the numerous cases that are ranged up and down the nave. The gewgaws of all Time are here, in precious metals, glass, china, ivory, and every other material that could be wrought into curious and beautiful shapes; great basins and dishes of embossed gold from the Queen's sideboard, or from the beaufets of noblemen; vessels set with precious stones; the pastoral staffs of prelates, some of them made of silver or gold, and enriched with gems, and what have been found in the tombs of the bishops; state swords, and silver maces; the rich plate of colleges, elaborately wrought, — great cups, salvers, tureens, that have been presented by loving sons to their Alma Mater; the heirlooms of old families, treasured from generation to generation, and hitherto only to be seen by favored friends; famous historical jewels, some of which are painted in the portraits of the historical men and women that hang on the walls; numerous specimens of the beautiful old Venetian glass, some of which looks

44

so fragile that it is a wonder how it could bear
even the weight of the wine, that used to be
poured into it, without breaking. These are
the glasses that tested poison, by being shattered into fragments at its touch. The strangest and ugliest old crockery, pictured over with
monstrosities, — the Palissy ware, embossed
with vegetables, fishes, lobsters, that look absolutely real; the delicate Sèvres china, each piece
made inestimable by pictures from a master's
hand; — in short, it is a despair and misery to
see so much that is curious and beautiful, and
to feel that far the greater portion of it will slip
out of the memory, and be as if we had never
seen it. But I mean to look again and again
at these things. We soon perceive that the
present day does not engross all the taste and
ingenuity that has ever existed in the mind of
man; that, in fact, we are a barren age in that
respect.

August 20. — I went to the Exhibition on
Monday, and again yesterday, and measurably
enjoyed both visits. I continue to think, however, that a picture cannot be fully enjoyed except by long and intimate acquaintance with it,
nor can I quite understand what the enjoyment
of a connoisseur is. He is not usually, I think,
a man of deep, poetic feeling, and does not deal
with the picture through his heart, nor set it in

a poem, nor comprehend it morally. If it be a landscape, he is not entitled to judge of it by his intimacy with nature; if a picture of human action, he has no experience nor sympathy of life's deeper passages. However, as my acquaintance with pictures increases, I find myself recognizing more and more the merit of the acknowledged masters of the art; but possibly it is only because I adopt the wrong principles which may have been laid down by the connoisseurs. But there can be no mistake about Murillo, — not that I am worthy to admire him yet, however.

Seeing the many pictures of Holy Families, and the Virgin and Child, which have been painted for churches and convents, the idea occurs, that it was in this way that the poor monks and nuns gratified, as far as they could, their natural longing for earthly happiness. It was not Mary and her heavenly Child that they really beheld, or wished for; but an earthly mother rejoicing over her baby, and displaying it probably to the world as an object worthy to be admired by kings, — as Mary does in the Adoration of the Magi. Every mother, I suppose, feels as if her first child deserved everybody's worship.

I left the Exhibition at three o'clock, and went to Manchester, where I sought out Mr. C—— S—— in his little office. He greeted

46

me warmly, and at five we took the omnibus
for his house, about four miles from town. He
seems to be on pleasant terms with his neighbors,
for almost everybody that got into the omnibus
exchanged kindly greetings with him, and indeed his kindly, simple, genial nature comes
out so evidently that it would be difficult not to
like him.   His house stands, with others, in a
green park, — a small, pretty, semi-detached
suburban residence of brick, with a lawn and
garden round it.   In close vicinity, there is a
deep clough or dell, as shaggy and wild as a
poet could wish, and with a little stream running
through it, as much as five miles long.

.   .   .   .

The interior of the house is very pretty, and
nicely, even handsomely and almost sumptu-
ously, furnished ; and I was very glad to find
him so comfortable.   His recognition as a poet
has been hearty enough to give him a feeling of
success, for he showed me various tokens of the
estimation in which he is held, — for instance,
a presentation copy of Southey's works, in
which the latter had written "Amicus amico, —
poeta poetæ."   He said that Southey had always
been most kind to him. . . . There were various other testimonials from people of note,
American as well as English.   In his parlor
there is a good oil painting of himself, and in
the drawing-room a very fine crayon sketch,

wherein his face, handsome and agreeable, is lighted up with all a poet's ecstasy; likewise a large and fine engraving from the picture. The government has recognized his poetic merit by a pension of fifty pounds, — a small sum, it is true, but enough to mark him out as one who has deserved well of his country. . . . The man himself is very good and lovable. . . . I was able to gratify him by saying that I had recently seen many favorable notices of his poems in the American newspapers; an edition having been published a few months since on our side of the ocean. He was much pleased at this, and asked me to send him the notices. . . .

August 30. — I have been two or three times to the Exhibition since my last date, and enjoy it more as I become familiar with it. There is supposed to be about a third of the good pictures here which England contains; and it is said that the Tory nobility and gentry have contributed to it much more freely and largely than the Whigs. The Duke of Devonshire, for instance, seems to have sent nothing. Mr. Ticknor, the Spanish historian, whom I met yesterday, observed that we should not think quite so much of this Exhibition as the English do after we have been to Italy, although it is a good school in which to gain a preparatory knowledge of the different styles of art. I am glad to hear that there are better things still to be seen.   Nevertheless, I should suppose that certain painters are better represented here than they ever have been or will be elsewhere.   Vandyke, certainly, can be seen nowhere else so well ; Rembrandt and Rubens have satisfactory specimens ; and the whole series of English pictorial achievement is shown more perfectly than within any other walls.   Perhaps it would be wise to devote myself to the study of this latter, and leave the foreigners to be studied on their own soil.   Murillo can hardly have done better than in the pictures by him which we see here.   There is nothing of Raphael's here that is impressive.   Titian has some noble portraits, but little else that I care to see. In all these old masters, Murillo only excepted, it is very rare, I must say, to find· any trace of natural feeling and passion ; and I am weary of naked goddesses who never had any real life and warmth in the painter's imagination, — or, if so, it was the impure warmth of an unchaste woman, who sat for him.

Last week I dined at Mr. F. Heywood's, to meet Mr. Adolphus, the author of a critical work on the Waverley Novels, published long ago, and intended to prove, from internal evidence, that they were written by Sir Walter Scott. . . . His wife was likewise of the party, . . . and also a young Spanish lady, their niece, and daughter of a Spaniard of literary note.   She herself has literary tastes and ability, and is well known to Prescott, whom, I believe, she has assisted in his historical researches, and also to Professor Ticknor; and furthermore she is very handsome and unlike an English damsel, very youthful and maidenlike; and her manners have an ardor and enthusiasm that were pleasant to see, especially as she spoke warmly of my writings; and yet I should wrong her if I left the impression of her being forth-putting and obtrusive, for it was not the fact in the least. She speaks English like a native, insomuch that I should never have suspected her to be anything else.

.   .   .   .

My nerves recently have not been in an exactly quiet and normal state. I begin to weary of England and need another clime.

.   .   .   .

September 6. — I think I paid my last visit to the Exhibition, and feel as if I had had enough of it, although I have got but a small part of the profit it might have afforded me. But pictures are certainly quite other things to me now from what they were at my first visit; it seems even as if there were a sort of illumination within them, that makes me see them more distinctly. Speaking of pictures, the miniature of Anne of Cleves is here, on the faith of which Henry VIII. married her; also, the picture of the Infanta of Spain, which Buckingham brought over to Charles I. while Prince of Wales. This has a delicate rosy prettiness.

One rather interesting portion of the Exhibition is the Refreshment-room, or rather rooms; for very much space is allowed both to the first and second classes. I have looked most at the latter, because there John Bull and his wife may be seen in full gulp and guzzle, swallowing vast quantities of cold boiled beef, thoroughly moistened with porter or bitter ale; and very good meat and drink it is.

At my last visit, on Friday, I met Judge Pollock of Liverpool, who introduced to me a gentleman in a gray slouched hat as Mr. Du Val, an artist, resident in Manchester; and Mr. Du Val invited me to dine with him at six o'clock. So I went to Carlton Grove, his residence, and found it a very pretty house with its own lawn and shrubbery about it. . . . There was a mellow fire in the grate, which made the drawing-room very cosy and pleasant, as the dusk came on before dinner. Mr. Du Val looked like an artist, and like a remarkable man. . . . We had very good talk, chiefly about the Exhibition, and Du Val spoke generously and intelligently of his brother-artists. He says that England might furnish five exhibitions, each one as rich as the present. I find that the most famous picture here is one that I have hardly looked at,

The Three Marys, by Annibal Caracci.   In the
drawing-room there were several pictures and
sketches by Du Val, one of which I especially
liked, — a misty, moonlight picture of the Mersey near Seacombe.   I never saw painted such
genuine moonlight. . . .

I took my leave at half past ten, and found
my cab at the door, and my cabman snugly
asleep inside of it ; and when Mr. Du Val awoke
him, he proved to be quite drunk, insomuch
that I hesitated whether to let him clamber upon
the box, or to take post myself, and drive the
cabman home.   However, I propounded two
questions to him : first, whether his horse would
go of his own accord ; and, secondly, whether
he himself was invariably drunk at that time of
night, because, if it were his normal state, I
should be safer with him drunk than sober.
Being satisfied on these points, I got in, and
was driven home without accident or adventure;
except, indeed, that the cabman drew up and
opened the door for me to alight at a vacant lot
on Stratford Road, just as if there had been a
house and home and cheerful lighted windows
in that vacancy.   On my remonstrance he resumed the whip and reins, and reached Boston
Terrace at last ; and, thanking me for an extra
sixpence as well as he could speak, he begged
me to inquire for " Little John" whenever I
next wanted a cab.   Cabmen are, as a body, the

most ill-natured and ungenial men in the world; but this poor little man was excellently good-humored.

Speaking of the former rudeness of manners, now gradually refining away, of the Manchester people, Judge ——— said that, when he first knew Manchester, women, meeting his wife in the street, would take hold of her dress and say, "Ah, three and sixpence a yard!" The men were very rough, after the old Lancashire fashion. They have always, however, been a musical people, and this may have been a germ of refinement in them. They are still much more simple and natural than the Liverpool people, who love the aristocracy, and whom they heartily despise. It is singular that the great Art Exhibition should have come to pass in the rudest great town in England.

LEAMINGTON. — *Lansdowne Circus, September* 10.—We have become quite weary of our small, mean, uncomfortable, and unbeautiful lodgings at Chorlton Road, with poor and scanty furniture within doors, and no better prospect from the parlor windows than a mud-puddle, larger than most English lakes, on a vacant building-lot opposite our house. The Exhibition, too, was fast becoming a bore; for you must really love a picture, in order to tolerate the sight of it many times. Moreover, the smoky and sooty

air of that abominable Manchester affected my
wife's throat disadvantageously ; so, on a Tuesday morning, we struck our tent and set forth
again, regretting to leave nothing except the
kind disposition of Mrs. Honey, our house-
keeper.   I do not remember meeting with any
other lodging-house keeper who did not grow
hateful and fearful on short acquaintance ; but
I attribute this, not so much to the people themselves, as, primarily, to the unfair and ungen-
erous conduct of some of their English guests,
who feel so sure of being cheated that they always behave as if in an enemy's country, and
therefore they find it one.

The rain poured down upon us as we drove
away in two cabs, laden with mountainous luggage, to the London Road station ; and the
whole day was grim with cloud and moist with
showers.   We went by way of Birmingham, and
stayed three hours at the great dreary station
there, — waiting for the train to Leamington,
whither Fanny had gone forward the day before
to secure lodgings for us (as she is English, and
understands the matter). . . . We all were tired
and dull by the time we reached the Leamington station, where a note from Fanny gave us
the address of our lodgings. Lansdowne Circus
is really delightful after that ugly and grimy
suburb of Manchester. Indeed, there could
not possibly be a greater contrast than between

Leamington and Manchester, — the latter built only for dirty uses, and scarcely intended as a habitation for man ; the former so cleanly, so set out with shade trees, so regular in its streets, so neatly paved, its houses so prettily contrived and nicely stuccoed, that it does not look like a portion of the workaday world.

· · · · · · · ·

KENILWORTH, *September* 13. — The weather was very uncertain through the last week, and yesterday morning, too, was misty and sunless ; notwithstanding which we took the rail for Kenilworth before eleven. The distance from Leamington is less than five miles, and at the Kenilworth station we found a little bit of an omnibus, into which we packed ourselves, together with two ladies, one of whom, at least, was an American. I begin to agree partly with the English, that we are not a people of elegant manners. At all events, there is sometimes a bare, hard, meagre sort of deportment, especially in our women, that has not its parallel elsewhere. But perhaps what sets off this kind of behavior, and brings it into *alto relievo*, is the fact of such uncultivated persons travelling abroad, and going to see sights that would not be interesting except to people of some education and refinement.

We saw but little of the village of Kenilworth,

passing through it sidelong fashion, in the omnibus; but I learn that it has between three and
four thousand inhabitants, and is of immemorial
antiquity.   We saw a few old, gabled, and tim-
ber-framed houses; but generally the town was
of modern aspect, although less so in the immediate vicinity of the castle gate, across the road
from which there was an inn, with bowling-
greens, and a little bunch of houses and shops.
Apart from the high road there is a gate-house,
ancient, but in excellent repair, towered, tur-
reted and battlemented, and looking like a castle
in itself.   Until Cromwell's time, the entrance
to the castle used to be beneath an arch that
passed through this structure; but the gate-
house being granted to one of the Parliament
officers, he converted it into a residence, and apparently added on a couple of gables, which now
look quite as venerable as the rest of the edifice.
Admission within the outer grounds of the castle
is now obtained through a little wicket close beside the gate-house, at which sat one or two old
men, who touched their hats to us in humble
willingness to accept a fee.   One of them had
guide-books for sale; and, finding that we were
not to be bothered by a cicerone, we bought one
of his books.

The ruins are perhaps two hundred yards from
the gate-house and the road, and the space between is a pasture for sheep, which also browse

in the inner court, and shelter themselves in the
dungeons and state apartments of the castle.
Goats would be fitter occupants, because they
would climb to the tops of the crumbling towers, and nibble the weeds and shrubbery that
grow there.   The first part of the castle which
we reach is called Cæsar's Tower, being the oldest portion of the ruins, and still very stalwart
and massive, and built of red freestone, like all
the rest.   Cæsar's Tower being on the right,
Leicester's Buildings, erected by the Earl of
Leicester, Queen Elizabeth's favorite, are on the
left ; and between these two formerly stood other
structures which have now as entirely disappeared as if they had never existed ; and through
the wide gap, thus opened, appears the grassy
inner court, surrounded on three sides by half-
fallen towers and shattered walls.   Some of these
were erected by John of Gaunt ; and among
these ruins is the Banqueting-Hall, — or rather
was, — for it has now neither floor nor roof, but
only the broken stonework of some tall, arched
windows, and the beautiful old ivied arch of the
entrance-way, now inaccessible from the ground.
The ivy is very abundant about the ruins, and
hangs its green curtains quite from top to bottom of some of the windows.   There are likewise very large and aged trees within the castle,
there being no roof nor pavement anywhere, except in some dungeon-like nooks ; so that the

trees having soil and air enough, and being shel-
tered from unfriendly blasts, can grow as if in a
nursery.   Hawthorn, however, next to ivy, is
the great ornament and comforter of these desolate ruins.   I have not seen so much nor such
thriving hawthorn anywhere else, — in the
court, high up on crumbly heights, on the sod
that carpets roofless rooms, — everywhere, indeed, and now rejoicing in plentiful crops of red
berries.   The ivy is even more wonderfully luxuriant ; its trunks being, in some places, two or
three feet in diameter, and forming real buttresses against the walls, which are actually supported and vastly strengthened by this parasite,
that clung to them at first only for its own convenience, and now holds them up, lest it should
be ruined by their fall.   Thus an abuse has
strangely grown into a use, and I think we may
sometimes see the same fact, morally, in English
matters.   There is something very curious in the
close, firm grip which the ivy fixes upon the wall,
closer and closer for centuries.   Neither is it at
all nice as to what it clutches, in its necessity for
support.   I saw in the outer court an old haw-
thorn-tree, to which a plant of ivy had married
itself, and the ivy trunk and the hawthorn trunk
were now absolutely incorporated, and in their
close embrace you could not tell which was
which.

At one end of the Banqueting-Hall there are

two large bay-windows, one of which looks into the inner court, and the other affords a view of the surrounding country. The former is called Queen Elizabeth's Dressing-room. Beyond the Banqueting-Hall is what is called the Strong Tower, up to the top of which we climbed principally by the aid of the stones that have tumbled down from it. A lady sat halfway down the crumbly descent, within the castle, on a camp-stool, and before an easel, sketching this tower, on the summit of which we sat. She said it was Amy Robsart's Tower; and within it, open to the day, and quite accessible, we saw a room that we were free to imagine had been occupied by her. I do not find that these associations of real scenes with fictitious events greatly heighten the charm of them.

By this time the sun had come out brightly, and with such warmth that we were glad to sit down in the shadow. Several sightseers were now rambling about, and among them some schoolboys, who kept scrambling up to points whither no other animal, except a goat, would have ventured. Their shouts and the sunshine made the old castle cheerful; and what with the ivy and the hawthorn, and the other old trees, it was very beautiful and picturesque. But a castle does not make nearly so interesting and impressive a ruin as an abbey, because the latter was built for beauty, and on a plan in which deep thought and feeling were involved; and having once been a grand and beautiful work, it continues grand and beautiful through all the successive stages of its decay. But a castle is rudely piled together for strength and other material conveniences; and, having served these ends, it has nothing left to fall back upon, but crumbles into shapeless masses, which are often as little picturesque as a pile of bricks. Without the ivy and the shrubbery, this huge Kenilworth would not be a pleasant object, except for one or two window-frames, with broken tracery, in the Banqueting-Hall. . . .

We stayed from eleven till two, and identified the various parts of the castle as well as we could by the guide-book. The ruins are very extensive, though less so than I should have imagined, considering that seven acres were included within the castle wall. But a large part of the structures have been taken away to build houses in Kenilworth village and elsewhere, and much, too, to make roads with, and a good deal lies under the green turf in the courtyards, inner and outer. As we returned to the gate, my wife and Una went into the gate-house to see an old chimney-piece, and other antiquities; and Julian and I proceeded a little way round the outer wall, and saw the remains of the moat, and Lin's Tower, — a real and shattered fabric of John of Gaunt.

The omnibus now drove up, and one of the
old men at the gate came hobbling up to open
the door, and was rewarded with a sixpence, and
we drove down to the King's Head. . . . We
then walked out and bought prints of the castle,
and inquired our way to the church and to the
ruins of the Priory. The latter, so far as we
could discover them, are very few and uninteresting; and the church, though it has a venerable exterior, and an aged spire, has been so
modernized within, and in so plain a fashion, as
to have lost what beauty it may once have had.
There were a few brasses and mural monuments,
one of which was a marble group of a dying
woman and her family, by Westmacott. The
sexton was a cheerful little man, but knew very
little about his church, and nothing of the remains of the Priory. The day was spent very
pleasantly amid this beautiful green English
scenery, these fine old Warwickshire trees, and
broad, gently swelling fields.

LIVERPOOL, *September* 17. — I took the train
for Rugby, and thence to Liverpool. The most
noticeable character at Mrs. Blodgett's now is
Mr. T——, a Yankee, who has seen the world,
and gathered much information and experience
already, though still a young man, — a handsome man with black curly hair, a dark, intelligent, bright face, and rather cold blue eyes, but

a very pleasant air and address. His observing faculties are very strongly developed in his forehead, and his reflective ones seem to be adequate to making some, if not the deepest, use of what he sees. He has voyaged and travelled almost all over the world, and has recently published a book of his peregrinations, which has been well received. He is of exceeding fluent talk, though rather too much inclined to unfold the secret springs of action in Louis Napoleon and other potentates, and to tell of revolutions that are coming at some unlooked-for moment, but soon. Still I believe in his wisdom and foresight about as much as in any other man's. There are no such things. He is a merchant, and meditates settling in London, and making a colossal fortune there during the next ten or twenty years; that being the period during which London is to hold the exchanges of the world, and to continue its metropolis. After that, New York is to be the world's queen city.

There is likewise here a young American, named A——, who has been at a German University, and favors us with descriptions of his student life there, which seems chiefly to have consisted in drinking beer and fighting duels. He shows a cut on his nose as a trophy of these combats. He has with him a dog of St. Bernard, who is a much more remarkable character than himself, — an immense dog, a noble and gentle creature; and really it touches my heart that his master is going to take him from his native snow-mountain to a Southern plantation to die. Mr. A—— says that there are now but five of these dogs extant at the convent; there having, within two or three years, been a disease among them, with which this dog also has suffered. His master has a certificate of his genuineness, and of himself being the rightful purchaser; and he says that as he descended the mountain, every peasant along the road stopped him, and would have compelled him to give up the dog had he not produced this proof of property. The neighboring mountaineers are very jealous of the breed being taken away, considering them of such importance to their own safety. This huge animal, the very biggest dog I ever saw, though only eleven months old, and not so high by two or three inches as he will be, allows Mr. —— to play with him, and take him on his shoulders (he weighs, at least, a hundred pounds), like any lapdog.

LEAMINGTON. — *Lansdowne Circus, October* 10. — I returned hither from Liverpool last week, and have spent the time idly since then, reposing myself after the four years of unnatural restraint in the Consulate. Being already pretty well acquainted with the neighborhood of Leamington, I have little or nothing to record about the prettiest, cheerfullest, cleanest of English towns.

.   .   .   .

On Saturday we took the rail for Coventry, about a half-hour's travel distant. I had been there before, more than two years ago. . . . No doubt I described it on my first visit; and it is not remarkable enough to be worth two descriptions, — a large town of crooked and irregular streets and lanes, not looking nearly so ancient as it is, because of new brick and stuccoed fronts which have been plastered over its antiquity; although still there are interspersed the peaked gables of old-fashioned, timber-built houses; or an archway of worn stone, which, if you pass through it, shows like an avenue from the present to the past; for just in the rear of the new-fangled aspect lurks the old arrangement of courtyards, and rustiness, and grimness, that would not be suspected from the exterior.

.   .   .   .

Right across the narrow street stands St. Michael's Church with its tall, tall tower and spire. The body of the church has been almost entirely recased with stone since I was here before; but the tower still retains its antiquity, and is decorated with statues that look down from their lofty niches seemingly in good preservation. The tower and spire are most stately and beautiful, the whole church very noble. We went in, and found that the vulgar plaster of Cromwell's time has been scraped from the pillars and arches, leaving them all as fresh and splendid as if just made.

We looked also into Trinity Church, which stands close by St. Michael's, separated only, I think, by the churchard. We also visited St. John's Church, which is very venerable as regards its exterior, the stone being worn and smoothed — if not roughened, rather — by centuries of storm and fitful weather. This wear and tear, however, has almost ceased to be a charm to my mind, comparatively to what it was when I first began to see old buildings. Within, the church is spoiled by wooden galleries, built across the beautiful pointed arches.

We saw nothing else particularly worthy of remark except Ford's Hospital, in Grey Friars' Street. It has an Elizabethan front of timber and plaster, facing on the street, with two or three peaked gables in a row, beneath which is a low, arched entrance, giving admission into a small paved quadrangle, open to the sky above, but surrounded by the walls, lozenge-paned windows, and gables of the Hospital. The quadrangle is but a few paces in width, and perhaps twenty in length; and, through a half-closed doorway, at the farther end, there was a glimpse into a garden. Just within the entrance, through an open door, we saw the neat and comfortable apartment of the Matron of the Hospital; and, along the quadrangle, on each side, there were three or four doors, through which we glanced into little rooms, each containing a fireplace, a bed, a chair or two, — a little, homely, domestic scene, with one old woman in the midst of it; one old woman in each room. They are destitute widows, who have their lodgings and home here, — a small room for each one to sleep, cook, and be at home in, — and three and sixpence a week to feed and clothe themselves with, — a cloak being the only garment bestowed on them. When one of the sisterhood dies, each old woman has to pay twopence towards the funeral; and so they slowly starve and wither out of life, and claim each their twopence contribution in turn. I am afraid they have a very dismal time.

There is an old man's hospital in another part of the town, on a similar plan. A collection of sombre and lifelike tales might be written on the idea of giving the experiences of these Hospitallers, male and female; and they might be supposed to be written by the Matron of one, who had acquired literary taste and practice as a governess, — and by the Master of the other, a retired school-usher.

It was market-day in Coventry, and far adown the street leading from it there were booths and stalls, and apples, pears, toys, books, — among

which I saw my Twice-Told Tales, with an
awful portrait of myself as frontispiece, — and
various country produce, offered for sale by
men, women, and girls. The scene looked lively,
but had not much vivacity in it.

.   .   .   .

October 27. — The autumn has advanced pro-
gressively, and is now fairly established, though
still there is much green foliage, in spite of many
brown trees, and an enormous quantity of withered leaves, too damp to rustle, strewing the
paths, — whence, however, they are continually
swept up and carried off in wheelbarrows, either
for neatness or for the agricultural worth, as
manure, of even a withered leaf. The pastures
look just as green as ever, — a deep, bright
verdure, that seems almost sunshine in itself,
however sombre the sky may be. The little
plats of grass and flowers, in front of our circle
of houses, might still do credit to an American
midsummer; for I have seen beautiful roses
here within a day or two; and dahlias, asters,
and such autumnal flowers, are plentiful; and
I have no doubt that the old year's flowers
will bloom till those of the New Year appear.
Really, the English winter is not so terrible as
ours.

.   .   .   .

October 30. — Wednesday was one of the most beautiful of all days, and gilded almost throughout with the precious English sunshine, — the most delightful sunshine ever made, both for its positive fine qualities and because we seldom get it without too great an admixture of water. We made no use of this lovely day, except to walk to an Arboretum and Pinetum on the outskirts of the town. Una and Mrs. Shepard made an excursion to Guy's Cliff.

[Here comes in the visit to Leicester's Hospital and Redfern's Shop, and St. Mary's Church, printed in Our Old Home. — S. H.]

From Redfern's we went back to the marketplace, expecting to find Julian at the Museum, but the keeper said he had gone away. We went into this Museum, which contains the collections in Natural History, etc., of a county society. It is very well arranged, and is rich in specimens of ornithology, among which was an albatross, huge beyond imagination. I do not think that Coleridge could have known the size of the fowl when he caused it to be hung round the neck of his Ancient Mariner. There were a great many humming-birds from various parts of the world, and some of their breasts actually gleamed and shone as with the brightest lustre of sunset. Also many strange fishes, and a huge pike taken from the river Avon, and so long that I wonder how he could turn himself about

in such a little river as the Avon is near Warwick. A great curiosity was a bunch of skeleton
leaves and flowers, prepared by a young lady,
and preserving all the most delicate fibres of
the plant, looking like inconceivably fine lace-
work, white as snow, while the substance was
quite taken away. In another room there were
minerals, shells, and a splendid collection of
fossils, among which were remains of antedilu-
vian creatures, several feet long. In still another
room we saw some historical curiosities, — the
most interesting of which were two locks of
reddish-brown hair, one from the head and one
from the beard of Edward IV. They were fastened to a manuscript letter which authenticates
the hair as having been taken from King Edward's tomb in 1789. Near these relics was a
seal of the great Earl of Warwick, the mighty
king-maker; also a sword from Bosworth Field,
smaller and shorter than those now in use; for
indeed, swords seem to have increased in length,
weight, and formidable aspect, now that the weapon has almost ceased to be used in actual warfare. The short Roman sword was probably
more murderous than any weapon of the same
species, except the bowie-knife. Here, too, were
Parliamentary cannon-balls, etc. . . .

[The visit to Whitnash intervenes here. —
S. H.]

LONDON, 24 *Great Russell Street, November* 10. We have been thinking and negotiating about taking lodgings in London lately, and this morning we left Leamington and reached London with no other misadventure than that of leaving the great bulk of our luggage behind us, — the van which we hired to take it to the railway station having broken down under its prodigious weight, in the middle of the street. On our journey we saw nothing particularly worthy of note, — but everywhere the immortal verdure of England, scarcely less perfect than in June, so far as the fields are concerned, though the foliage of the trees presents pretty much the same hues as those of our own forests, after the gayety and gorgeousness have departed from them.

Our lodgings are in close vicinity to the British Museum, which is the great advantage we took them for.

I felt restless and uncomfortable, and soon strolled forth, without any definite object, and walked as far as Charing Cross. Very dull and dreary the city looked, and not in the least lively, even where the throng was thickest and most brisk. As I trudged along, my reflection was, that never was there a dingier, uglier, less picturesque city than London; and that it is really wonderful that so much brick and stone, for centuries together, should have been built up with so poor a result. Yet these old names of

the city — Fleet Street, Ludgate Hill, the Strand
— used to throw a glory over these homely precincts when I first saw them, and still do so in
a less degree.   Where Farringdon Street opens
upon Fleet Street, moreover, I had a glimpse
of St. Paul's, along Ludgate Street, in the gathering dimness, and felt as if I saw an old friend.
In that neighborhood — speaking of old friends
— I met Mr. Parker, of Boston, who told me
sad news of a friend whom I love as much as if
I had known him for a lifetime, though he is,
indeed, but of two or three years' standing.   He
said that my friend's bankruptcy is in to-day's
Gazette.   Of all men on earth, I had rather
this misfortune should have happened to any
other; but I hope and think he has sturdiness
and buoyancy enough to rise up beneath it.
I cannot conceive of his face otherwise than
with a glow on it, like that of the sun at noonday.

Before I reached our lodgings, the dusk settled into the streets, and a mist bedewed and
bedamped me, and I went astray, as is usual
with me, and had to inquire my way; indeed,
except in the principal thoroughfares, London
is so miserably lighted that it is impossible to
recognize one's whereabouts.   On my arrival I
found our parlor looking cheerful with a brisk
fire; . . . but the first day or two in new lodgings is at best an uncomfortable time.   Fanny

has just come in with more unhappy news about
——.   Pray Heaven it may not be true ! . . .
Troubles are a sociable brotherhood ; they love
to come hand in hand, or sometimes, even, to
come side by side with long looked-for and
hoped-for good fortune. . . .

November 11.—This morning we all went
to the British Museum, always a most wearisome and depressing task to me.   I strolled
through the lower rooms with a good degree of
interest, looking at the antique sculptures, some
of which were doubtless grand and beautiful in
their day. . . . The Egyptian remains are, on
the whole, the more satisfactory ; for, though
inconceivably ugly, they are at least miracles
of size and ponderosity, — for example, a hand
and arm of polished granite, as much as ten feet
in length.   The upper rooms, containing mil-
lions of specimens of Natural History in all departments, really made my heart ache with a pain
and woe that I have never felt anywhere but
in the British Museum, and I hurried through
them as rapidly as I could persuade Julian to
follow me.   We had left the rest of the party
still intent on the Grecian sculptures, — and
though Julian was much interested in the vast
collection of shells, he chose to quit the Museum with me in the prospect of a stroll about
London.   He seems to have my own passion

for thronged streets, and the utmost bustle of human life.

We went first to the railway station, in quest of our luggage, which we found. Then we made a pretty straight course down to Holborn, and through Newgate Street, stopping a few moments to look through the iron fence at the Christ's Hospital boys, in their long blue coats and yellow petticoats and stockings. It was between twelve and one o'clock; and I suppose this was their hour of play, for they were running about the enclosed space, chasing and overthrowing one another, without their caps, with their yellow petticoats tucked up, and all in immense activity and enjoyment. They were eminently a healthy and handsome set of boys.

Then we went into Cheapside, where I called at Mr. Bennett's shop, to inquire what are the facts about ———. When I mentioned his name, Mr. Bennett shook his head and expressed great sorrow; but, on further talk, I found that he referred only to the failure, and had heard nothing about the other rumor. It cannot, therefore, be true; for Bennett lives in his neighborhood, and could not have remained ignorant of such a calamity. There must be some mistake; none, however, in regard to the failure, it having been announced in the Times.

From Bennett's shop, — which is so near the steeple of Bow Church that it would tumble

upon it if it fell over — we strolled still east-
ward, aiming at London Bridge; but missed it,
and bewildered ourselves among many dingy
and frowzy streets and lanes. I bore towards
the right, however, knowing that that course
must ultimately bring me to the Thames; and
at last I saw before me ramparts, towers, circular and square, with battlemented summits, large
sweeps and curves of fortification, as well as
straight and massive walls and chimneys behind
them (all a great confusion — to my eye), of
ancient and more modern structure, and four
loftier turrets rising in the midst; the whole great
space surrounded by a broad, dry moat, which
now seemed to be used as an ornamental walk,
bordered partly with trees. This was the Tower;
but seen from a different and more picturesque
point of view than I have heretofore gained of
it. Being so convenient for a visit, I determined to go in. At the outer gate, which is not
a part of the fortification, a sentinel walks to and
fro, besides whom there was a warder, in the rich
old costume of Henry VIII.'s time, looking
very gorgeous indeed, — as much so as scarlet
and gold can make him.

. . . .

As Julian and I were not going to look at the
Jewel-room, we loitered about in the open space,
before the White Tower, while the tall, slender,
white-haired, gentlemanly warder led the rest of

the party into that apartment. We found what
one might take for a square in a town, with
gabled houses lifting their peaks on one side,
and various edifices enclosing the other sides,
and the great White Tower, — now more black
than white, — rising venerable, and rather picturesque than otherwise, the most prominent object in the scene. I have no plan nor available
idea of it whatever in my mind, but it seems
really to be a town within itself, with streets,
avenues, and all that pertains to human life.
There were soldiers going through their exercise in the open space, and along at the base of
the White Tower lay a great many cannon and
mortars, some of which were of Turkish manufacture, and immensely long and ponderous.
Others, likewise of mighty size, had once belonged to the famous ship Great Harry, and
had lain for ages under the sea. Others were
East Indian. Several were beautiful specimens
of workmanship. The mortars — some so large
that a fair-sized man might easily be rammed
into them — held their great mouths slanting
upward to the sky, and mostly contained a quantity of rain-water. While we were looking at
these warlike toys, — for I suppose not one of
them will ever thunder in earnest again, — the
warder reappeared with his ladies, and, leading
us all to a certain part of the open space, he
struck his foot on the small stones with which

it is paved, and told us that we were standing on the spot where Anne Boleyn and Catharine Howard were beheaded. It is not exactly in the centre of the square, but on a line with one of the angles of the White Tower. I forgot to mention that the middle of the open space is occupied by a marble statue of Wellington, which appeared to me very poor and laboriously spirited.

Lastly the warder led us under the Bloody Tower, and by the side of the Wakefield Tower, and showed us the Traitor's Gate, which is now closed up, so as to afford no access to the Thames. No ; we first visited the Beauchamp Tower, famous as the prison of many historical personages. Some of its former occupants have left their initials or names, and inscriptions of piety and patience, cut deep into the freestone of the walls, together with devices — as a crucifix, for instance — neatly and skilfully done. This room has a long, deep fireplace ; it is chiefly lighted by a large window, which, I fancy, must have been made in modern times ; but there are four narrow apertures, throwing in a little light through deep alcoves in the thickness of the octagon wall. One would expect such a room to be picturesque ; but it is really not of striking aspect, being low, with a plastered ceiling, — the beams just showing through the plaster, — a boarded floor, and the walls being washed over with a buff color. A warder sat within a railing, by the great window, with sixpenny books to sell, containing transcripts of the inscriptions on the walls.

We now left the Tower, and made our way deviously westward, passing St. Paul's, which looked magnificently and beautifully, so huge and dusky as it was, with here and there a space on its vast form where the original whiteness of the marble came out like a streak of moonshine amid the blackness with which time has made it grander than it was in its newness. It is a most noble edifice; and I delight, too, in the statues that crown some of its heights, and in the wreaths of sculpture which are hung around it.

.   .   .   .

November 12. — This morning began with such fog, that at the window of my chamber, lighted only from a small courtyard, enclosed by high, dingy walls, I could hardly see to dress. It kept alternately darkening, and then brightening a little, and darkening again, so much that we could but just discern the opposite houses; but at eleven or thereabouts it grew so much clearer that we resolved to venture out. Our plan for the day was to go in the first place to Westminster Abbey, and to the National Gallery, if we should find time. . . . The fog dark-

ened again as we went down Regent Street, and
the Duke of York's Column was but barely visible, looming vaguely before us; nor, from Pall
Mall, was Nelson's Pillar much more distinct,
though methought his statue stood aloft in a
somewhat clearer atmosphere than ours.   Passing Whitehall, however, we could scarcely see
Inigo Jones's Banqueting-House, on the other
side of the street; and the towers and turrets
of the new Houses of Parliament were all but
invisible, as was the Abbey itself; so that we
really were in some doubt whither we were going.   We found our way to Poets' Corner, however, and entered those holy precincts, which
looked very dusky and grim in the smoky
light. . . . I was strongly impressed with the
perception that very commonplace people com-
pose the great bulk of society in the home of
the illustrious dead.   It is wonderful how few
names there are that one cares anything about
a hundred years after their departure ; but perhaps each generation acts in good faith in canon-
izing its own men. . . . But the fame of the
buried person does not make the marble live,
— the marble keeps merely a cold and sad memory of a man who would else be forgotten. No
man who needs a monument ever ought to have
one.

. . . .

The painted windows of the Abbey, though

mostly modern, are exceedingly rich and beautiful ; and I do think that human art has invented
no other such magnificent method of adornment
as this.

.　.　.　.　.　.　.　.

Our final visit to-day was to the National
Gallery, where I came to the conclusion that
Murillo's St. John was the most lovely picture
I had ever seen, and that there never was a
painter who has really made the world richer,
except Murillo.

.　.　.　.　.　.　.　.

November 12. — This morning we issued
forth, and found the atmosphere chill and almost frosty, tingling upon our cheeks. . . . The
gateway of Somerset House attracted us, and
we walked round its spacious quadrangle, en-
countering many government clerks hurrying to
their various offices.　At least, I presumed them
to be so.　This is certainly a handsome square
of buildings, with its Grecian façades and pillars,
and its sculptured bas-reliefs, and the group of
statuary in the midst of the court.　Besides the
part of the edifice that rises above ground, there
appear to be two subterranean stories below the
surface.　From Somerset House we pursued our
way through Temple Bar, but missed it, and
therefore entered by the passage from what was
formerly Alsatia, but which now seems to be a

very respectable and humdrum part of London. We came immediately to the Temple Gardens, which we walked quite round. The grass is still green, but the trees are leafless, and had an aspect of not being very robust, even at more genial seasons of the year. There were, however, large quantities of brilliant chrysanthemums, golden and of all hues, blooming gorgeously all about the borders; and several gardeners were at work, tending these flowers, and sheltering them from the weather. I noticed no roses, nor even rosebushes, in the spot where the factions of York and Lancaster plucked their two hostile flowers.

Leaving these grounds, we went to the Hall of the Middle Temple, where we knocked at the portal, and, finding it not fastened, thrust it open. A boy appeared within, and the porter or keeper, at a distance, along the inner passage, called to us to enter; and, opening the door of the great hall, left us to view it till he should be at leisure to attend to us. Truly it is a most magnificent apartment; very lofty, — so lofty, indeed, that the antique oak roof was quite hidden, as regarded all its details, in the sombre gloom that brooded under its rafters. The hall was lighted by four great windows, I think, on each of the two sides, descending halfway from the ceiling to the floor, leaving all beneath enclosed by oaken panelling, which, on three sides,

was carved with escutcheons of such members
of the society as have held the office of reader.
There is likewise, in a large recess or transept,
a great window, occupying the full height of
the hall, and splendidly emblazoned with the
arms of the Templars who have attained to the
dignity of Chief Justices.   The other windows
are pictured in like manner, with coats of arms
of local dignities connected with the Temple ;
and besides all these there are arched lights,
high towards the roof, at either end, full of richly
and chastely colored glass, and all the illumination that the great hall had came through these
glorious panes, and they seemed the richer for
the sombreness in which we stood.   I cannot
describe, or even intimate, the effect of this
transparent glory, glowing down upon us in
that gloomy depth of the hall.   The screen at
the lower end was of carved oak, very dark and
highly polished, and as old as Queen Elizabeth's
time.   The keeper told us that the story of the
Armada was said to be represented in these
carvings, but in the imperfect light we could
trace nothing of it out.   Along the length of
the apartment were set two oaken tables for the
students of law to dine upon ; and on the dais,
at the upper end, there was a cross-table for the
big-wigs of the society ; the latter being provided with comfortable chairs, and the former
with oaken benches. From a notification posted

near the door, I gathered that the cost of dinners is two shillings to each gentleman, including, as the attendant told me, ale and wine.   I am reluctant to leave this hall without expressing how grave, how grand, how sombre, and how magnificent I feel it to be. As regards historical association, it was a favorite dancing hall of Queen Elizabeth, and Sir Christopher Hatton danced himself into her good graces there.

We next went to the Temple Church, and, finding the door ajar, made free to enter beneath its Norman arches, which admitted us into a circular vestibule, very ancient and beautiful. In the body of the church beyond we saw a boy sitting, but nobody either forbade or invited our entrance. On the floor of the vestibule lay about half a score of Templars, — the representatives of the warlike priest who built this church and formerly held these precincts, — all in chain armor, grasping their swords, and with their shields beside them.   Except two or three, they lay cross-legged, in token that they had really fought for the Holy Sepulchre. I think I have seen nowhere else such well-preserved monumental knights as these. We proceeded into the interior of the church, and were greatly impressed with its wonderful beauty, — the roof springing, as it were, in a harmonious and accordant fountain, out of the clustered pillars that support its groined arches ; and these pillars, immense as they are, are polished like so many gems.   They are of Purbeck marble, and, if I mistake not, had been covered with plaster for ages, until latterly redeemed and beautified anew. But the glory of the church is its old painted windows ; and, positively, those great spaces over the chancel appeared to be set with all manner of precious stones, — or it was as if the many-colored radiance of heaven were breaking upon us, — or as if we saw the wings of angels, storied over with richly tinted pictures of holy things.   But it is idle to talk of this marvellous adornment ; it is to be seen and wondered at, not written about.   Before we left the church the porter made his appearance, in time to receive his fee, — which somebody, indeed, is always ready to stretch out his hand for.   And so ended our visit to the Temple, which, by the bye, though close to the midmost bustle of London, is as quiet as if it were always Sunday there.

We now went to St. Paul's. Una and Miss Shepard ascended to the Whispering Gallery, and we, sitting under the dome, at the base of one of the pillars, saw them far above us, looking very indistinct, for those misty upper depths seemed almost to be hung with clouds.   This cathedral, I think, does not profit by gloom, but requires cheerful sunshine to show it to the best advantage.   The statues and sculptures in St. Paul's are mostly covered with years of dust, and look thereby very grim and ugly ; but there are few memories there from which I should care to brush away the dust, they being, in nine cases out of ten, naval and military heroes of second or third class merit.   I really remember no literary celebrity admitted solely on that account, except Dr. Johnson.   The Crimean War has supplied two or three monuments, chiefly mural tablets ; and doubtless more of the same excrescences will yet come out upon the walls.   One thing that I newly noticed was the beautiful shape of the great covered marble vase that serves for a font.

From St. Paul's we went down Cheapside, and, turning into King Street, visited Guild-hall, which we found in process of decoration for a public ball, to take place next week.   It looked rather gewgawish than gorgeous, being hung with flags of all nations, and adorned with military trophies ; and the scene was repeated by a range of looking-glasses at one end of the room.   The execrably painted windows really shocked us by their vulgar glare, after those of the Temple Hall and Church ; yet, a few years ago, I might very likely have thought them beautiful.   Our own national banner, I must remember to say, was hanging in Guild-hall, but with only ten Stars, and an insufficient number of Stripes.

November 15. — Yesterday morning we went to London Bridge and along Lower Thames Street, and quickly found ourselves in Billingsgate Market, — a dirty, evil-smelling, crowded precinct, thronged with people carrying fish on their heads, and lined with fish-shops and fish-stalls, and pervaded with a fishy odor. The footwalk was narrow, — as indeed was the whole street, — and filthy to travel upon ; and we had to elbow our way among rough men and slatternly women, and to guard our heads from the contact of fish-trays ; very ugly, grimy, and misty, moreover, is Billingsgate Market, and though we heard none of the foul language of which it is supposed to be the fountain-head, yet it has its own peculiarities of behavior. For instance, Una tells me that one man, staring at her and her governess as they passed, cried out, "What beauties ! " — another, looking under her veil, greeted her with, " Good-morning, my love ! " We were in advance, and heard nothing of these civilities. Struggling through this fishy purgatory, we caught sight of the Tower, as we drew near the end of the street ; and I put all my party under charge of one of the Trump Cards, not being myself inclined to make the rounds of the small part of the fortress that is shown, so soon after my late visit.

When they departed with the warder, I set

out by myself to wander about the exterior of the Tower, looking with interest at what I suppose to be Tower Hill, — a slight elevation of the large open space into which Great Tower Street opens; though, perhaps, what is now called Trinity Square may have been a part of Tower Hill, and possibly the precise spot where the executions took place. Keeping to the right, round the Tower, I found the moat quite surrounded by a fence of iron rails, excluding me from a pleasant gravel-path, among flowers and shrubbery, on the inside, where I could see nursery-maids giving children their airings. Possibly these may have been the privileged inhabitants of the Tower, which certainly might contain the population of a large village. The aspect of the fortress has so much that is new and modern about it that it can hardly be called picturesque, and yet it seems unfair to withhold that epithet from such a collection of gray ramparts. I followed the iron fence quite round the outer grounds, till it approached the Thames, and in this direction the moat and the pleasure-ground terminate in a narrow graveyard, which extends beneath the walls, and looks neglected and shaggy with long grass. It appeared to contain graves enough, but only a few tombstones, of which I could read the inscription of but one; it commemorated a Mr. George Gibson, a person of no note, nor ap-

parently connected with the place. St. Katharine's Dock lies along the Thames, in this vicinity; and while on one side of me were the
Tower, the quiet gravel-path and the shaggy
graveyard, on the other were draymen and their
horses, dock laborers, sailors, empty puncheons,
and a miscellaneous spectacle of life, — including organ-grinders, men roasting chestnuts over
small ovens on the sidewalk, boys and women
with boards or wheelbarrows of apples, oyster-
stands, besides peddlers of small wares, dirty
children at play, and other figures and things
that a Dutch painter would seize upon.

I went a little way into St. Katharine's Dock,
and found it crowded with great ships; then,
returning, I strolled along the range of shops
that front towards this side of the Tower. They
have all something to do with ships, sailors, and
commerce; being for the sale of ships' stores,
nautical instruments, arms, clothing, together
with a tavern and grog-shop at every other
door; bookstalls, too, covered with cheap novels
and song-books; cigar-shops in great numbers;
and everywhere were sailors, and here and there
a soldier, and children at the doorsteps, and
women showing themselves at the doors or
windows of their domiciles. These latter figures, however, pertain rather to the street up
which I walked, penetrating into the interior of
this region, which, I think, is Blackwall — no,

I forget what its name is.   At all events, it has an ancient and most grimy and rough look, with its old gabled houses, each of them the seat of some petty trade and business in its basement story.   Among these I saw one house with three or four peaks along its front, — a second story projecting over the basement, and the whole clapboarded over. . . . There was a butcher's stall in the lower story, with a front open to the street, in the ancient fashion, which seems to be retained only by butchers' shops. This part of London having escaped the Great Fire, I suppose there may be many relics of architectural antiquity hereabouts.

At the end of an hour I went back to the Refreshment-room, within the outer gate of the Tower, where the rest of us shortly appeared. We now returned westward by way of Great Tower Street, Eastcheap, and Cannon Street, and, entering St. Paul's, sat down beneath the misty dome to rest ourselves.   The muffled roar of the city, as we heard it there, is very soothing, and keeps one listening to it, somewhat as the flow of a river keeps us looking at it.   It is a grand and quiet sound; and, ever and anon, a distant door slammed somewhere in the cathedral, and reverberated long and heavily, like the roll of thunder or the boom of cannon.   Every noise that is loud enough to be heard in so vast an edifice melts into the

no idea is to be developed from the use of glass as a building material, instead of brick and stone. It will have its own rules and its own results; but meanwhile, even the present Palace is positively a very beautiful object. On entering we found the atmosphere chill and comfortless, — more so, it seemed to me, than the open air itself. It was not a genial day; though now and then the sun gleamed out, and once caused fine effects in the glass-work of a crystal fountain in one of the courts.

We were under Mr. Silsbee's guidance for the day, . . . and first we looked at the sculpture, which is composed chiefly of casts or copies of the most famous statues of all ages, and likewise of those crumbs and little fragments which have fallen from Time's jaw, — and half-picked bones, as it were, that have been gathered up from spots where he has feasted full, — torsos, heads and broken limbs, some of them half worn away, as if they had been rolled over and over in the sea. I saw nothing in the sculptural way, either modern or antique, that impressed me so much as a statue of a nude mother by a French artist. In a sitting posture, with one knee over the other, she was clasping her highest knee with both hands; and in the hollow cradle thus formed by her arms lay two sweet little babies, as snug and close to her heart as if they had not yet been born, — two little love-blossoms, — and the mother encircling them and pervading them with love. But an infinite pathos and strange terror are given to this group by some faint bas-reliefs on the pedestal, indicating that the happy mother is Eve, and Cain and Abel the two innocent babes.

Then we went to the Alhambra, which looks like an enchanted palace. If it had been a sunny day, I should have enjoyed it more; but it was miserable to shiver and shake in the Court of the Lions, and in those chambers which were contrived as places of refuge from a fervid temperature. Furthermore, it is not quite agreeable to see such clever specimens of stage decoration; they are so very good that it gets to be past a joke, without becoming actual earnest. I had not a similar feeling in respect to the reproduction of mediæval statues, arches, doorways, all brilliantly colored as in the days of their first glory; yet I do not know but that the first is as little objectionable as the last. Certainly, in both cases, scenes and objects of a past age are here more vividly presented to the dullest mind than without such material facilities they could possibly be brought before the most powerful imagination. Truly, the Crystal Palace, in all its departments, offers wonderful means of education. I marvel what will come of it. Among the things that

I admired most was Benvenuto Cellini's statue of Perseus holding the head of Medusa, and standing over her headless and still writhing body, out of which, at the severed neck, gushed a vast exuberance of snakes. Likewise a sitting statue by Michel Angelo, of one of the Medici, full of dignity and grace and reposeful might. Also the bronze gate of a baptistery in Florence, carved all over with relievos of Scripture subjects, executed in the most lifelike and expressive manner. The cast itself was a miracle of art. I should have taken it for the genuine original bronze.

We then wandered into the House of Diomed, which seemed to me a dismal abode, affording no possibility of comfort. We sat down in one of the rooms, on an iron bench, very cold.

It being by this time two o'clock, we went to the Refreshment-room and lunched — and before we had finished our repast, my wife discovered that she had lost her sable tippet, which she had been carrying on her arm. Mr. Silsbee most kindly and obligingly immediately went in quest of it, . . . but to no purpose. . . .

Upon entering the Tropical Saloon, we found a most welcome and delightful change of temperature among those gigantic leaves of banyan-trees, and the broad expanse of water-plants floating on lakes, and spacious aviaries, where birds of brilliant plumage sported and sang amid such foliage as they knew at home. Howbeit, the atmosphere was a little faint and sickish, perhaps owing to the odor of the half-tepid water. The most remarkable object here was the trunk of a tree, huge beyond imagination, — a pine-tree from California. It was only the stripped-off bark, however, which had been conveyed hither in segments, and put together again beyond the height of the palace roof; and the hollow interior circle of the tree was large enough to contain fifty people, I should think. We entered and sat down in all the remoteness from one another that is attainable in a good-sized drawing-room. We then ascended the gallery to get a view of this vast tree from a more elevated position, and found it looked even bigger from above. Then we loitered slowly along the gallery as far as it extended, and afterwards descended into the nave; for it was getting dusk, and a horn had sounded, and a bell rung a warning to such as delayed in the remote regions of the building. Mr. Silsbee again most kindly went in quest of the sables, but still without success. . . . I have not much enjoyed the Crystal Palace, but think it a great and admirable achievement.

November 19. — On Tuesday evening Mr. Silsbee came to read some letters which he has written to his friends, chiefly giving his observations on Art, together with descriptions of Venice and other cities on the Continent. They were very good, and indicate much sensibility and talent. After the reading we had a little oyster-supper and wine.

I had written a note to ———, and received an answer indicating that he was much weighed down by his financial misfortune. . . . However, he desired me to come and see him ; so yesterday morning I wended my way down into the city, and after various reluctant circumlocutions arrived at his house. The interior looked confused and dismal.

.   .   .   .

It seems to me nobody else runs such risks as a man of business, because he risks everything. Every other man, into whatever depth of poverty he may sink, has still something left, be he author, scholar, handicraftman, or what not ; the merchant has nothing.

We parted with a long and strong grasp of the hand, and ——— promised to come and see us soon.

On my way home I called at Trübner's in Paternoster Row. . . . I waited a few minutes, he being busy with a tail, muscular, English-built man, who, after he had taken leave, Trübner told me was Charles Reade. I once met him at an evening party, but should have been glad to meet him again, now that I appreciate him so much better after reading Never too Late to Mend.

December 6. — All these days, since my last date, have been marked by nothing very well worthy of detail and description. I have walked the streets a great deal in the dull November days, and always take a certain pleasure in being in the midst of human life, — as closely encompassed by it as it is possible to be anywhere in this world ; and in that way of viewing it there is a dull and sombre enjoyment always to be had in Holborn, Fleet Street, Cheapside, and the other busiest parts of London. It is human life ; it is this material world ; it is a grim and heavy reality. I have never had the same sense of being surrounded by materialisms and hemmed in with the grossness of this earthly existence anywhere else ; these broad, crowded streets are so evidently the veins and arteries of an enormous city. London is evidenced in every one of them, just as a megatherium is in each of its separate bones, even if they be small ones. Thus I never fail of a sort of self-congratulation in finding myself, for instance, passing along Ludgate Hill ; but, in spite of this, it is really an ungladdened life to wander through these huge, thronged ways, over a pavement foul with

mud, ground into it by a million of footsteps;
jostling against people who do not seem to be
individuals, but all one mass, so homogeneous
is the street-walking aspect of them; the roar
of vehicles pervading me, — wearisome cabs and
omnibuses; everywhere the dingy brick edifices
heaving themselves up, and shutting out all but
a strip of sullen cloud, that serves London for
a sky, — in short, a general impression of grime
and sordidness; and at this season always a fog
scattered along the vista of streets, sometimes
so densely as almost to spiritualize the materi-
alism, and make the scene resemble the other
world of worldly people, gross even in ghostli-
ness. It is strange how little splendor and brilliancy one sees in London, — in the city almost
none, though some in the shops of Regent
Street. My wife has had a season of indisposition within the last few weeks, so that my rambles have generally been solitary, or with Julian
only for a companion. I think my only excursion with my wife was a week ago, when we
went to Lincoln's Inn Fields, which truly are
almost fields right in the heart of London, and
as retired and secluded as if the surrounding
city were a forest, and its heavy roar were the
wind among the branches. We gained admission into the noble Hall, which is modern, but
built in antique style, and stately and beautiful
exceedingly. I have forgotten all but the gen-

eral effect, with its lofty oaken roof, its panelled walls, with the windows high above, and the great arched window at one end full of painted coats of arms, which the light glorifies in passing through them, as if each were the escutcheon of some illustrious personage. Thence we went to the chapel of Lincoln's Inn, where, on entering, we found a class of young choristers receiving instruction from their music-master, while the organ accompanied their strains. These young, clear, fresh, elastic voices are wonderfully beautiful; they are like those of women, yet have something more birdlike and aspiring, more like what one conceives of the singing of angels. As for the singing of saints and blessed spirits that have once been human, it never can resemble that of these young voices; for no duration of heavenly enjoyments will ever quite take the mortal sadness out of it.

In this chapel we saw some painted windows of the time of James I., a period much subsequent to the age when painted glass was in its glory; but the pictures of Scriptural people in these windows were certainly very fine, — the figures being as large as life, and the faces having much expression. The sunshine came in through some of them, and produced a beautiful effect, almost as if the painted forms were the glorified spirits of those holy personages.

After leaving Lincoln's Inn, we looked at

Gray's Inn, which is a great, quiet domain, quadrangle beyond quadrangle, close beside Holborn, and a large space of greensward enclosed within it. It is very strange to find so much of ancient quietude right in the monster city's very jaws, which yet the monster shall not eat up, — right in its very belly, indeed, which yet, in all these ages, it shall not digest and convert into the same substance as the rest of its bustling streets. Nothing else in London is so like the effect of a spell, as to pass under one of these archways, and find yourself transported from the jumble, mob, tumult, uproar, as of an age of week-days condensed into the present hour, into what seems an eternal sabbath. Thence we went into Staples Inn, I think it was, — which has a front upon Holborn of four or five ancient gables in a row, and a low arch under the impending story, admitting you into a paved quadrangle, beyond which you have the vista of another. I do not understand that the residences and chambers in these Inns of Court are now exclusively let to lawyers; though such inhabitants certainly seem to preponderate there.

Since then Julian and I walked down into the Strand, and found ourselves unexpectedly mixed up with a crowd that grew denser as we approached Charing Cross, and became absolutely impermeable when we attempted to make our way to Whitehall. The wicket in the gate of

Northumberland House, by the bye, was open, and gave me a glimpse of the front of the edifice within, — a very partial glimpse, however, and that obstructed by the solid person of a foot-man, who, with some women, was passing out from within. The crowd was a real English crowd, perfectly undemonstrative, and entirely decorous, being composed mostly of well-dressed people, and largely of women. The cause of the assemblage was the opening of Parliament by the Queen, but we were too late for any chance of seeing her Majesty. However, we extricated ourselves from the multitude, and, going along Pall Mall, got into the Park by the steps at the foot of the Duke of York's Column, and thence went to the Whitehall Gateway, outside of which we found the Horse-Guards drawn up : a regi-ment of black horses and burnished cuirasses. On our way thither an open carriage came through the gateway into the Park, conveying two ladies in court dresses ; and another splen-did chariot pressed out through the gateway, — the coachman in a cocked hat and scarlet and gold embroidery, and two other scarlet and gold figures hanging behind. It was one of the Queen's carriages, but seemed to have nobody in it. I have forgotten to mention what, I think, produced more effect on me than anything else, namely, the clash of the bells from the steeple of St. Martin's Church and those of St. Mar-garet.   Really, London seemed to cry out through them, and bid welcome to the Queen.

December 7. — This being a muddy and dismal day, I went only to the British Museum, which is but a short walk down the street (Great Russell Street).   I have now visited it often enough to be on more familiar terms with it than at first, and therefore do not feel myself so weighed down by the many things to be seen.   I have ceased to expect or hope or wish to devour and digest the whole enormous collection; so I content myself with individual things, and succeed in getting now and then a little honey from them.   Unless I were studying some particular branch of history or science or art, this is the best that can be done with the British Museum.

I went first to-day into the Townley Gallery, and so along through all the ancient sculpture, and was glad to find myself able to sympathize more than heretofore with the forms of grace and beauty which are preserved there, — poor, maimed immortalities as they are, — headless and legless trunks, godlike cripples, faces beautiful and broken-nosed, — heroic shapes which have stood so long, or lain prostrate so long, in the open air, that even the atmosphere of Greece has almost dissolved the external layer of the marble ; and yet, however much they be worn away, or battered and shattered, the grace and nobility seems as deep in them as the very heart of the stone. It cannot be destroyed, except by grinding them to powder. In short, I do really believe that there was an excellence in ancient sculpture, which has yet a potency to educate and refine the minds of those who look at it even so carelessly and casually as I do. As regards the frieze of the Parthenon, I must remark that the horses represented on it, though they show great spirit and lifelikeness, are rather of the pony species than what would be considered fine horses now. Doubtless, modern breeding has wrought a difference in the animal. Flaxman, in his outlines, seems to have imitated these classic steeds of the Parthenon, and thus has produced horses that always appeared to me affected and diminutively monstrous.

From the classic sculpture, I passed through an Assyrian room, where the walls are lined with great slabs of marble sculptured in bas-relief with scenes in the life of Sennacherib, I believe; very ugly, to be sure, yet artistically done in their own style, and in wonderfully good preservation. Indeed, if the chisel had cut its last stroke in them yesterday, the work could not be more sharp and distinct. In glass cases, in this room, are little relics and scraps of utensils, and a great deal of fragmentary rubbish, dug up by Layard in his researches, — things that it is hard to call anything but trash, but which yet may be of

great significance as indicating the modes of life
of a long-past race. I remember nothing particularly just now, except some pieces of broken
glass, iridescent with certainly the most beautiful hues in the world, — indescribably beautiful,
and unimaginably, unless one can conceive of
the colors of the rainbow, and a thousand glorious sunsets, and the autumnal forest leaves of
America, all condensed upon a little fragment
of a glass cup, — and that, too, without becoming in the least glaring or flagrant, but mildly
glorious, as we may fancy the shifting hues of an
angel's wing may be. I think this chaste splendor will glow in my memory for years to come.
It is the effect of time, and cannot be imitated
by any known process of art. I have seen it in
specimens of old Roman glass, which has been
famous here in England ; but never in anything
is there the brilliancy of these Oriental fragments. How strange that decay, in dark places
and underground, and where there are a bil-
lion chances to one that nobody will ever see
its handiwork, should produce these beautiful
effects ! The glass seems to become perfectly
brittle, so that it would vanish, like a soap-bub-
ble, if touched.

Ascending the stairs, I went through the halls
of fossil remains, — which I care little for,
though one of them is a human skeleton in
limestone, — and through several rooms of min-

eralogical specimens, including all the gems in the world, among which is seen, not the Koh-i-noor itself, but a facsimile of it in crystal. I think the aerolites are as interesting as anything in this department, and one piece of pure iron, laid against the wall of the room, weighs about fourteen hundred pounds. Whence could it have come? If these aerolites are bits of other planets, how happen they to be always iron? But I know no more of this than if I were a philosopher.

Then I went through rooms of shells and fishes, and reptiles and tortoises, crocodiles and alligators and insects, including all manner of butterflies, some of which had wings precisely like leaves, a little withered and faded, even the skeleton and fibres of the leaves represented; and immense hairy spiders, covering, with the whole circumference of their legs, a space as big as a saucer; and centipedes little less than a foot long; and winged insects that look like jointed twigs of a tree. In America, I remember, when I lived in Lenox, I found an insect of this species, and at first really mistook it for a twig. It was smaller than these specimens in the Museum. I suppose every creature, almost, that runs or creeps or swims or flies, is represented in this collection of Natural History; and it puzzles me to think what they were all made for, though it is quite as mysterious why man himself was made.

By and by I entered the room of Egyptian mummies, of which there are a good many, one of which, the body of a priestess, is unrolled, except the innermost layer of linen. The outline of her face is perfectly visible. Mummies of cats, dogs, snakes, and children are in the wall-cases, together with a vast many articles of Egyptian manufacture and use, — even children's toys; bread, too, in flat cakes; grapes, that have turned to raisins in the grave; queerest of all, methinks, a curly wig, that is supposed to have belonged to a woman, — together with the wooden box that held it. The hair is brown, and the wig is as perfect as if it had been made for some now living dowager.

From Egypt we pass into rooms containing vases and other articles of Grecian and Roman workmanship, and funeral urns, and beads, and rings, none of them very beautiful. I saw some splendid specimens, however, at a former visit, when I obtained admission to a room not indiscriminately shown to visitors. What chiefly interested me in that room was a cast taken from the face of Cromwell after death; representing a wide-mouthed, long-chinned, uncomely visage, with a triangular English nose in the very centre. There were various other curiosities, which I fancied were safe in my memory, but they do not now come uppermost.

To return to my to-day's progress through the Museum: next to the classic rooms are the collections of Saxon and British and early English antiquities, the earlier portions of which are not very interesting to me, possessing little or no beauty in themselves, and indicating a kind of life too remote from our own to be readily sympathized with.   Who cares for glass beads and copper brooches, and knives, spear-heads, and swords, all so rusty that they look as much like pieces of old iron hoop as anything else? The bed of the Thames has been a rich treasury of antiquities, from the time of the Roman Conquest downwards; it seems to preserve bronze in considerable perfection, but not iron.

Among the mediæval relics, the carvings in ivory are often very exquisite and elaborate. There are likewise caskets and coffers, and a thousand other Old World ornamental works; but I saw so many and such superior specimens of them at the Manchester Exhibition, that I shall say nothing of them here.   The seal-ring of Mary Queen of Scots is in one of the cases; it must have been a thumb-ring, judging from its size, and it has a dark stone, engraved with armorial bearings.   In another case is the magic glass formerly used by Dr. Dee, and in which, if I rightly remember, used to be seen pro-

phetic visions or figures of persons and scenes
at a distance.   It is a round ball of glass or crystal, slightly tinged with a pinkish hue, and
about as big as a small apple, or a little bigger
than an egg would be if perfectly round. This
ancient humbug kept me looking at it perhaps
ten minutes; and I saw my own face dimly in
it, but no other vision. Lastly, I passed through
the Ethnographical Rooms; but I care little
for the varieties of the human race, — all that
is really important and interesting being found
in our own variety. Perhaps equally in any
other. This brought me to the head of one of
the staircases, descending which I entered the
library.

Here — not to speak of the noble rooms and
halls — there are numberless treasures beyond
all price; too valuable in their way for me to
select any one as more curious and valuable
than many others. Letters of statesmen and
warriors of all nations, and several centuries
back, — among which, long as it has taken Europe to produce them, I saw none so illustrious as those of Washington, nor more so than
Franklin's, whom America gave to the world in
her nonage; and epistles of poets and artists,
and of kings, too, whose chirography appears to
have been much better than I should have expected from fingers so often cramped in iron
gauntlets. In another case there were the ori-

ginal autograph copies of several famous works, — for example, that of Pope's Homer, written on the backs of letters, the direction and seals of which appear in the midst of "the Tale of Troy divine," which also is much scratched and interlined with Pope's corrections; a manuscript of one of Ben Johnson's masques; of the Sentimental Journey, written in much more careful and formal style than might be expected, the book pretending to be a harum-scarum; of Walter Scott's Kenilworth, bearing such an aspect of straightforward diligence that I shall hardly think of it again as a romance; — in short, I may as well drop the whole matter here.

All through the long vista of the king's library, we came to cases in which — with their pages open beneath the glass — we see books worth their weight in gold, either for their uniqueness or their beauty, or because they have belonged to illustrious men, and have their autographs in them. The copy of the English translation of Montaigne, containing the strange scrawl of Shakespeare's autograph, is here. Bacon's name is in another book; Queen Elizabeth's in another; and there is a little devotional volume, with Lady Jane Grey's writing in it. She is supposed to have taken it to the scaffold with her. Here, too, I saw a copy, which was printed at a Venetian press at the time, of the challenge which the Admirable

Crichton caused to be posted on the church
doors of Venice, defying all the scholars of Italy
to encounter him. But if I mentioned one
thing, I find fault with myself for not putting
down fifty others just as interesting, — and,
after all, there is an official catalogue, no doubt,
of the whole.

As I do not mean to fill any more pages with
the British Museum, I will just mention the
hall of Egyptian antiquities, on the ground-
floor of the edifice, though I did not pass
through it to-day. They consist of things that
would be very ugly and contemptible if they
were not so immensely magnified; but it is
impossible not to acknowledge a certain grandeur, resulting from the scale on which those
strange old sculptors wrought. For instance,
there is a granite fist of prodigious size, at least
a yard across, and looking as if it were doubled
in the face of Time, defying him to destroy it.
All the rest of the statue to which it belonged
seems to have vanished; but this fist will certainly outlast the Museum, and whatever else
it contains, unless it be some similar Egyptian
ponderosity. There is a beetle, wrought out
of immensely hard black stone, as big as a hogs-
head. It is satisfactory to see a thing so big and
heavy. Then there are huge stone sarcophagi,
engraved with hieroglyphics within and without,
all as good as new, though their age is reckoned

by thousands of years. These great coffins are of vast weight and mass, insomuch that when once the accurately fitting lids were shut down, there might have seemed little chance of their being lifted again till the Resurrection. I positively like these coffins, they are so faithfully made, and so black and stern, — and polished to such a nicety, only to be buried forever; for the workmen and the kings who were laid to sleep within could never have dreamed of the British Museum.

There is a deity named Pasht, who sits in the hall, very big, very grave, carved of black stone, and very ludicrous, wearing a dog's head. I will just mention the Rosetta Stone, with a Greek inscription, and another in Egyptian characters which gave the clew to a whole field of history; and shall pretermit all further handling of this unwieldy subject.

In all the rooms I saw people of the poorer classes, some of whom seemed to view the objects intelligently, and to take a genuine interest in them. A poor man in London has great opportunities of cultivating himself if he will only make the best of them; and such an institution as the British Museum can hardly fail to attract, as the magnet does steel, the minds that are likeliest to be benefited by it in its various departments. I saw many children there, and come ragged boys.

It deserves to be noticed that some small figures of Indian Thugs, represented as engaged in their profession and handiwork of cajoling and strangling travellers, have been removed from the place which they formerly occupied in the part of the Museum shown to the general public. They are now in the more private room, and the reason of their withdrawal is, that, according to the Chaplain of Newgate, the practice of garroting was suggested to the English thieves by this representation of Indian Thugs. It is edifying, after what I have written in the preceding paragraph, to find that the only lesson known to have been inculcated here is that of a new mode of outrage.

December 8. — This morning, when it was time to rise, there was but a glimmering of daylight, and we had candles on the breakfast-table at nearly ten o'clock. All abroad there was a dense dim fog brooding through the atmosphere, insomuch that we could hardly see across the street. At eleven o'clock I went out into the midst of the fog bank, which for the moment seemed a little more interfused with daylight; for there seem to be continual changes in the density of this dim medium, which varies so much that now you can but just see your hand before you, and a moment afterwards you can see the cabs dashing out of the duskiness a

score of yards off. It is seldom or never, moreover, an unmitigated gloom, but appears to be
mixed up with sunshine in different proportions; sometimes only one part sun to a thousand of smoke and fog, and sometimes sunshine
enough to give the whole mass a coppery hue.
This would have been a bright sunny day but
for the interference of the fog; and before I
had been out long, I actually saw the sun looking red and rayless, much like the millionth
magnification of a new halfpenny.

I was bound towards Bennoch's; for he had
written a note to apologize for not visiting us,
and I had promised to call and see him to-day.

.   .   .   .

I went to Marlborough House to look at
the English pictures, which I care more about
seeing, here in England, than those of foreign
artists, because the latter will be found more
numerously and better on the Continent. I saw
many pictures that pleased me; nothing that
impressed me very strongly. Pictorial talent
seems to be abundant enough, up to a certain
point; pictorial genius, I should judge, is among
the rarest of gifts. To be sure, I very likely
might not recognize it where it existed; and yet
it ought to have the power of making itself
known even to the uninstructed mind, as literary genius does. If it exist only for connoisseurs, it is a very suspicious matter. I looked

at all Turner's pictures, and at many of his drawings ; and must again confess myself wholly unable to understand more than a very few of
them.   Even those few are tantalizing.   At a
certain distance you discern what appears to be
a grand and beautiful picture, which you shall
admire and enjoy infinitely if you can get within
the range of distinct vision.   You come nearer,
and find only blotches of color and dabs of the
brush, meaning nothing when you look closely,
and meaning a mystery at the point where the
painter intended to station you.   Some landscapes there were, indeed, full of imaginative
beauty, and of the better truth etherealized out
of the prosaic truth of nature ; only it was still
impossible actually to see it.   There was a mist
over it ; or it was like a tract of beautiful dream-
land, seen dimly through sleep, and glimmering
out of sight, if looked upon with wide-open eyes.
These were the more satisfactory specimens.
There were many others which I could not comprehend in the remotest degree ; not even so
far as to conjecture whether they purported to
represent earth, sea, or sky.   In fact, I should
not have known them to be pictures at all, but
might have supposed that the artist had been
trying his brush on the canvas, mixing up all
sorts of hues, but principally white paint, and
now and then producing an agreeable harmony
of color without particularly intending it.   Now

that I have done my best to understand them without an interpreter, I mean to buy Ruskin's pamphlet at my next visit, and look at them through his eyes. But I do not think that I can be driven out of the idea that a picture ought to have something in common with what the spectator sees in nature.

Marlborough House may be converted, I think, into a very handsome residence for the young Prince of Wales. The entrance from the courtyard is into a large, square central hall, the painted ceiling of which is at the whole height of the edifice, and has a gallery on one side, whence it would be pleasant to look down on a festal scene below. The rooms are of fine proportions, with vaulted ceilings, and with fireplaces and mantelpieces of great beauty, adorned with pillars and terminal figures of white and of variegated marble ; and in the centre of each mantel-piece there is a marble tablet, exquisitely sculptured with classical designs, done in such high relief that the figures are sometimes almost disengaged from the background. One of the subjects was Androcles, or whatever was his name, taking the thorn out of the lion's foot. I suppose these works are of the era of the first old Duke and Duchess. After all, however, for some reason or other, the house does not at first strike you as a noble and princely one, and you have to convince yourself of it by examining it more in detail.

On leaving Marlborough House I stepped for a few moments into the National Gallery, and looked, among other things, at the Turners and Claudes that hung there side by side. These pictures, I think, are quite the most comprehensible of Turner's productions; but I must say I prefer the Claudes. The latter catches " the light that never was on sea or land " without taking you quite away from nature for it. Nevertheless, I will not be quite certain that I care for any painter except Murillo, whose St. John I should like to own. As far as my own pleasure is concerned, I could not say as much for any other picture; for I have always found an infinite weariness and disgust resulting from a picture being too frequently before my eyes. I had rather see a basilisk, for instance, than the very best of those old, familiar pictures in the Boston Athenæum; and most of those in the National Gallery might soon affect me in the same way.

From the Gallery I almost groped my way towards the city, for the fog seemed to grow denser and denser as I advanced; and when I reached St. Paul's, the sunny intermixture above spoken of was at its minimum, so that the smoke-cloud grew really black about the dome

and pinnacles, and the statues of saints looked
down dimly from their standpoints on high. It
was very grand, however, to see the pillars and
porticos, and the huge bulk of the edifice, heaving up its dome from an obscure foundation
into yet more shadowy obscurity; and by the
time I reached the corner of the churchyard
nearest Cheapside, the whole vast cathedral had
utterly vanished, leaving " not a wrack behind,"
unless those thick, dark vapors were the elements of which it had been composed, and into
which it had again dissolved. It is good to
think, nevertheless, — and I gladly accept the
analogy and the moral, — that the cathedral was
really there, and as substantial as ever, though
those earthly mists had hidden it from mortal
eyes.

I found —— in better spirits than when I saw
him last, but his misfortune has been too real
not to affect him long and deeply. He was cheerful, however, and his face shone with almost its
old lustre. It has still the cheeriest glow that
I ever saw in any human countenance.

.   .   .   .

I went home by way of Holborn, and the
fog was denser than ever, — very black, indeed
more more like a distillation of mud than anything else ; the ghost of mud, — the spiritual-
ized medium of departed mud, through which
the dead citizens of London probably tread in

the Hades whither they are translated. So
heavy was the gloom, that gas was lighted in all
the shop windows ; and the little charcoal fur-
naces of the women and boys, roasting chestnuts, threw a ruddy, misty glow around them.
And yet I liked it. This fog seems an atmosphere proper to huge, grimy London ; as proper to London as that light neither of the sun
nor moon is to the New Jerusalem.

On reaching home, I found the same fog diffused through the drawing-room, though how
it could have got in is a mystery. Since nightfall, however, the atmosphere is clear again.

December 20. — Here we are still in London,
at least a month longer than we expected, and
at the very dreariest and dullest season of the
year. Had I thought of it sooner, I might
have found interesting people enough to know,
even when all London is said to be out of town ;
but meditating a stay only of a week or two (on
our way to Rome), it did not seem worth while
to seek acquaintances.

I have been out only for one evening ; and
that was at Dr. ——'s, who had been attending
all the children in the measles. (Their illness
was what detained us.) He is a homœopathist,
and is known in scientific or general literature ;
at all events, a sensible and enlightened man,
with an un-English freedom of mind on some

points.   For example, he is a Swedenborgian,
and a believer in modern spiritualism.   He
showed me some drawings that had been made
under the spiritual influence by a miniature-
painter who possesses no imaginative power of
his own, and is merely a good mechanical and
literal copyist ; but these drawings, representing
angels and allegorical people, were done by an
influence which directed the artist's hand, he
not knowing what his next touch would be, nor
what the final result.   The sketches certainly
did show a high and fine expressiveness, if
examined in a trustful mood.   Dr. —— also
spoke of Mr. Harris, the American poet of
spiritualism, as being the best poet of the day ;
and he produced his works in several volumes,
and showed me songs, and paragraphs of longer
poems, in support of his opinion.   They
seemed to me to have a certain light and splendor, but not to possess much power, either passionate or intellectual.   Mr. Harris is the medium of deceased poets, Milton and Lord Byron
among the rest ; and Dr. —— said that Lady
Byron — who is a devoted admirer of her husband, in spite of their conjugal troubles — pronounced some of these posthumous strains to
be worthy of his living genius.   Then the Doc-
tor spoke of various strange experiences which
he himself has had in these spiritual matters ;
for he has witnessed the miraculous perform-

ances of Home, the American medium, and he has seen with his own eyes, and felt with his own touch, those ghostly hands and arms the reality of which has been certified to me by other beholders.   Dr. —— tells me that they are cold, and that it is a somewhat awful matter to see and feel them.   I should think so, indeed.   Do I believe in these wonders?   Of course; for how is it possible to doubt either the solemn word or the sober observation of a learned and sensible man like Dr. ——?   But again, do I really believe it?   Of course not; for I cannot consent to have heaven and earth, this world and the next, beaten up together like the white and yolk of an egg, merely out of respect to Dr. ——'s sanity and integrity.   I would not believe my own sight, nor touch of the spiritual hands; and it would take deeper and higher strains than those of Mr. Harris to convince me.   I think I *might* yield to higher poetry or heavenlier wisdom than mortals in the flesh have ever sung or uttered.   Meanwhile, this matter of spiritualism is surely the strangest that ever was heard of; and yet I feel unaccountably little interest in it, — a sluggish disgust, and repugnance to meddle with it, — insomuch that I hardly feel as if it were worth this page or two in my not very eventful journal.   One or two of the ladies present at Dr. ——'s little party seemed to be mediums.

I have made several visits to the picture galleries since my last date; and I think it fair towards my own powers of appreciation to record that I begin to appreciate Turner's pictures rather better than at first. Not that I have anything to recant as respects those strange, white-grounded performances in the chambers at the Marlborough House; but some of his happier productions (a large landscape illustrative of Childe Harold, for instance) seem to me to have more magic in them than any other pictures. I admire, too, that misty morning landscape in the National Gallery; and no doubt his very monstrosities are such as only he could have painted, and may have an infinite value for those who can appreciate the genius in them.

The shops in London begin to show some tokens of approaching Christmas; especially the toy shops, and the confectioners' — the latter ornamenting their windows with a profusion of bon-bons and all manner of pygmy figures in sugar; the former exhibiting Christmas trees hung with rich and gaudy fruit. At the butchers' shops, there is a great display of fat carcasses, and an abundance of game at the poulterers'. We think of going to the Crystal Palace to spend the festival day and eat our Christmas dinner; but, do what we may, we shall have no home feeling or fireside enjoyment. I am weary, weary of London and of

England, and can judge now how the old Loyal-
ists must have felt, condemned to pine out their
lives here, when the Revolution had robbed
them of their native country.   And yet there
is still a pleasure, being in this dingy, smoky,
midmost haunt of men ; and I trudge through
Fleet Street and Ludgate Street and along
Cheapside with an enjoyment as great as I ever
felt in a wood-path at home ; and I have come
to know these streets as well, I believe, as I
ever knew Washington Street in Boston, or
even Essex Street in my stupid old native town.
For Piccadilly or for Regent Street, though more
brilliant promenades, I do not care nearly so
much.

December 27. — Still leading an idle life,
which, however, may not be quite thrown away,
as I see some things, and think many thoughts.

The other day we went to Westminster Abbey,
and through the chapels ; and it being as sunny
a day as could well be in London, and in December, we could judge, in some small degree,
what must have been the splendor of those
tombs and monuments when first erected there.

I presume I was sufficiently minute in de-
scribing my first visit to the chapels, so I shall
only mention the stiff figure of a lady of Queen
Elizabeth's court, reclining on the point of her
elbow under a mural arch through all these

dusty years ; . . . and the old coronation chair, with the stone of Scone beneath the seat, and the wood-work cut and scratched all over with names and initials. . . .

I continue to go to the picture galleries. I have an idea that the face of Murillo's St. John has a certain mischievous intelligence in it. This has impressed me almost from the first. It is a boy's face, very beautiful and very pleasant too, but with an expression that one might fairly suspect to be roguish if seen in the face of a living boy.

About equestrian statues, as those of various kings at Charing Cross, and otherwhere about London, and of the Duke of Wellington opposite Apsley House, and in front of the Exchange, it strikes me as absurd, the idea of putting a man on horseback on a place where one movement of the steed forward or backward or sideways would infallibly break his own and his rider's neck. The English sculptors generally seem to have been aware of this absurdity, and have endeavored to lessen it by making the horse as quiet as a cab-horse on the stand, instead of rearing rampant, like the bronze group of Jackson at Washington. The statue of Wellington at the Piccadilly corner of the Park has a stately and imposing effect, seen from far distances, in approaching either through the Green Park or from the Oxford Street corner of Hyde Park.

January 3, 1858. — On Thursday we had the pleasure of a call from Mr. Coventry Patmore, to whom Dr. Wilkinson gave me a letter of introduction, and on whom I had called twice at the British Museum without finding him. We had read his Betrothal and Angel in the House with unusual pleasure and sympathy, and therefore were very glad to make his personal acquaintance. He is a man of much more youthful aspect than I had expected, . . . a slender person to be an Englishman, though not remarkably so had he been an American ; with an intelligent, pleasant, and sensitive face, — a man very evidently of refined feelings and cultivated mind. . . . He is very simple and agreeable in his manners ; a little shy, yet perfectly frank, and easy to meet on real grounds. . . . He said that his wife had proposed to come with him, and had, indeed, accompanied him to town, but was kept away. . . . We were very sorry for this, because Mr. Patmore seems to acknowledge her as the real Angel in the House, although he says she herself ignores all connection with the poem. It is well for her to do so, and for her husband to feel that the character is her real portrait; and both, I suppose, are right. It is a most beautiful and original poem, — a poem for happy married people to read together, and to understand by the light of their own past and present life ; but

I doubt whether the generality of English people are capable of appreciating it.   I told Mr. Patmore that I thought his popularity in America would be greater than at home, and he said that it was already so ; and he appeared to estimate highly his American fame, and also our general gift of quicker and more subtle recognition of genius than the English public. . . . We mutually gratified each other by expressing high admiration of one another's works, and Mr. Patmore regretted that in the few days of our further stay here we should not have time to visit him at his home.   It would really give me pleasure to do so. . . . I expressed a hope of seeing him in Italy during our residence there, and he seemed to think it possible, as his friend, and our countryman, Thomas Buchanan Read, had asked him to come thither and be his guest. He took his leave, shaking hands with all of us because he saw that we were of his own people, recognizing him as a true poet.   He has since given me the new edition of his poems, with a kind note.

We are now making preparations for our departure, which we expect will take place on Tuesday ; and yesterday I went to our Minister's to arrange about the passport.   The very moment I rang at his door, it swung open, and the porter ushered me with great courtesy into the anteroom ; not that he knew me, or anything about me, except that I was an American citizen. This is the deference which an American servant of the public finds it expedient to show to his sovereigns. Thank Heaven, I am a sovereign again, and no longer a servant; and really it is very singular how I look down upon our ambassadors and dignitaries of all sorts — not excepting the President himself. I doubt whether this is altogether a good influence of our mode of government.

I did not see, and in fact declined seeing, the Minister himself, but only his son, the Secretary of Legation, and a Dr. P——, an American traveller just from the Continent. He gave a fearful account of the difficulties that beset a person landing with much luggage in Italy, and especially at Civita Vecchia, the very port at which we intended to debark. I have been so long in England that it seems a cold and shivery thing to go anywhere else.

Bennoch came to take tea with us on the 5th, it being his first visit since we came to London, and likewise his farewell visit on our leaving for the Continent.

. . . .

On his departure, Julian and I walked a good way down Oxford Street and Holborn with him, and I took leave of him with the kindest wishes for his welfare.

PARIS. — *Hôtel de Louvre, January 6,
1858.* — On Tuesday morning, our
dozen trunks and half-dozen carpet-bags
being all ready packed and labelled, we began
to prepare for our journey two or three hours
before light. Two cabs were at the door by
half past six, and at seven we set out for the
London Bridge station, while it was still dark
and bitterly cold. There were already many
people in the streets, growing more numerous
as we drove cityward; and, in Newgate Street,
there was such a number of market-carts, that
we almost came to a deadlock with some of
them. At the station we found several persons
who were apparently going in the same train
with us, sitting round the fire of the waiting-
room. Since I came to England there has
hardly been a morning when I should have less
willingly bestirred myself before daylight; so
sharp and inclement was the atmosphere. We
started at half past eight, having taken through
tickets to Paris by way of Folkestone and Boulogne. A foot-warmer (a long, flat, tin utensil,
full of hot water) was put into the carriage just
before we started; but it did not make us more
than half comfortable, and the frost soon began
to cloud the windows and shut out the prospect,

126

so that we could only glance at the green fields
—immortally green, whatever winter can do
against them — and, at here and there, a stream
or pool with the ice forming on its borders. It
was the first cold weather of a very mild season.
The snow began to fall in scattered and almost
invisible flakes; and it seemed as if we had
stayed our English welcome out, and were to
find nothing genial and hospitable there any
more.

At Folkestone we were deposited at a railway station close upon a shingly beach, on which
the sea broke in foam, and which Julian reported
as strewn with shells and star-fish; behind was
the town, with an old church in the midst; and
close at hand the pier, where lay the steamer in
which we were to embark. But the air was so
wintry that I had no heart to explore the town,
or pick up shells with Julian on the beach; so
we kept within doors during the two hours of
our stay, now and then looking out of the windows at a fishing-boat or two, as they pitched
and rolled with an ugly and irregular motion,
such as the British Channel generally communi-
cates to the craft that navigate it.

At about one o'clock we went on board, and
were soon under steam, at a rate that quickly
showed a long line of the white cliffs of Albion
behind us. It is a very dusky white, by the
bye, and the cliffs themselves do not seem, at a

distance, to be of imposing height, and have too even an outline to be picturesque.

As we increased our distance from England, the French coast came more and more distinctly in sight, with a low, wavy outline, not very well worth looking at, except because it was the coast of France.   Indeed, I looked at it but little ; for the wind was bleak and boisterous, and I went down into the cabin, where I found the fire very comfortable, and several people were stretched on sofas in a state of placid wretchedness. . . . I have never suffered from sea-sickness, but had been somewhat apprehensive of this rough strait between England and France, which seems to have more potency over people's stomachs than ten times the extent of sea in other quarters.   Our passage was of two hours, at the end of which we landed on French soil, and found ourselves immediately in the clutches of the custom-house officers, — who, however, merely made a momentary examination of my passport, and allowed us to pass without opening even one of our carpet-bags.   The great bulk of our luggage had been registered through to Paris, for examination after our arrival there.

We left Boulogne in about an hour after our arrival, when it was already a darkening twilight. The weather had grown colder than ever, since our arrival in sunny France, and the night was now setting in, wickedly black and dreary.   The frost hardened upon the carriage windows in such thickness that I could scarcely scratch a peep-hole through it; but, from such glimpses as I could catch, the aspect of the country seemed pretty much to resemble the December aspect of my dear native land, — broad, bare, brown fields, with streaks of snow at the foot of ridges, and along fences, or in the furrows of ploughed soil. There was ice wherever there happened to be water to form it.

We had feet-warmers in the carriage, but the cold crept in, nevertheless; and I do not remember hardly in my life a more disagreeable short journey than this, my first advance into French territory. My impression of France will always be that it is an arctic region. At any season of the year, the tract over which we passed yesterday must be an uninteresting one as regards its natural features; and the only adornment, as far as I could observe, which art has given it consists in straight rows of very stiff-looking and slender-stemmed trees. In the dusk they resembled poplar-trees.

Weary and frost-bitten, — morally, if not physically, — we reached Amiens in three or four hours, and here I underwent much annoyance from the French railway officials and attendants, who, I believe, did not mean to incommode me, but rather to forward my purposes as far as they well could. If they would speak slowly and distinctly I might understand them well enough, being perfectly familiar with the written language, and knowing the principles of its pronunciation; but, in their customary rapid utterance, it sounds like a string of mere gabble. When left to myself, therefore, I got into great difficulties. . . . It gives a taciturn personage like myself a new conception as to the value of speech, even to him, when he finds himself unable either to speak or understand.

Finally, being advised on all hands to go to the Hôtel de Rhin, we were carried thither in an omnibus, rattling over a rough pavement, through an invisible and frozen town; and, on our arrival, were ushered into a handsome *salon*, as chill as a tomb. They made a little bit of a wood fire for us in a low and deep chimney-hole, which let a hundred times more heat escape up the flue than it sent into the room.

In the morning we sallied forth to see the Cathedral.

The aspect of the old French town was very different from anything English; whiter, infinitely cleaner; higher and narrower houses, the entrance to most of them seeming to be through a great gateway affording admission into a central courtyard; a public square, with a statue in the middle, and another statue in a neighboring street. We met priests in three-cornered hats, long frock-coats, and knee-breeches ; also soldiers and gendarmes, and peasants and children, clattering over the pavements in wooden shoes.

It makes a great impression of outlandishness to see the signs over the shop doors in a foreign tongue. If the cold had not been such as to dull my sense of novelty, and make all my perceptions torpid, I should have taken in a set of new impressions, and enjoyed them very much. As it was, I cared little for what I saw, but yet had life enough left to enjoy the Cathedral of Amiens, which has many features unlike those of English cathedrals.

It stands in the midst of the cold, white town, and has a high-shouldered look to a spectator accustomed to the minsters of England, which cover a great space of ground in proportion to their height. The impression the latter gives is of magnitude and mass ; this French Cathedral strikes one as lofty. The exterior is venerable, though but little time-worn by the action of the atmosphere ; and statues still keep their places in numerous niches, almost as perfect as when first placed there in the thirteenth century. The principal doors are deep, elaborately wrought, pointed arches ; — and the interior seemed to us, at the moment, as grand as any that we had seen, and to afford as vast an idea of included space ; it being of such an airy height,

and with no screen betwixt the chancel and
nave, as in all the English cathedrals.   We saw
the differences, too, between a church in which
the same form of worship for which it was originally built is still kept up, and those of England, where it has been superseded for centuries ;
for here, in the recess of every arch of the side-
aisles, beneath each lofty window, there was a
chapel dedicated to some saint, and adorned
with great marble sculptures of the crucifixion,
and with pictures, execrably bad, in all cases,
and various kinds of gilding and ornamentation.
Immensely tall wax candles stand upon the altars
of these chapels, and before one sat a woman,
with a great supply of tapers, one of which was
burning.   I suppose these were to be lighted
as offerings to the saints, by the true believers.
Artificial flowers were hung at some of the
shrines, or placed under glass.   In every chapel,
moreover, there was a confessional, — a little
oaken structure, about as big as a sentry-box,
with a closed part for the priest to sit in, and an
open one for the penitent to kneel at, and speak
through the open-work of the priest's closet.
Monuments, mural and others, to long-departed
worthies, and images of the Saviour, the Virgin,
and saints, were numerous everywhere about the
church ; and in the chancel there was a great
deal of quaint and curious sculpture, fencing in
the Holy of Holies, where the high altar stands.

There is not much painted glass; one or two
very rich and beautiful rose-windows, however,
that looked antique; and the great eastern window, which, I think, is modern. The pavement
has, probably, never been renewed, as one piece
of work, since the structure was erected, and is
foot-worn by the successive generations, though
still in excellent repair.   I saw one of the small,
square stones in it, bearing the date of 1597,
and no doubt there are a thousand older ones.
It was gratifying to find the Cathedral in such
good condition, without any traces of recent
repair; and it is perhaps a mark of difference
between French and English character, that the
Revolution in the former country, though all
religious worship disappears before it, does not
seem to have caused such violence to ecclesiastical monuments as the Reformation and the reign
of Puritanism in the latter. I did not see a mu-
tilated shrine, or even a broken-nosed image, in
the whole Cathedral.   But, probably, the very
rage of the English fanatics against idolatrous
tokens, and their smashing blows at them, were
symptoms of sincerer religious faith than the
French were capable of.   These last did not
care enough about their Saviour to beat down
his crucified image; and they preserved the
works of sacred art, for the sake only of what
beauty there was in them.

While we were in the Cathedral, we saw several persons kneeling at their devotions on the steps of the chancel and elsewhere. One dipped his fingers in the holy water at the entrance: by the bye, I looked into the stone basin that held it, and saw it full of ice. Could not all that sanctity at least keep it thawed? Priests, — jolly, fat, mean-looking fellows, in white robes, — went hither and thither, but did not interrupt or accost us.

There were other peculiarities, which I suppose I shall see more of in my visits to other churches, but now we were all glad to make our stay as brief as possible, the atmosphere of the Cathedral being so bleak, and its stone pavement so icy cold beneath our feet. We returned to the hotel, and the chambermaid brought me a book, in which she asked me to inscribe my name, age, profession, country, destination, and the authorization under which I travelled. After the freedom of an English hotel, so much greater than even that of an American one, where they make you disclose your name, this is not so pleasant.

We left Amiens at half past one; and I can tell as little of the country between that place and Paris, as between Boulogne and Amiens. The windows of our railway carriage were already frosted with French breath when we got into it, and the ice grew thicker and thicker continually. I tried, at various times, to rub a peep-

hole through, as before; but the ice immediately
shot its crystallized tracery over it again; and,
indeed, there was little or nothing to make it
worth while to look out, so bleak was the scene.
Now and then a château, too far off for its
characteristics to be discerned; now and then a
church, with a tall gray tower, and a little peak
atop; here and there a village or a town, which
we could not well see. At sunset, there was just
that clear, cold, wintry sky which I remember
so well in America, but have never seen in England.

At five we reached Paris, and were suffered
to take a carriage to the Hôtel de Louvre, without any examination of the little luggage we had
with us. Arriving, we took a suite of apartments
and the waiter immediately lighted a wax candle
in each separate room.

We might have dined at the *table d'hôte*, but
preferred the restaurant connected with and
within the hotel. All the dishes were very delicate, and a vast change from the simple English
system, with its joints, shoulders, beefsteaks, and
chops; but I doubt whether English cookery,
for the very reason that it is so simple, is not
better for men's moral and spiritual nature than
French. In the former case, you know that you
are gratifying your animal needs and propensi-
ties, and are duly ashamed of it; but, in dealing
with these French delicacies, you delude your-

self into the idea that you are cultivating your
taste while satisfying your appetite.   This last,
however, it requires a good deal of perseverance
to accomplish.

In the Cathedral at Amiens there were printed
lists of acts of devotion posted on the columns,
such as prayers at the shrines of certain saints,
whereby plenary indulgences might be gained.
It is to be observed, however, that all these external forms were necessarily accompanied with
true penitence and religious devotion.

Hôtel de Louvre, January 8. — It was so fearfully cold this morning that I really felt little
or no curiosity to see the city. . . . Until after
one o'clock, therefore, I knew nothing of Paris
except the lights which I had seen beneath our
window the evening before, far, far downward
in the narrow Rue St. Honoré, and the rumble
of the wheels, which continued later than I was
awake to hear it, and began again before dawn.
I could see, too, tall houses, that seemed to be
occupied in every story, and that had windows
on the steep roofs.   One of these houses is six
stories high.   This Rue St. Honoré is one of
the old streets in Paris, and is that in which
Henry IV. was assassinated ; but it has not, in
this part of it, the aspect of antiquity.

After one o'clock we all went out and walked
along the Rue de Rivoli. . . . We are here,

right in the midst of Paris, and close to whatever is best known to those who hear or read about it, — the Louvre being across the street, the Palais Royal but a little way off, the Tuileries joining to the Louvre, the Place de la Concorde just beyond, verging on which is the Champs Elysées.   We looked about us for a suitable place to dine, and soon found the Restaurant des Echelles, where we entered at a venture, and were courteously received.   It has a handsomely furnished saloon, much set off with gilding and mirrors; and appears to be frequented by English and Americans; its *carte*, a bound volume, being printed in English as well as French. . . .

It was now nearly four o'clock, and too late to visit the galleries of the Louvre, or to do anything else but walk a little way along the street. The splendor of Paris, so far as I have seen, takes me altogether by surprise: such stately edifices, prolonging themselves in unwearying magnificence and beauty, and, ever and anon, a long vista of a street, with a column rising at the end of it, or a triumphal arch, wrought in memory of some grand event.   The light stone or stucco, wholly untarnished by smoke and soot, puts London to the blush, if a blush could be seen on its dingy face ; but, indeed, London is not to be mentioned with, nor compared even with Paris.   I never knew what a palace was till

I had a glimpse of the Louvre and Tuileries; never had my idea of a city been gratified till I trod those stately streets.   The life of the scene, too, is infinitely more picturesque than that of London, with its monstrous throng of grave faces and black coats, — whereas there you see soldiers and priests, policemen in cocked hats, Zouaves with turbans, long mantles, and bronzed, half Moorish faces; and a great many people whom you perceive to be outside of your experience, and know them ugly to look at, and fancy them villanous.   Truly, I have no sympathies towards the French people; their eyes do not win me, nor do their glances melt and mingle with mine.   But they do grand and beautiful things in the architectural way; and I am grateful for it.   The Place de la Concorde is a most splendid square, large enough for a nation to erect trophies in of all its triumphs; and on one side of it is the Tuileries, on the opposite side the Champs Elysées, and on a third the Seine, adown which we saw large cakes of ice floating, beneath the arches of a bridge.   The Champs Elysées, so far as I saw it, had not a grassy soil beneath its trees, but the bare earth, white and dusty.   The very dust, if I saw nothing else, would assure me that I was out of England.

We had time only to take this little walk, when it began to grow dusk; and, being so pitilessly cold, we hurried back to our hotel.

Thus far, I think, what I have seen of Paris is wholly unlike what I expected; but very like an imaginary picture which I had conceived of St. Petersburg, — new, bright, magnificent, and desperately cold.

A great part of this architectural splendor is due to the present Emperor, who has wrought a great change in the aspect of the city within a very few years. A traveller, if he looks at the thing selfishly, ought to wish him a long reign and arbitrary power, since he makes it his policy to illustrate his capital with palatial edifices, which are, however, better for a stranger to look at than for his own people to pay for.

We have spent to-day chiefly in seeing some of the galleries of the Louvre. I must confess that the vast and beautiful edifice struck me far more than the pictures, sculpture, and curiosities which it contains, — the shell more than the kernel inside; such noble suites of rooms and halls were those through which we first passed, containing Egyptian, and, farther onward, Greek and Roman antiquities; the walls cased in variegated marbles; the ceilings glowing with beautiful frescos; the whole extended into infinite vistas by mirrors that seemed like vacancy, and multiplied everything forever. The picture rooms are not so brilliant, and the pictures themselves did not greatly win upon me in this one day. Many artists were employed

in copying them, especially in the rooms hung
with the productions of French painters.   Not
a few of these copyists were females ; most of
them were young men, picturesquely mustached
and bearded ; but some were elderly, who, it
was pitiful to think, had passed through life
without so much success as now to paint pictures of their own.

From the pictures we went into a suite of
rooms where are preserved many relics of the
ancient and later kings of France ; more relics
of the elder ones, indeed, than I supposed had
remained extant through the Revolution. The
French seem to like to keep memorials of whatever they do, and of whatever their forefathers
have done, even if it be ever so little to their
credit ; and perhaps they do not take matters
sufficiently to heart to detest anything that has
ever happened. What surprised me most were
the golden sceptre and the magnificent sword
and other gorgeous relics of Charlemagne, —
a person whom I had always associated with a
sheepskin cloak. There were suits of armor
and weapons that had been worn and handled
by a great many of the French kings ; and a
religious book that had belonged to St. Louis ;
a dressing-glass, most richly set with precious
stones, which formerly stood on the toilet-table
of Catherine de' Medici, and in which I saw my
own face where hers had been.   And there were

a thousand other treasures, just as well worth mentioning as these.   If each monarch could have been summoned from Hades to claim his own relics, we should have had the halls full of the old Childerics, Charleses, Bourbons and Capets, Henrys and Louises, snatching with ghostly hands at sceptres, swords, armor, and mantles ; and Napoleon would have seen, apparently, almost everything that personally belonged to him, — his coat, his cocked hats, his camp-desk, his field-bed, his knives, forks, and plates, and even a lock of his hair.   I must let it all go.   These things cannot be reproduced by pen and ink.

Hôtel de Louvre, January 9. — . . . Last evening Mr. Fezandie called.   He spoke very freely respecting the Emperor, and the hatred entertained against him in France ; but said that he is more powerful, that is, more firmly fixed as a ruler, than ever the first Napoleon was.   We, who look back upon the first Napoleon as one of the eternal facts of the past, a great boulder in history, cannot well estimate how momentary and unsubstantial the great Captain may have appeared to those who beheld his rise out of obscurity.   They never, perhaps, took the reality of his career fairly into their minds, before it was over.   The present Emperor, I believe, has already been as long in possession of the supreme power as his uncle was. I should like to see him, and may, perhaps, do so, as he is our neighbor across the way.

This morning Miss ——, the celebrated astronomical lady, called. She had brought a letter of introduction to me, while consul; and her purpose now was to see if we could take her as one of our party to Rome, whither she likewise is bound. We readily consented, for she seems to be a simple, strong, healthy-humored woman, who will not fling herself as a burden on our shoulders; and my only wonder is that a person evidently so able to take care of herself should wish to have an escort.

We issued forth at about eleven, and went down the Rue St. Honoré, which is narrow, and has houses of five or six stories on either side, between which runs the street like a gully in a rock. One face of our hotel borders and looks on this street. After going a good way, we came to an intersection with another street, the name of which I forget; but, at this point, Ravaillac sprang at the carriage of Henry IV. and plunged his dagger into him. As we went down the Rue St. Honoré, it grew more and more thronged, and with a meaner class of people. The houses still were high, and without the shabbiness of exterior that distinguishes the old part of London, — being of light-colored stone ; but I never saw anything that so much came up to my idea of a swarming city as this narrow, crowded, and rambling street.

Thence we turned into the Rue St. Denis, which is one of the oldest streets in Paris, and is said to have been first marked out by the track of the saint's footsteps, where, after his martyrdom, he walked along it, with his head under his arm, in quest of a burial-place. This legend may account for any crookedness of the street; for it could not reasonably be asked of a headless man that he should walk straight.

Through some other indirections we at last found the Rue Bergère, down which I went with Julian in quest of Hottinguer & Co., the bankers, while the rest of us went along the Boulevards, towards the church of the Madeleine. . . . This business accomplished, Julian and I threaded our way back, and overtook the rest of the party, still a good distance from the Madeleine. I know not why the Boulevards are called so. They are a succession of broad walks through broad streets, and were much thronged with people, most of whom appeared to be bent more on pleasure than business. The sun, long before this, had come out brightly, and gave us the first genial and comfortable sensations which we have had in Paris.

Approaching the Madeleine, we found it a most beautiful church, that might have been

adapted from Heathenism to Catholicism; for
on each side there is a range of magnificent pillars, unequalled except by those of the Parthenon.   A mourning coach, arrayed in black and
silver, was drawn up at the steps, and the front
of the church was hung with black cloth, which
covered the whole entrance.   However, seeing
the people going in, we entered along with
them. Glorious and gorgeous is the Madeleine.
The entrance to the nave is beneath a most
stately arch; and three arches of equal height
open from the nave to the side-aisles; and at
the end of the nave is another great arch, rising,
with a vaulted half-dome, over the high altar.
The pillars supporting these arches are Corinthian, with richly sculptured capitals; and wherever gilding might adorn the church, it is lavished like sunshine; and within the sweeps of
the arches there are fresco paintings of sacred
subjects, and a beautiful picture covers the hollow of the vault over the altar; all this, besides
much sculpture; and especially a group above
and around the high altar, representing the Mag-
dalen smiling down upon angels and archan-
gels, some of whom are kneeling, and shadow-
ing themselves with their heavy marble wings.
There is no such thing as making my page glow
with the most distant idea of the magnificence
of this church, in its details and in its whole.
It was founded a hundred or two hundred years

ago ; then Bonaparte contemplated transform-
ing it into a Temple of Victory, or building it
anew as one. The restored Bourbon remade it
into a church ; but it still has a heathenish look,
and will never lose it.

When we entered we saw a crowd of people,
all pressing forward towards the high altar, before which burned a hundred wax lights, some
of which were six or seven feet high ; and, altogether, they shone like a galaxy of stars. In the
middle of the nave, moreover, there was another
galaxy of wax candles burning around an immense pall of black velvet, embroidered with
silver, which seemed to cover, not only a coffin,
but a sarcophagus, or something still more huge.
The organ was rumbling forth a deep, lugubri-
ous bass, accompanied with heavy chanting of
priests, out of which sometimes rose the clear,
young voices of choristers, like light flashing out
of the gloom. The church, between the arches,
along the nave, and round the altar, was hung
with broad expanses of black cloth ; and all the
priests had their sacred vestments covered with
black. They looked exceedingly well ; I never
saw anything half so well got up on the stage.
Some of these ecclesiastical figures were very
stately and noble, and knelt and bowed, and
bore aloft the cross, and swung the censers in a
way that I liked to see. The ceremonies of the
Catholic Church were a superb work of art, or

perhaps a true growth of man's religious nature ; and so long as men felt their original meaning, they must have been full of awe and glory. Being of another parish, I looked on coldly, but not irreverently, and was glad to see the funeral service so well performed, and very glad when it was over. What struck me as singular, the person who performed the part usually performed by a verger, keeping order among the audience, wore a golden-embroidered scarf, a cocked hat, and, I believe, a sword, and had the air of a military man.

Before the close of the service a contribution box — or, rather, a black velvet bag — was handed about by this military verger ; and I gave Julian a franc to put in, though I did not in the least know for what.

Issuing from the church, we inquired of two or three persons who was the distinguished defunct at whose obsequies we had been assisting, for we had some hope that it might be Rachel, who died last week, and is still above ground. But it proved to be only a Madame Mentel, or some such name, whom nobody had ever before heard of. I forgot to say that her coffin was taken from beneath the illuminated hall, and carried out of the church before us.

When we left the Madeleine we took our way to the Place de la Concorde, and thence through the Elysian Fields (which, I suppose, are the French idea of heaven) to Bonaparte's triumphal arch. The Champs Elysées may look pretty in summer; though I suspect they must be somewhat dry and artificial at whatever season, — the trees being slender and scraggy, and requiring to be renewed every few years. The soil is not genial to them. The strangest peculiarity of this place, however, to eyes fresh from moist and verdant England, is, that there is not one blade of grass in all the Elysian Fields, nothing but hard clay, now covered with white dust. It gives the whole scene the air of being a contrivance of man, in which nature has either not been invited to take any part, or has declined to do so. There were merry-go-rounds, wooden horses, and other provision for children's amusements among the trees; and booths, and tables of cakes and candy-women; and restaurants on the borders of the wood; but very few people there; and doubtless we can form no idea of what the scene might become when alive with French gayety and vivacity.

As we walked onward the Triumphal Arch began to loom up in the distance, looking huge and massive, though still a long way off. It was not, however, till we stood almost beneath it that we really felt the grandeur of this great arch, including so large a space of the blue sky in its airy sweep. At a distance, it impresses the spectator with its solidity; nearer, with the lofty vacancy beneath it.   There is a spiral staircase within one of its immense limbs ; and, climbing steadily upward, lighted by a lantern which the door-keeper's wife gave us, we had a bird's-eye view of Paris, much obscured by smoke or mist. Several interminable avenues shoot with painful directness right towards it.

On our way homeward we visited the Place Vendôme, in the centre of which is a tall column, sculptured from top to bottom, all over the pedestal, and all over the shaft, and with Napoleon himself on the summit.   The shaft is wreathed round and round about with representations of what, as far as I could distinguish, seemed to be the Emperor's victories.   It has a very rich effect.   At the foot of the column we saw wreaths of artificial flowers, suspended there, no doubt, by some admirer of Napoleon, still ardent enough to expend a franc or two in this way.

Hôtel de Louvre, January 10. — We had purposed going to the Cathedral of Notre Dame today, but the weather and walking were too unfavorable for a distant expedition ; so we merely went across the street to the Louvre. . . .

Our principal object this morning was to see the pencil drawings by eminent artists. Of these the Louvre has a very rich collection, occupying many apartments, and comprising sketches

148

by Annibal Caracci, Claude, Raphael, Leonardo da Vinci, Michel Angelo, Rubens, Rembrandt, and almost all the other great masters, whether French, Italian, Dutch, or whatever else; the earliest drawings of their great pictures, when they had the glory of their pristine idea directly before their minds' eye, — that idea which inevitably became overlaid with their own handling of it in the finished painting. No doubt, the painters themselves had often a happiness in these rude, off-hand sketches which they never felt again in the same work, and which resulted in disappointment, after they had done their best. To an artist, the collection must be most deeply interesting: to myself, it was merely curious, and soon grew wearisome.

In the same suite of apartments, there is a collection of miniatures, some of them very exquisite, and absolutely lifelike, on their small scale. I observed two of Franklin, both good and picturesque, one of them especially so, with its cloud-like white hair. I do not think we have produced a man so interesting to contemplate, in many points of view, as he. Most of our great men are of a character that I find it impossible to warm into life by thought, or by lavishing any amount of sympathy upon them. Not so Franklin, who had a great deal of common and uncommon human nature in him.

Much of the time, while my wife was looking at the drawings, I sat observing the crowd of Sunday visitors. They were generally of a lower class than those of week days : private soldiers in a variety of uniforms, and, for the most part, ugly little men, but decorous and well behaved. I saw medals on many of their breasts, denoting Crimean service ; some were the English medal, with Queen Victoria's head upon it. A blue coat, with red, baggy trousers, was the most usual uniform. Some had short-breasted coats, made in the same style as those of the first Napoleon, which we had seen in the preceding rooms. The policemen, distributed pretty abundantly about the rooms, themselves looked military, wearing cocked hats and swords. There were many women of the middling classes ; some, evidently, of the lowest, but clean and decent, in colored gowns and caps ; and laboring men, citizens, Sunday gentlemen, young artists, too, no doubt looking with educated eyes at these art treasures, and I think, as a general thing, each man was mated with a woman. The soldiers, however, came in pairs or little squads, accompanied by women. I did not much like any of the French faces, and yet I am not sure that there is not more resemblance between them and the American physiognomy, than between the latter and the English. The women are not pretty, but in all ranks above the lowest they have a

trained expression that supplies the place of
beauty.

I was wearied to death with the drawings, and
began to have that dreary and desperate feeling
which has often come upon me when the sights
last longer than my capacity for receiving them.
As our time in Paris, however, is brief and precious, we next inquired our way to the galleries
of sculpture, and these alone are of astounding
extent, reaching, I should think, all round one
quadrangle of the Louvre, on the basement floor.
Hall after hall opened interminably before us,
and on either side of us, paved and encrusted
with variegated and beautifully polished marble,
relieved against which stand the antique statues
and groups, interspersed with great urns and
vases, sarcophagi, altars, tablets, busts of historic
personages, and all manner of shapes of marble
which consummate art has transmuted into precious stones.   Not that I really did feel much
impressed by any of this sculpture then, nor saw
more than two or three things which I thought
very beautiful ; but whether it be good or no, I
suppose the world has nothing better, unless it
be a few world-renowned statues in Italy.   I was
even more struck by the skill and ingenuity of
the French in arranging these sculptural remains,
than by the value of the sculptures themselves.
The galleries, I should judge, have been recently
prepared, and on a magnificent system, — the

adornments being yet by no means completed, — for besides the floor and wall-casings of rich, polished marble, the vaulted ceilings of some of the apartments are painted in fresco, causing them to glow as if the sky were opened. It must be owned, however, that the statuary, often time-worn and darkened from its original brilliancy by weather-stains, does not suit well as furniture for such splendid rooms. When we see a per-fection of modern finish around them, we recog-nize that most of these statues had been thrown down from their pedestals, hundreds of years ago, and have been battered and externally de-graded; and though whatever spiritual beauty they ever had may still remain, yet this is not made more apparent by the contrast betwixt the new gloss of modern upholstery, and their tar-nished, even if immortal grace. I rather think the English have given really the more hospit-able reception to the maimed Theseus, and his broken-nosed, broken-legged, headless compan-ions, because flouting them with no gorgeous fittings up.

By this time poor Julian (who, with his taste for art yet undeveloped, is the companion of all our visits to sculpture and picture galleries) was wofully hungry, and for bread we had given him a stone, — not one stone, but a thousand. We returned to the hotel, and it being too damp and raw to go to our Restaurant des Echelles, we

dined at the hotel.   In my opinion it would require less time to cultivate our gastronomic taste
than taste of any other kind ; and, on the whole,
I am not sure that a man would not be wise to
afford himself a little discipline in this line.   It
is certainly throwing away the bounties of Providence, to treat them as the English do, producing from better materials than the French have
to work upon nothing but sirloins, joints, joints,
steaks, steaks, steaks, chops, chops, chops, chops!
We had a soup to-day, in which twenty kinds
of vegetables were represented, and manifested
each its own aroma ; a fillet of stewed beef, and
a fowl, in some sort of delicate fricassee.   We
had a bottle of Chablis, and renewed ourselves,
at the close of the banquet, with a plate of
Chateaubriand ice.   It was all very good, and
we respected ourselves far more than if we had
eaten a quantity of red roast beef; but I am not
quite sure that we were right. . . .

Among the relics of kings and princes, I do
not know that there was anything more interesting than a little brass cannon, two or three
inches long, which had been a toy of the unfor-
tunate Dauphin, son of Louis XVI.   There
was a map, — a hemisphere of the world, —
which his father had drawn for this poor boy ;
very neatly done, too.   The sword of Louis
XVI., a magnificent rapier, with a beautifully
damasked blade ; and a jewelled scabbard, but

without a hilt, is likewise preserved, as is the hilt of Henry IV.'s sword.   But it is useless to begin a catalogue of these things.   What a collection it is, including Charlemagne's sword and sceptre, and the last Dauphin's little toy cannon, and so much between the two !

Hôtel de Louvre, January 11. — This was another chill, raw day, characterized by a spitefulness of atmosphere which I do not remember ever to have experienced in my own dear country.   We meant to have visited the Hôtel des Invalides, but Julian and I walked to the Rivoli, the Place de la Concorde, the Champs Elysées, and to the Place de Beaujon, and to the residence of the American minister, where I wished to arrange about my passport.   After speaking with the Secretary of Legation, we were ushered into the minister's private room, where he received me with great kindness.   Mr. —— is an old gentleman with a white head, and a large, florid face, which has an expression of amiability, not unmingled with a certain dignity. He did not rise from his armchair to greet me, — a lack of ceremony which I imputed to the gout, feeling it impossible that he should have willingly failed in courtesy to one of his twenty-five million sovereigns.   In response to some remark of mine about the shabby way in which our government treats its officials pecuniarily, he gave a detailed account of his own troubles on that score; then expressed a hope that I had made a good thing out of my consulate, and inquired whether I had received a hint to resign; to which I replied that, for various reasons, I had resigned of my own accord, and before Mr. Buchanan's inauguration. We agreed, however, in disapproving the system of periodical change in our foreign officials; and I remarked that a consul or an ambassador ought to be a citizen both of his native country and of the one in which he resided; and that his possibility of beneficent influence depended largely on his being so. Apropos to which Mr. —— said that he had once asked a diplomatic friend of long experience what was the first duty of a minister. "To love his own country, and to watch over its interests," answered the diplomatist. "And his second duty?" asked Mr. ——. "To love and to promote the interests of the country to which he is accredited," said his friend. This is a very Christian and sensible view of the matter; but it can scarcely have happened once in our whole diplomatic history, that a minister can have had time to overcome his first rude and ignorant prejudice against the country of his mission; and if there were any suspicion of his having done so, it would be held abundantly sufficient ground for his recall. I like Mr. ——, a good-hearted, sensible old man.

Julian and I returned along the Champs Elysées, and, crossing the Seine, kept on our way by the river's brink, looking at the titles of books on the long lines of stalls that extend between the bridges.   Novels, fairy tales, dream books, treatises of behavior and etiquette, collections of *bon-mots* and of songs, were interspersed with volumes in the old style of calf and gilt binding, the works of the classics of French literature.   A good many persons, of the poor classes, and of those apparently well to do, stopped transitorily to look at these books. On the other side of the street was a range of tall edifices with shops beneath, and the quick stir of French life hurrying, and babbling, and swarming along the sidewalk.   We passed two or three bridges, occurring at short intervals, and at last we recrossed the Seine by a bridge which oversteps the river, from a point near the National Institute, and reaches the other side, not far from the Louvre. . . .

Though the day was so disagreeable, we thought it best not to lose the remainder of it, and therefore set out to visit the Cathedral of Notre Dame.   We took a fiacre in the Place de Carrousel, and drove to the door.   On entering, we found the interior miserably shut off from view by the stagings erected for the purpose of repairs.   Penetrating from the nave towards the chancel, an official personage signified to us that we must first purchase a ticket for each grown person, at the price of half a franc each. This expenditure admitted us into the sacristy, where we were taken in charge by a guide, who came down upon us with an avalanche or cataract of French, descriptive of a great many treasures deposited in this chapel. I understood hardly more than one word in ten, but gathered doubtfully that a bullet which was shown us was the one that killed the late Archbishop of Paris, on the floor of the Cathedral. [But this was a mistake. It was the archbishop who was killed in the insurrection of 1848. Two joints of his backbone were also shown.] Also, that some gorgeously embroidered vestments, which he drew forth, had been used at the coronation of Napoleon I. There were two large, full-length portraits hanging aloft in the sacristy, and a gold or silver gilt, or, at all events, gilt image, of the Virgin, as large as life, standing on a pedestal. The guide had much to say about these, but, understanding him so imperfectly, I have nothing to record.

The guide's supervision of us seemed not to extend beyond this sacristy, on quitting which he gave us permission to go where we pleased, only intimating a hope that we would not forget him; so I gave him half a franc, though thereby violating an inhibition on the printed ticket of entrance.

We had been much disappointed at first by the apparently narrow limits of the interior of this famous church; but now, as we made our way round the choir, gazing into chapel after chapel, each with its painted window, its crucifix, its pictures, its confessional, and afterwards came back into the nave, where arch rises above arch to the lofty roof, we came to the conclusion that it was very sumptuous.   It is the greatest of pities that its grandeur and solemnity should just now be so infinitely marred by the workmen's boards, timber, and ladders occupying the whole centre of the edifice, and screening all its best effects.   It seems to have been already most richly ornamented, its roof being painted, and the capitals of the pillars gilded, and their shafts illuminated in fresco; and no doubt it will shine out gorgeously when all the repairs and adornments shall be completed.   Even now it gave to my actual sight what I have often tried to imagine in my visits to the English cathedrals, — the pristine glory of those edifices, when they stood glowing with gold and picture, fresh from the architects' and adorners' hands.

The interior loftiness of Notre Dame, moreover, gives it a sublimity which would swallow up anything that might look gewgawy in its ornamentation, were we to consider it window by window, or pillar by pillar.   It is an advantage of these vast edifices, rising over us and spread-

ing about us in such a firmamental way, that we
cannot spoil them by any pettiness of our own,
but that they receive (or absorb) our pettiness
into their own immensity. Every little fantasy
finds its place and propriety in them, like a flower
on the earth's broad bosom.

When we emerged from the Cathedral, we
found it beginning to rain or snow, or both ; and,
as we had dismissed our fiacre at the door, and
could find no other, we were at a loss what to
do. We stood a few moments on the steps
of the Hôtel Dieu, looking up at the front of
Notre Dame, with its twin towers, and its three
deep-pointed arches, piercing through a great
thickness of stone, and throwing a cavern-like
gloom around these entrances. The front is very
rich. Though so huge, and all of gray stone,
it is carved and fretted with statues and innumerable devices, as cunningly as any ivory casket
in which relics are kept ; but its size did not so
much impress me. . . .

Hôtel de Louvre, January 12.— This has been
a bright day as regards weather ; but I have
done little or nothing worth recording. After
breakfast, I set out in quest of the consul, and
found him up a court, at 51 Rue Cammartin,
in an office rather smaller, I think, than mine
at Liverpool ; but, to say the truth, a little better furnished. I was received in the outer apart-

ment by an elderly, brisk-looking man, in whose air, respectful and subservient, and yet with a kind of authority in it, I recognized the vice-consul. He introduced me to Mr. ——, who sat writing in an inner room ; a very gentle-manly, courteous, cool man of the world, whom I should take to be an excellent person for con-sul at Paris. He tells me that he has resided here some years, although his occupancy of the consulate dates only from November last. Con-sulting him respecting my passport, he gave me what appear good reasons why I should get all the necessary *visés* here ; for example, that the *visé* of a minister carries more weight than that of a consul ; and especially that an Austrian con-sul will never *visé* a passport unless he sees his minister's name upon it. Mr. —— has trav-elled much in Italy, and ought to be able to give me sound advice. His opinion was, that at this season of the year I had better go by steamer to Città Vecchia, instead of landing at Leghorn, and thence journeying to Rome. On this point I shall decide when the time comes. As I left the office the vice-consul informed me that there was a charge of five francs and some sous for the consul's *visé*, a tax which surprised me, — the whole business of passports having been taken from consuls before I quitted office, and the consular fee having been annulled even earlier. However, no doubt Mr. —— had a fair claim

The Cathedral of Notre Dame, Paris

to my five francs; but, really, it is not half so pleasant to pay a consular fee as it used to be to receive it.

Afterwards I walked to Notre Dame, the rich front of which I viewed with more attention than yesterday. There are whole histories, carved in stone figures, within the vaulted arches of the three entrances in this west front, and twelve apostles in a row above, and as much other sculpture as would take a month to see. We then walked quite round it, but I had no sense of immensity from it, not even that of great height, as from many of the cathedrals in England. It stands very near the Seine; indeed, if I mistake not, it is on an island formed by two branches of the river. Behind it is what seems to be a small public ground (or garden, if a space entirely denuded of grass or other green thing except a few trees can be called so), with benches, and a monument in the midst. This quarter of the city looks old, and appears to be inhabited by poor people, and to be busied about small and petty affairs; the most picturesque business that I saw being that of the old woman who sells crucifixes of pearl and of wood at the cathedral door. We bought two of these yesterday.

I must again speak of the horrible muddiness, not only of this part of the city, but of all Paris, so far as I have traversed it to-day. My ways, since I came to Europe, have often lain through nastiness, but I never before saw a pavement so universally overspread with mud-padding as that of Paris. It is difficult to imagine where so much filth can come from.

After dinner I walked through the gardens of the Tuileries ; but as dusk was coming on, and as I was afraid of being shut up within the iron railing, I did not have time to examine them particularly. There are wide, intersecting walks, fountains, broad basins, and many statues ; but almost the whole surface of the gardens is barren earth, instead of the verdure that would beautify an English pleasure-ground of this sort. In the summer it has doubtless an agreeable shade ; but at this season the naked branches look meagre, and sprout from slender trunks. Like the trees in the Champs Elysées, those, I presume, in the gardens of the Tuileries need renewing every few years. The same is true of the human race, — families becoming extinct after a generation or two of residence in Paris. Nothing really thrives here ; man and vegetables have but an artificial life, like flowers stuck in a little mould, but never taking root. I am quite tired of Paris, and long for a home more than ever.

MARSEILLES, *Hôtel d' Angleterre, January* 15. — On Tuesday morning (12th) we took our departure from the Hôtel de Louvre. It is a most excellent and perfectly ordered hotel, and I have not seen a more magnificent hall in any palace than the dining - saloon, with its profuse gilding, and its ceiling, painted in compartments ; so that when the chandeliers are all alight, it looks a fit place for princes to banquet in, and not very fit for the few Americans whom I saw scattered at its long tables.

By the bye, as we drove to the railway, we passed through the public square where the Bastille formerly stood ; and in the centre of it now stands a column, surmounted by a golden figure of Mercury (I think), which seems to be just on the point of casting itself from a gilt ball into the air. This statue is so buoyant, that the spectator feels quite willing to trust it to the viewless element, being as sure that it would be borne up as that a bird would fly.

Our first day's journey was wholly without interest, through a country entirely flat, and looking wretchedly brown and barren. There were rows of trees, very slender, very prim and formal ; there was ice wherever there happened to be any water to form it ; there were occasional villages, compact little streets or masses of stone or plastered cottages, very dirty and with gable ends and earthen roofs ; and a succession of this same landscape was all that we saw, whenever we rubbed away the congelation

163

of our breath from the carriage windows. Thus we rode on all day long, from eleven o'clock, with hardly a five minutes' stop, till long after dark, when we came to Dijon, where there was a halt of twenty-five minutes for dinner. Then we set forth again, and rumbled forward, through cold and darkness without, until we reached Lyons at about ten o'clock. We left our luggage at the railway station, and took an omnibus for the Hôtel de Provence, which we chose at a venture, among a score of other hotels.

As this hotel was a little off the direct route of the omnibus, the driver set us down at the corner of a street, and pointed to some lights, which he said designated the Hôtel de Provence ; and thither we proceeded, all seven of us, taking along a few carpet-bags and shawls, our equipage for the night. The porter of the hotel met us near its doorway, and ushered us through an arch into the inner quadrangle, and then up some old and worn steps, — very broad and appearing to be the principal staircase. At the first landing-place, an old woman and a waiter or two received us ; and we went up two or three more flights of the same broad and worn stone staircases. What we could see of the house looked very old, and had the musty odor with which I first became acquainted at Chester.

After ascending to the proper level, we were conducted along a corridor, paved with octag-

onal earthen tiles; on one side were windows,
looking into the courtyard; on the other, doors
opening into the sleeping-chambers.   The corridor was of immense length, and seemed still
to lengthen itself before us, as the glimmer of
our conductor's candle went farther and farther
into the obscurity.   Our own chamber was at
a vast distance along this passage; those of the
rest of the party were on the hither side; but
all this immense suite of rooms appeared to communicate by doors from one to another, like the
chambers through which the reader wanders at
midnight, in Mrs. Radcliffe's romances.   And
they were really splendid rooms, though of an
old fashion, lofty, spacious, with floors of oak
or other wood, inlaid in squares and crosses, and
waxed till they were slippery, but without carpets.   Our own sleeping-room had a deep fireplace, in which we ordered a fire, and asked if
there were not some saloon already warmed
where we could get a cup of tea.

Hereupon the waiter led us back along the
endless corridor, and down the old stone staircases, and out into the quadrangle, and jour-
neyed with us along an exterior arcade, and
finally threw open the door of the *salle à manger*,
which proved to be a room of lofty height, with
a vaulted roof, a stone floor, and interior spa-
ciousness sufficient for a baronial hall, the whole
bearing the same aspect of times gone by that

characterized the rest of the house. There were two or three tables covered with white cloth, and we sat down at one of them and had our tea. Finally we wended back to our sleeping-rooms, — a considerable journey, so endless seemed the ancient hotel. I should like to know its history.

The fire made our great chamber look comfortable, and the fireplace threw out the heat better than the little square hole over which we cowered in one saloon at the Hôtel de Louvre. . . .

In the morning we began our preparations for starting at ten. Issuing into the corridor, I found a soldier of the line, pacing to and fro there as sentinel. Another was posted in another corridor, into which I wandered by mistake; another stood in the inner courtyard, and another at the *porte-cochère*. They were not there the night before, and I know not whence nor why they came, unless that some officer of rank may have taken up his quarters at the hotel. Miss M—— says she heard at Paris that a considerable number of troops had recently been drawn together at Lyons, in consequence of symptoms of disaffection that have recently shown themselves here.

Before breakfast I went out to catch a momentary glimpse of the city. The street in which our hotel stands is near a large public square; in the centre is a bronze equestrian statue of Louis XIV.; and the square itself is called the Place de Louis le Grand. I wonder where this statue hid itself while the Revolution was raging in Lyons, and when the guillotine, perhaps, stood on that very spot.

The square was surrounded by stately buildings, but had what seemed to be barracks for soldiers, — at any rate, mean little huts, deforming its ample space; and a soldier was on guard before the statue of Louis le Grand. It was a cold, misty morning, and a fog lay throughout the area, so that I could scarcely see from one side of it to the other.

Returning towards our hotel, I saw that it had an immense front, along which ran in gigantic letters, its title, — "Hôtel de Provence et des Ambassadeurs." The excellence of the hotel lay rather in the faded pomp of its sleeping-rooms, and the vastness of its *salle à manger*, than in anything very good to eat or drink.

We left it, after a poor breakfast, and went to the railway station. Looking at the mountainous heap of our luggage the night before, we had missed a great carpet-bag; and we now found that Miss M——'s trunk had been substituted for it, and, there being the proper number of packages as registered, it was impossible to convince the officials that anything was wrong. We, of course, began to generalize forthwith, and pronounce the incident to be characteristic

of French morality.   They love a certain system and external correctness, but do not trouble
themselves to be deeply in the right ; and Miss
M—— suggested that there used to be parallel
cases in the French Revolution, when, so long
as the assigned number were sent out of prison
to be guillotined, the jailer did not much care
whether they were the persons designated by
the tribunal or not.   At all events, we could
get no satisfaction about the carpet-bag, and
shall very probably be compelled to leave Marseilles without it.

This day's ride was through a far more picturesque country than that we saw yesterday.
Heights began to rise imminent above our way
with sometimes a ruined castle wall upon them ;
on our left the rail-track kept close to the hills ;
on the other side there was the level bottom of
a valley, with heights descending upon it a mile
or a few miles away.   Farther off we could see
blue hills, shouldering high above the interme-
diate ones, and themselves worthy to be called
mountains.   These hills arranged themselves in
beautiful groups, affording openings between
them, and vistas of what lay beyond, and gorges
which I suppose held a great deal of romantic
scenery.   By and by a river made its appearance, flowing swiftly in the same direction that
we were travelling,—a beautiful and cleanly
river, with white pebbly shores, and itself **of a**

peculiar blue. It rushed along very fast, sometimes whitening over shallow descents, and even
in its calmer intervals its surface was all covered
with whirls and eddies, indicating that it dashed
onward in haste. I do not now know the name
of this river, but have set it down as the "Ar-
rowy Rhone." It kept us company a long while,
and I think we did not part with it as long as
daylight remained. I have seldom seen hill
scenery that struck me more than some that we
saw to-day, and the old feudal towers and old
villages at their feet ; and the old churches, with
spires shaped just like extinguishers, gave it an
interest accumulating from many centuries past.

Still going southward, the vineyards began
to border our track, together with what I at
first took to be orchards, but soon found were
plantations of olive-trees, which grow to a much
larger size than I supposed, and look almost
exactly like very crabbed and eccentric apple-
trees. Neither they nor the vineyards add
anything to the picturesqueness of the landscape.

On the whole, I should have been delighted
with all this scenery if it had not looked so
bleak, barren, brown, and bare ; so like the wintry New England before the snow has fallen.
It was very cold, too ; ice along the borders of
streams, even among the vineyards and olives.
The houses are of rather a different shape here

than farther northward, their roofs being not nearly so sloping. They are almost invariably covered with white plaster ; the farmhouses have their outbuildings in connection with the dwelling, — the whole surrounding three sides of a quadrangle.

We travelled far into the night, swallowed a cold and hasty dinner at Avignon, and reached Marseilles sorely wearied, at about eleven o'clock. We took a cab to the Hôtel d'Angleterre (two cabs, to be quite accurate), and find it a very poor place.

To go back a little : as the sun went down, we looked out of the window of our railway carriage, and saw a sky that reminded us of what we used to see day after day in America, and what we have not seen since ; and, after sunset, the horizon burned and glowed with rich crimson and orange lustre, looking at once warm and cold. After it grew dark, the stars brightened, and Miss M—— from her window pointed out some of the planets to the children, she being as familiar with them as a gardener with his flowers. They were as bright as diamonds.

We had a wretched breakfast, and Julian and I then went to the railway station to see about our luggage. On our walk back we went astray, passing by a triumphal arch, erected by the Marseillaise, in honor of Louis Napoleon ;

but we inquired our way of old women and soldiers, who were very kind and courteous, — especially the latter, — and were directed aright.
We came to a large, oblong, public place, set
with trees, but devoid of grass, like all public places in France.   In the middle of it was
a bronze statue of an ecclesiastical personage,
stretching forth his hands in the attitude of addressing the people or of throwing a benediction over them.   It was some archbishop, who
had distinguished himself by his humanity and
devotedness during the plague of 1720.   At
the moment of our arrival the piazza was quite
thronged with people, who seemed to be talking amongst themselves with considerable earnestness, though without any actual excitement.
They were smoking cigars ; and we judged that
they were only loitering here for the sake of
the sunshine, having no fires at home, and nothing to do.   Some looked like gentlemen,
others like peasants ; most of them I should
have taken for the lazzaroni of this Southern
city, — men with cloth caps, like the classic lib-
erty-cap, or with wide-awake hats.   There were
one or two women of the lower classes, without bonnets, the elder ones with white caps,
the younger bareheaded.   I have hardly seen
a lady in Marseilles ; and I suspect, it being a
commercial city, and dirty to the last degree,
ill-built, narrow-streeted, and sometimes pesti-

lential, there are few or no families of gentility
resident here.

Returning to the hotel, we found the rest of
the party ready to go out; so we all issued
forth in a body, and inquired our way to the
telegraph-office, in order to send my message
about the carpet-bag. In a street through which
we had to pass (and which seemed to be the Exchange, or its precincts), there was a crowd even
denser, yes, much denser, than that which we
saw in the square of the archbishop's statue;
and each man was talking to his neighbor in a
vivid, animated way, as if business were very
brisk to-day.

At the telegraph - office, we discovered the
cause that had brought out these many people.
There had been attempts on the Emperor's life,
— unsuccessful, as they seem fated to be, though
some mischief was done to those near him. I
rather think the good people of Marseilles were
glad of the attempt, as an item of news and
gossip, and did not very greatly care whether it
were successful or no. It seemed to have roused
their vivacity rather than their interest. The
only account I have seen of it was in the brief
public despatch from the Syndic (or whatever
he be) of Paris to the chief authority of Mar-
seiiles, which was printed and posted in various
conspicuous places. The only chance of knowing the truth with any fulness of detail would

be to come across an English paper. We have
had a banner hoisted half-mast in front of our
hotel to-day as a token, the head-waiter tells
me, of sympathy and sorrow for the General
and other persons who were slain by this trea-
sonable attempt.

Julian and I now wandered by ourselves
along a circular line of quays, having on one
side of us a thick forest of masts, while on the
other was a sweep of shops, bookstalls, sailors'
restaurants and drinking-houses, fruit sellers,
candy-women, and all manner of open-air deal-
ers and peddlers; little children playing, and
jumping the rope, and such a babble and bustle
as I never saw or heard before; the sun lying
along the whole sweep, very hot, and evidently
very grateful to those who basked in it. Whenever I passed into the shade, immediately from
too warm I became too cold. The sunshine
was like hot air; the shade, like the touch of
cold steel; sharp, hard, yet exhilarating. From
the broad street of the quays, narrow, thread-
like lanes pierced up between the edifices, calling themselves streets, yet so narrow that a
person in the middle could almost touch the
houses on either hand. They ascended steeply,
bordered on each side by long, contiguous walls
of high houses, and from the time of their first
being built, could never have had a gleam of
sunshine in them, — always in shadow, always

unutterably nasty, and often pestiferous. The
nastiness which I saw in Marseilles exceeds my
heretofore experience. There is dirt in the
hotel, and everywhere else ; and it evidently
troubles nobody, — no more than if all the
people were pigs in a pigsty. . . .

Passing by all this sweep of quays, Julian and
I ascended to an elevated walk, overlooking the
harbor, and far beyond it ; for here we had our
first view of the Mediterranean, blue as heaven
and bright with sunshine. It was a bay, widening forth into the open deep, and bordered
with heights and bold, picturesque headlands,
some of which had either fortresses or convents
on them. Several boats and one brig were under
sail, making their way towards the port. I have
never seen a finer sea view. Behind the town
there seemed to be a mountainous landscape,
imperfectly visible, in consequence of the intervening edifices.

Steamer Calabrese, January 17. — If I had
remained at Marseilles, I might have found
many peculiarities and characteristics of that
Southern city to notice ; but I fear that these
will not be recorded if I leave them till I touch
the soil of Italy. Indeed, I doubt whether there
be anything really worth recording in the little
distinctions between one nation and another ;
at any rate, after the first novelty is over, new

things seem equally commonplace with the old.
There is but one little interval when the mind
is in such a state that it can catch the fleeting
aroma of a new scene. And it is always so
much pleasanter to enjoy this delicious newness
than to attempt arresting it, that it requires
great force of will to insist with one's self upon
sitting down to write. I can do nothing with
Marseilles, especially here on the Mediterranean, long after nightfall, and when the steamer
is pitching in a pretty lively way.

(Later). — I walked out with Julian yesterday morning, and reached the outskirts of the
city, whence we could see the bold and picturesque heights that surround Marseilles as
with a semicircular wall. They rise into peaks,
and the town, being on their lower slope, descends from them towards the sea with a gradual sweep. Adown the streets that descend
these declivities come little rivulets, running
along over the pavement, close to the sidewalks,
as over a pebbly bed ; and though they look
vastly like kennels, I saw women washing linen
in these streams, and others dipping up the
water for household purposes. The women appear very much in public at Marseilles. In the
squares and places you see half a dozen of them
together, sitting in a social circle on the bot-
toms of upturned baskets, knitting, talking, and
enjoying the public sunshine, as if it were their

own household fire. Not one in a thousand of them, probably, ever has a household fire for the purpose of keeping themselves warm, but only to do their little cookery ; and when there is sunshine they take advantage of it, and in the short season of rain and frost they shrug their shoulders, put on what warm garments they have, and get through the winter somewhat as grasshoppers and butterflies do, — being summer insects like them. This certainly is a very keen and cutting air, sharp as a razor, and I saw ice along the borders of the little rivulets almost at noonday. To be sure, it is midwinter, and yet in the sunshine I found myself uncomfortably warm, but in the shade the air was like the touch of death itself. I do not like the climate.

There are a great number of public places in Marseilles, several of which are adorned with statues or fountains, or triumphal arches or columns, and set out with trees, and otherwise furnished as a kind of drawing-rooms, where the populace may meet together and gossip. I never before heard from human lips anything like this bustle and babble, this thousand-fold talk which you hear all round about you in the crowd of a public square ; so entirely different is it from the dulness of a crowd in England, where, as a rule, everybody is silent, and hardly half a dozen monosyllables will come from the lips of a thousand people. In Marseilles, on the contrary, a stream of unbroken talk seems to bubble from the lips of every individual. A great many interesting scenes take place in these squares. From the window of our hotel (which looked into the Place Royal) I saw a juggler displaying his art to a crowd, who stood in a regular square about him, none pretending to press nearer than the prescribed limit. While the juggler wrought his miracles his wife supplied him with his magic materials out of a box; and when the exhibition was over she packed up the white cloth with which his table was covered, together with cups, cards, balls, and whatever else, and they took their departure.

I have been struck with the idle curiosity, and, at the same time, the courtesy and kindness, of the populace of Marseilles, and I meant to exemplify it by recording how Miss S——and I attracted their notice, and became the centre of a crowd of at least fifty of them, while doing no more remarkable thing than settling with a cab-driver. But really this pitch and swell is getting too bad, and I shall go to bed, as the best chance of keeping myself in an equable state.

ROME. — 37 *Palazzo Larazani, Via Porta Pinciana, January* 24. — We left Marseilles in the Neapolitan steamer Calabrese, as noticed above, a week ago this morning. There was no fault to be found with the steamer, which was very clean and comfortable, contrary to what we had understood beforehand ; except for the coolness of the air (and I know not that this was greater than that of the Atlantic in July), our voyage would have been very pleasant ; but for myself, I enjoyed nothing, having a cold upon me, or a low fever, or something else that took the light and warmth out of everything.

I went to bed immediately after my last record, and was rocked to sleep pleasantly enough by the billows of the Mediterranean ; and, coming on deck about sunrise next morning, found the steamer approaching Genoa. We saw the city, lying at the foot of a range of hills, and stretching a little way up their slopes, the hills sweeping round it in the segment of a circle, and looking like an island rising abruptly out of the sèa ; for no connection with the mainland was visible on either side. There was snow scattered on their summits, and streaking their sides a good way down. They looked bold, and barren, and brown, except where the snow whitened them. The city did not impress me with much expectation of size or splendor. Shortly after coming into the port our whole party landed, and we found ourselves at once in the midst of a crowd of cab-drivers, hotel-runners, and commissionaires, who assaulted us with a volley of French, Italian, and broken

English, which beat pitilessly about our ears;
for really it seemed as if all the dictionaries in
the world had been torn to pieces, and blown
around us by a hurricane. Such a pother! We
took a commissionaire, a respectable-looking
man, in a cloak, who said his name was Salvator Rosa; and he engaged to show us whatever
was interesting in Genoa.

In the first place he took us through narrow
streets to an old church, the name of which I
have forgotten, and indeed, its peculiar features; but I know that I found it preëminently
magnificent, — its whole interior being encased
in polished marble, of various kinds and colors,
its ceiling painted, and its chapels adorned with
pictures. However, this church was dazzled
out of sight by the Cathedral of San Lorenzo,
to which we were afterwards conducted, whose
exterior front is covered with alternate slabs of
black and white marble, which were brought,
either in whole or in part, from Jerusalem.
Within, there was a prodigious richness of precious marbles, and a pillar, if I mistake not,
from Solomon's Temple; and a picture of the
Virgin by St. Luke; and others (rather more
intrinsically valuable, I imagine), by old masters, set in superb marble frames, within the
arches of the chapels. I used to try to imagine
how the English cathedrals must have looked
in their primeval glory, before the Reforma-

tion, and before the whitewash of Cromwell's
time had overlaid their marble pillars; but I
never imagined anything at all approaching what
my eyes now beheld: this sheen of polished
and variegated marble covering every inch of
its walls; this glow of brilliant frescos all over
the roof, and up within the domes; these beautiful pictures by great masters, painted for the
places which they now occupied, and making
an actual portion of the edifice; this wealth of
silver, gold, and gems, that adorned the shrines
of the saints, before which wax candles burned,
and were kept burning, I suppose, from year's
end to year's end; in short, there is no imagin-
ing nor remembering a hundredth part of the
rich details.   And even the Cathedral (though
I give it up as indescribable) was nothing at all
in comparison with a church to which the commissionaire afterwards led us; a church that had
been built four or five hundred years ago, by a
pirate, in expiation of his sins, and out of the
profit of his rapine.   This last edifice, in its interior, absolutely shone with burnished gold,
and glowed with pictures; its walls were a quarry
of precious stones, so valuable were the marbles
out of which they were wrought; its columns
and pillars were of inconceivable costliness; its
pavement was a mosaic of wonderful beauty,
and there were four twisted pillars made out of
stalactites.   Perhaps the best way to form some

dim conception of it is to fancy a little casket, inlaid inside with precious stones, so that there shall not a hair's-breadth be left un-precious-stoned, and then to conceive this little bit of a casket increased to the magnitude of a great church, without losing anything of the excessive glory that was compressed into its original small compass, but all its pretty lustre made sublime by the consequent immensity. At any rate, nobody who has not seen a church like this can imagine what a gorgeous religion it was that reared it.

In the Cathedral, and in all the churches, we saw priests and many persons kneeling at their devotions ; and our Salvator Rosa, whenever we passed a chapel or shrine, failed not to touch the pavement with one knee, crossing himself the while ; and once, when a priest was going through some form of devotion, he stopped a few moments to share in it.

He conducted us, too, to the Balbi Palace, the stateliest and most sumptuous residence, but not more so than another which he afterwards showed us, nor perhaps than many others which exist in Genoa the Superb. The painted ceilings in these palaces are a glorious adornment ; the walls of the saloons, encrusted with various-colored marbles, give an idea of splendor which I never gained from anything else. The floors, laid in mosaic, seem too precious to tread upon. In the royal palace, many of the floors were of various woods, inlaid by an English artist, and they looked like a magnification of some exquisite piece of Tunbridge ware; but, in all respects, this palace was inferior to others which we saw. I say nothing of the immense pictorial treasures which hung upon the walls of all the rooms through which we passed; for I soon grew so weary of admirable things, that I could neither enjoy nor understand them. My receptive faculty is very limited, and when the utmost of its small capacity is full, I become perfectly miserable, and the more so the better worth seeing are the things I am forced to reject. I do not know a greater misery; to see sights, after such repletion, is to the mind what it would be to the body to have dainties forced down the throat long after the appetite was satiated.

All this while, whenever we emerged into the vault-like streets, we were wretchedly cold. The commissionaire took us to a sort of pleasure-garden, occupying the ascent of a hill, and presenting seven different views of the city, from as many stations. One of the objects pointed out to us was a large yellow house, on a hillside, in the outskirts of Genoa, which was formerly inhabited for six months by Charles Dickens. Looking down from the elevated part of the pleasure-gardens, we saw orange-trees beneath us, with the golden fruit hanging upon them, though their trunks were muffled in straw; and, still lower down, there was ice and snow.

Gladly (so far as I myself was concerned) we dismissed the commissionaire, after he had brought us to the Hotel of the Cross of Malta, where we dined; needlessly, as it proved, for another dinner awaited us after our return on board the boat.

We set sail for Leghorn before dark, and I retired early, feeling still more ill from my cold than the night before. The next morning we were in the crowded port of Leghorn. We all went ashore, with some idea of taking the rail for Pisa, which is within an hour's distance, and might have been seen in time for our departure with the steamer. But a necessary visit to a banker's, and afterwards some unnecessary formalities about our passports, kept us wandering through the streets nearly all day; and we saw nothing in the slightest degree interesting, except the tomb of Smollett, in the burial-place attached to the English Chapel. It is surrounded by an iron railing, and marked by a slender obelisk of white marble, the pattern of which is many times repeated over surrounding graves.

We went into a Jewish synagogue, — the interior cased in marbles, and surrounded with gal-

leries, resting upon arches above arches. There
were lights burning at the altar, and it looked
very like a Christian church; but it was dirty,
and had an odor not of sanctity.

In Leghorn, as everywhere else, we were
chilled to the heart, except when the sunshine
fell directly upon us; and we returned to the
steamer with a feeling as if we were getting back
to our home; for this life of wandering makes
a three days' residence in one place seem like
home.

We found several new passengers on board,
and among others a monk, in a long brown
frock of woollen cloth, with an immense cape,
and a little black covering over his tonsure. He
was a tall figure, with a gray beard, and might
have walked, just as he stood, out of a picture
by one of the old masters. This holy person addressed me very affably in Italian; but
we found it impossible to hold much conversation.

The evening was beautiful, with a bright
young moonlight, not yet sufficiently powerful
to overwhelm the stars, and as we walked the
deck, Miss M——— showed the children the con-
stellations, and told their names. Julian made a
slight mistake as to one of them, pointing it out
to me as " O'Brien's belt!"

Elba was presently in view, and we might
have seen many other interesting points, had it

not been for our steamer's practice of resting by day, and only pursuing its voyage by night.

The next morning we found ourselves in the harbor of Cività Vecchia, and, going ashore with our luggage, went through a blind turmoil with custom-house officers, inspectors of passports, soldiers, and vetturino people. My wife and I strayed a little through Cività Vecchia, and found its streets narrow, like clefts in a rock (which seems to be the fashion of Italian towns), and smelling nastily. I had made a bargain with a vetturino to send us to Rome in a carriage, with four horses, in eight hours; and as soon as the custom-house and passport people would let us, we started, lumbering slowly along with our mountain of luggage. We had heard rumors of robberies lately committed on this route; especially of a Nova Scotia bishop, who was detained on the road an hour and a half, and utterly pillaged; and certainly there was not a single mile of the dreary and desolate country over which we passed, where we might not have been robbed and murdered with impunity. Now and then, at long distances, we came to a structure that was either a prison, a tavern, or a barn, but did not look very much like either, being strongly built of stone, with iron-grated windows, and of ancient and rusty aspect. We kept along by the seashore a great part of the way, and stopped to feed our horses at a village, the

wretched street of which stands close along the
shore of the Mediterranean, its loose, dark sand
being made nasty by the vicinity. The vetturino cheated us, one of the horses giving out,
as he must have known it would do, halfway on
our journey; and we staggered on through cold
and darkness, and peril, too, if the banditti were
not a myth, — reaching Rome not much before
midnight. I perpetrated unheard-of briberies
on the custom-house officers at the gates, and
was permitted to pass through and establish myself at Spillman's Hotel, the only one where
we could gain admittance, and where we have
been half frozen, and have continued so ever
since.

And this is sunny Italy, and genial Rome!

*Palazzo Larazani, Via Porta Pinciana, Feb-
ruary* 3. — We have been in Rome a fortnight
to-day, or rather at eleven o'clock to-night; and
I have seldom or never spent so wretched a time
anywhere. Our impressions were very unfor-
tunate, arriving at midnight, half frozen in the
wintry rain, and being received into a cold and
cheerless hotel, where we shivered during two
or three days; meanwhile seeking lodgings
among the sunless, dreary alleys which are called
streets in Rome. One cold, bright day after another has pierced me to the heart, and cut me
in twain as with a sword, keen and sharp, and

poisoned at point and edge. I did not think that cold weather could have made me so very miserable. Having caught a feverish influenza, I was really glad of being muffled up comfortably in the fever heat. The atmosphere certainly has a peculiar quality of malignity. After a day or two we settled ourselves in a suite of ten rooms, comprehending one flat, or what is called the second piano of this house. The rooms, thus far, have been very uncomfortable, it being impossible to warm them by means of the deep, old-fashioned, inartificial fireplaces, unless we had the great logs of a New England forest to burn in them; so I have sat in my corner by the fireside with more clothes on than I ever wore before, and my thickest great-coat over all. In the middle of the day I generally venture out for an hour or two, but have only once been warm enough even in the sunshine, and out of the sun never at any time. I understand now the force of that story of Diogenes when he asked the Conqueror, as the only favor he could do him, to stand out of his sunshine, there being such a difference in these southern climes of Europe between sun and shade. If my wits had not been too much congealed, and my fingers too numb, I should like to have kept a minute journal of my feelings and impressions during the past fortnight. It would have shown modern Rome in an aspect in which it has never

yet been depicted. But I have now grown
somewhat acclimated, and the first freshness of
my discomfort has worn off, so that I shall never
be able to express how I dislike the place, and
how wretched I have been in it; and soon, I
suppose, warmer weather will come, and perhaps
reconcile me to Rome against my will. Cold,
narrow lanes, between tall, ugly, mean-looking,
whitewashed houses, — sour bread, pavements
most uncomfortable to the feet, enormous prices
for poor living; beggars, pickpockets, ancient
temples and broken monuments, and clothes
hanging to dry about them; French soldiers,
monks, and priests of every degree; a shabby
population, smoking bad cigars, — these would
have been some of the points of my description.
Of course there are better and truer things to
be said. . . .

It would be idle for me to attempt any sketches
of these famous sites and edifices, — St. Peter's,
for example, — which have been described by
a thousand people, though none of them have
ever given me an idea of what sort of place
Rome is. . . .

The Coliseum was very much what I had
preconceived it, though I was not prepared to
find it turned into a sort of Christian church,
with a pulpit on the verge of the open space.
. . . The French soldiers, who keep guard
within it, as in other public places in Rome,

have an excellent opportunity to secure the welfare of their souls.

February 7. — I cannot get fairly into the current of my journal since we arrived, and already I perceive that the nice peculiarities of Roman life are passing from my notice before I have recorded them. It is a very great pity.

During the past week I have plodded daily, for an hour or two, through the narrow, stony streets, that look worse than the worst backside lanes of any other city ; indescribably ugly and disagreeable they are, . . . without sidewalks, but provided with a line of larger square stones, set crosswise to each other, along which there is somewhat less uneasy walking. . . . Ever and anon, even in the meanest streets, — though, generally speaking, one can hardly be called meaner than another, — we pass a palace, extending far along the narrow way on a line with the other houses, but distinguished by its architectural windows, iron-barred on the basement story, and by its portal arch, through which we have glimpses, sometimes of a dirty courtyard, or perhaps of a clean, ornamented one, with trees, a colonnade, a fountain, and a statue in the vista ; though, more likely, it resembles the entrance to a stable, and may, perhaps, really be one. The lower regions of palaces come to strange uses in Rome. . . . In the basement

story of the Barberini Palace a regiment of
French soldiers (or soldiers of some kind [1])
seems to be quartered, while, no doubt, princes
have magnificent domiciles above. Be it palace
or whatever other dwelling, the inmates climb
through rubbish often to the comforts, such as
they may be, that await them above. I vainly
try to get down upon paper the dreariness, the
ugliness, shabbiness, un-homelikeness of a Roman street. It is also to be said that you cannot go far in any direction without coming to a
piazza, which is sometimes little more than a
widening and enlarging of the dingy street, with
the lofty façade of a church or basilica on one
side, and a fountain in the centre, where the
water squirts out of some fantastic piece of sculpture into a great stone basin. These fountains
are often of immense size and most elaborate
design. . . .

There are a great many of these fountain-
shapes, constructed under the orders of one
pope or another, in all parts of the city; and
only the very simplest, such as a jet springing
from a broad marble or porphyry vase, and falling back into it again, are really ornamental.
If an antiquary were to accompany me through
the streets, no doubt he would point out ten
thousand interesting objects that I now pass
over unnoticed, so general is the surface of plas-

1 We find them to be retainers of the Barberini family, not French.

ter and whitewash; but often I can see fragments of antiquity built into the walls, or perhaps a church that was a Roman temple, or a
basement of ponderous stones that were laid
above twenty centuries ago. It is strange how
our ideas of what antiquity is become altered
here in Rome; the sixteenth century, in which
many of the churches and fountains seem to
have been built or reëdified, seems close at
hand, even like our own days; a thousand
years, or the days of the latter empire, is but a
modern date, and scarcely interests us; and nothing is really venerable of a more recent epoch
than the reign of Constantine. And the Egyptian obelisks that stand in several of the piazzas
put even the Augustan or the Republican antiquities to shame. I remember reading in a New
York newspaper an account of one of the public buildings of that city, — a relic of " the olden
time," the writer called it; for it was erected in
1825! I am glad I saw the castles and Gothic
churches and cathedrals of England before visiting Rome — or I never could have felt that
delightful reverence for their gray and ivy-hung
antiquity after seeing these so much older remains. But, indeed, old things are not so beautiful in this dry climate and clear atmosphere as
in moist England. . . .

Whatever beauty there may be in a Roman
ruin is the remnant of what was beautiful ori-

ginally; whereas an English ruin is more beautiful often in its decay than even it was in its primal strength.   If we ever build such noble structures as these Roman ones, we can have just as good ruins, after two thousand years, in the United States; but we never can have a Furness Abbey or a Kenilworth.   The Corso, and perhaps some other streets, does not deserve all the vituperation which I have bestowed on the generality of Roman vias, though the Corso is narrow, not averaging more than nine paces, if so much, from sidewalk to sidewalk. But palace after palace stands along almost its whole extent, — not, however, that they make such architectural show on the street as palaces should.   The enclosed courts were perhaps the only parts of these edifices which the founders cared to enrich architecturally.   I think Linlithgow Palace, of which I saw the ruins during my last tour in Scotland, was built by an architect who had studied these Roman palaces. There was never any idea of domestic comfort, or of what we include in the name of home, at all implicated in such structures, they being generally built by wifeless and childless churchmen for the display of pictures and statuary in galleries and long suites of rooms.

I have not yet fairly begun the sightseeing of Rome.   I have been four or five times to St. Peter's, and always with pleasure, because there is such a delightful, summer-like warmth the moment we pass beneath the heavy, padded leather curtains that protect the entrances. It is almost impossible not to believe that this genial temperature is the result of furnace heat, — but, really, it is the warmth of last summer, which will be included within those massive walls, and in that vast immensity of space, till, six months hence, this winter's chill will just have made its way thither. It would be an excellent plan for a valetudinarian to lodge during the winter in St. Peter's, perhaps establishing his household in one of the papal tombs. I become, I think, more sensible of the size of St. Peter's, but am as yet far from being overwhelmed by it. It is not, as one expects, so big as all out-o'-doors, nor is its dome so immense as that of the firmament. It looked queer, however, the other day, to see a little ragged boy, the very least of human things, going round and kneeling at shrine after shrine, and a group of children standing on tiptoe to reach the vase of holy water. . . .

On coming out of St. Peter's at my last visit, I saw a great sheet of ice around the fountain on the right hand, and some little Romans awkwardly sliding on it. I, too, took a slide, just for the sake of doing what I never thought to do in Rome. This inclement weather, I should suppose, must make the whole city very miserable ; for the native Romans, I am told, never keep any fire, except for culinary purposes, even in the severest winter. They flee from their cheerless houses into the open air, and bring their firesides along with them in the shape of small earthen vases, or pipkins, with a handle by which they carry them up and down the streets, and so warm at least their hands with the lighted charcoal. I have had glimpses through open doorways into interiors, and saw them as dismal as tombs. Wherever I pass my summers, let me spend my winters in a cold country.

We went yesterday to the Pantheon. . . .

When I first came to Rome, I felt embarrassed and unwilling to pass, with my heresy, between a devotee and his saint ; for they often shoot their prayers at a shrine almost quite across the church. But there seems to be no violation of etiquette in so doing. A woman begged of us in the Pantheon, and accused my wife of impiety for not giving her an alms. . . . People of very decent appearance are often unexpectedly converted into beggars as you approach them; but in general they take a " No " at once.

February 9. — For three or four days it has been cloudy and rainy, which is the greater pity, as this should be the gayest and merriest

part of the Carnival.   I go out but little, —
yesterday only as far as Pakenham's and Hook-
er's bank, in the Piazza di Spagna, when I read
" Galignani " and the American papers.   At
last, after seeing in England more of my fel-
low-compatriots than ever before, I really am
disjoined from my country.

To-day I walked out along the Pincian Hill.
. . . As the clouds still threatened rain, I
deemed it my safest course to go to St. Peter's
for refuge.   Heavy and dull as the day was,
the effect of this great world of a church was
still brilliant in the interior, as if it had a sunshine of its own, as well as its own temperature ;
and, by and by, the sunshine of the outward
world came through the windows, hundreds of
feet aloft, and fell upon the beautiful inlaid
pavement. . . . Against a pillar, on one side
of the nave, is a mosaic copy of Raphael's
Transfiguration, fitly framed within a great arch
of gorgeous marble ; and, no doubt, the indestructible mosaic has preserved it far more completely than the fading and darkening tints in
which the artist painted it.   At any rate, it
seemed to me the one glorious picture that I
have ever seen.   The pillar nearest the great
entrance, on the left of the nave, supports the
monument to the Stuart family, where two
winged figures, with inverted torches, stand on
either side of a marble door, which is closed

forever.   It is an impressive monument, for you feel as if the last of the race had passed through that door.

Emerging from the church, I saw a French sergeant drilling his men in the piazza. These French soldiers are prominent objects everywhere about the city, and make up more of its sight and sound than anything else that lives. They stroll about individually ; they pace as sentinels in all the public places ; and they march up and down in squads, companies, and battalions, always with a very great din of drum, fife, and trumpet ; ten times the proportion of music that the same number of men would require elsewhere ; and it reverberates with ten times the noise, between the high edifices of these lanes, that it could make in broader streets. Nevertheless, I have no quarrel with the French soldiers ; they are fresh, healthy, smart, honest-looking young fellows enough, in blue coats and red trousers ; . . . and, at all events, they serve as an efficient police, making Rome as safe as London ; whereas, without them, it would very likely be a den of banditti.

On my way home I saw a few tokens of the Carnival, which is now in full progress ; though, as it was only about one o'clock, its frolics had not commenced for the day. . . . I question whether the Romans themselves take any great

interest in the Carnival. The balconies along
the Corso were almost entirely taken by English and Americans, or other foreigners.

As I approached the bridge of St. Angelo, I
saw several persons engaged, as I thought, in
fishing in the Tiber, with very strong lines;
but, on drawing nearer, I found that they were
trying to hook up the branches and twigs, and
other driftwood, which the recent rains might
have swept into the river. There was a little
heap of what looked chiefly like willow twigs,
the poor result of their labor. The hook was
a knot of wood, with the lopped-off branches
projecting in three or four prongs. The Tiber
has always the hue of a mud-puddle; but now,
after a heavy rain which has washed the clay
into it, it looks like pease soup. It is a broad
and rapid stream, eddying along as if it were
in haste to disgorge its impurities into the sea.
On the left side, where the city mostly is situated, the buildings hang directly over the
stream; on the other, where stand the Castle
of St. Angelo and the Church of St. Peter, the
town does not press so imminent upon the
shore. The banks are clayey, and look as if
the river had been digging them away for ages;
but I believe its bed is higher than of yore.

February 10. — I went out to-day, and, going along the Via Felice and the Via delle

Quattro Fontane, came unawares to the Basilica of Santa Maria Maggiore, on the summit of the Esquiline Hill. I entered it, without in the least knowing what church it was, and found myself in a broad and noble nave, both very simple and very grand. There was a long row of Ionic columns of marble, twenty or thereabouts on each side, supporting a flat roof. There were vaulted side-aisles, and, at the farther end, a bronze canopy over the high altar; and all along the length of the side-aisles were shrines with pictures, sculpture, and burning lamps; the whole church, too, was lined with marble; the roof was gilded; and yet the general effect of severe and noble simplicity triumphed over all the ornament. I should have taken it for a Roman temple, retaining nearly its pristine aspect; but Murray tells us that it was founded A. D. 342 by Pope Liberius, on the spot precisely marked out by a miraculous fall of snow in the month of August, and it has undergone many alterations since his time. But it is very fine, and gives the beholder the idea of vastness, which seems harder to attain than anything else. On the right hand, approaching the high altar, there is a chapel, separated from the rest of the church by an iron paling; and, being admitted into it with another party, I found it most elaborately magnificent. But one magnificence outshone

The Castle and Bridge of St. Angelo, Rome

another, and made itself the brightest conceivable for the moment. However, this chapel was as rich as the most precious marble could make it, in pillars and pilasters, and broad, polished slabs, covering the whole walls (except where there were splendid and glowing frescos; or where some monumental statuary or bas-relief, or mosaic picture, filled up an arched niche). Its architecture was a dome, resting on four great arches; and in size it would alone have been a church. In the centre of the mosaic pavement there was a flight of steps, down which we went, and saw a group in marble, representing the Nativity of Christ, which, judging by the unction with which our guide talked about it, must have been of peculiar sanctity. I hate to leave this chapel and church, without being able to say any one thing that may reflect a portion of their beauty, or of the feeling which they excite. Kneeling against many of the pillars there were persons in prayer, and I stepped softly, fearing lest my tread on the marble pavement should disturb them, — a needless precaution, however, for nobody seems to expect it, nor to be disturbed by the lack of it.

The situation of the church, I should suppose, is the loftiest in Rome: it has a fountain at one end, and a column at the other; but I did not pay particular attention to either, nor to the exterior of the church itself.

On my return, I turned aside from the Via delle Quattro Fontane into the Via Quirinalis, and was led by it into the Piazza di Monte Cavallo. The street through which I passed was broader, cleanlier, and statelier than most streets in Rome, and bordered by palaces; and the piazza had noble edifices around it, and a fountain, an obelisk, and two nude statues in the centre. The obelisk was, as the inscription indicated, a relic of Egypt; the basin of the fountain was an immense bowl of Oriental granite, into which poured a copious flood of water, discolored by the rain; the statues were colossal, — two beautiful young men, each holding a fiery steed. On the pedestal of one was the inscription, OPUS PHIDIÆ; on the other, OPUS PRAXITELIS. What a city is this, when one may stumble, by mere chance — at a street corner, as it were — on the works of two such sculptors! I do not know the authority on which these statues (Castor and Pollux, I presume) are attributed to Phidias and Praxiteles; but they impressed me as noble and godlike, and I feel inclined to take them for what they purport to be. On one side of the piazza is the Pontifical Palace; but, not being aware of this at the time, I did not look particularly at the edifice.

I came home by way of the Corso, which seemed a little enlivened by Carnival time; though, as it was not yet two o'clock, the fun had not begun for the day.   The rain throws a dreary damper on the festivities.

February 13. — Day before yesterday we took Julian and Rose in a carriage, and went to see the Carnival, by driving up and down the Corso.   It was as ugly a day, as respects weather, as has befallen us since we came to Rome, — cloudy, with an indecisive wet, which finally settled into a rain; and people say that such is generally the weather in Carnival time. There is very little to be said about the spectacle.   Sunshine would have improved it, no doubt; but a person must have very broad sunshine within himself to be joyous on such shallow provocation.   The street, at all events, would have looked rather brilliant under a sunny sky, the balconies being hung with bright-colored draperies, which were also flung out of some of the windows. . . .   Soon I had my first experience of the Carnival, in a handful of confetti, right slap in my face. . . .   Many of the ladies wore loose white dominoes, and some of the gentlemen had on defensive armor of blouses; and wire masks over the face were a protection for both sexes, — not a needless one, for I received a shot in my right eye which cost me many tears.   It seems to be a point of courtesy (though often disregarded by Americans and English) not to fling confetti at ladies, or at non-combatants, or quiet bystanders; and the engagements with these missiles were generally between open carriages, manned with youths, who were provided with confetti for such encounters, and with bouquets for the ladies. We had one real enemy on the Corso; for our former friend Mrs. T—— was there, and as often as we passed and repassed her, she favored us with a handful of lime. Two or three times somebody ran by the carriage and puffed forth a shower of winged seeds through a tube into our faces and over our clothes; and, in the course of the afternoon, we were hit with perhaps half a dozen sugar - plums. Possibly we may not have received our fair share of these last salutes, for Julian had on a black mask, which made him look like an imp of Satan, and drew many volleys of confetti that we might otherwise have escaped. A good many bouquets were flung at our little Rose, and at us generally. . . . This was what is called masking-day, when it is the rule to wear masks in the Corso, but the great majority of people appeared without them. . . . Two fantastic figures, with enormous heads, set round with frizzly hair, came and grinned into our carriage, and Julian tore out a handful of hair (which proved to be seaweed) from one of their heads, rather to the discomposure of the owner, who muttered his indignation in Italian. . . . On comparing notes with Julian and Rose, indeed with Una too, I find that they all enjoyed the Carnival much more than I did. Only the young ought to write descriptions of such scenes. My cold criticism chills the life out of it.

February 14. — Friday, 12th, was a sunny day, the first that we had had for some time; and my wife and I went forth to see sights as well as to make some calls that had long been due. We went first to the church of Santa Maria Maggiore, which I have already mentioned, and, on our return, we went to the Piazza di Monte Cavallo, and saw those admirable ancient statues of Castor and Pollux, which seem to me sons of the morning, and full of life and strength. The atmosphere, in such a length of time, has covered the marble surface of these statues with a gray rust, that envelops both the men and horses as with a garment; besides which, there are strange discolorations, such as patches of white moss on the elbows, and reddish streaks down the sides; but the glory of form overcomes all these defects of color. It is pleasant to observe how familiar some little birds are with these colossal statues, — hopping about on their heads and over their huge fists, and very likely they have nests in their ears or among their hair.

We called at the Barberini Palace, where

William Story has established himself and family for the next seven years or more, on the third piano, in apartments that afford a very fine outlook over Rome, and have the sun in them through most of the day.   Mrs. S—— invited us to her fancy ball, but we declined.

On the staircase ascending to their piano we saw the ancient Greek bas-relief of a lion, whence Canova is supposed to have taken the idea of his lions on the monument in St. Peter's. Afterwards we made two or three calls in the neighborhood of the Piazza di Spagna, finding only Mr. Hamilton Fish and family, at the Hôtel d'Europe, at home, and next visited the studio of Mr. C. G. Thompson, whom I knew in Boston.   He has very greatly improved since those days, and being always a man of delicate mind, and earnestly desiring excellence for its own sake, he has won himself the power of doing beautiful and elevated works. He is now meditating a series of pictures from Shakespeare's Tempest, the sketches of one or two of which he showed us, likewise a copy of a small Madonna, by Raphael, wrought with a minute faithfulness which it makes one a better man to observe. . . . Mr. Thompson is a true artist, and whatever his pictures have of beauty comes from very far beneath the surface; and this, I suppose, is one weighty reason why he has but moderate success.   I should like his pictures

for the mere color, even if they represented nothing.   His studio is in the Via Sistina; and,
at a little distance on the other side of the same
street, is William Story's, where we likewise
went, and found him at work on a sitting statue
of Cleopatra.

William Story looks quite as vivid, in a graver
way, as when I saw him last, a very young man.
His perplexing variety of talents and accomplish-
ments — he being a poet, a prose writer, a law-
yer, a painter, a musician, and a sculptor — seems
now to be concentrating itself into this latter
vocation, and I cannot see why he should not
achieve something very good.   He has a beautiful statue, already finished, of Goethe's Mar-
garet, pulling a flower to pieces to discover
whether Faust loves her; a very type of virgin-
ity and simplicity.   The statue of Cleopatra,
now only fourteen days advanced in the clay, is
as wide a step from the little maidenly Mar-
garet as any artist could take; it is a grand
subject, and he is conceiving it with depth and
power, and working it out with adequate skill.
He certainly is sensible of something deeper in
his art than merely to make beautiful nudities
and baptize them by classic names.   By the
bye, he told us several queer stories of American
visitors to his studio: one of them, after long
inspecting Cleopatra, into which he has put all
possible characteristics of her time and nation,

and of her own individuality, asked, "Have you baptized your statue yet?" as if the sculptor were waiting till his statue were finished before he chose the subject of it, — as, indeed, I should think many sculptors do. Another remarked of a statue of Hero, who is seeking Leander by torchlight, and in momentary expectation of finding his drowned body, "Is not the face a little sad?" Another time a whole party of Americans filed into his studio, and ranged themselves round his father's statue, and, after much silent examination, the spokesman of the party inquired, "Well, sir, what is this intended to represent?" William Story, in telling these little anecdotes, gave the Yankee twang to perfection. . . .

The statue of his father, his first work, is very noble, — as noble and fine a portrait-statue as I ever saw. In the outer room of his studio a stone-cutter, or whatever this kind of artisan is called, was at work, transferring the statue of Hero from the plaster-cast into marble; and already, though still in some respects a block of stone, there was a wonderful degree of expression in the face. It is not quite pleasant to think that the sculptor does not really do the whole labor on his statues, but that they are all but finished to his hand by merely mechanical people. It is generally only the finishing touches that are given by his own chisel.

Yesterday being another bright day, we went to the basilica of St. John Lateran, which is the basilica next in rank to St. Peter's, and has the precedence of it as regards certain sacred privileges.   It stands on a most noble site, on the outskirts of the city, commanding a view of the Sabine and Alban hills, blue in the distance, and some of them hoary with sunny snow.   The ruins of the Claudian aqueduct are close at hand. The church is connected with the Lateran palace and museum, so that the whole is one edifice ; but the façade of the church distinguishes it, and is very lofty and grand, — more so, it seems to me, than that of St. Peter's.   Under the portico is an old statue of Constantine, representing him as a very stout and sturdy personage.   The inside of the church disappointed me, though, no doubt, I should have been wonder-struck had I seen it a month ago.   We went into one of the chapels, which was very rich in colored marbles ; and, going down a winding staircase, found ourselves among the tombs and sarcophagi of the Corsini family, and in presence of a marble Pietà, very beautifully sculptured.   On the other side of the church we looked into the Torlonia Chapel, very rich and rather profusely gilded, but, as it seemed to me, not tawdry, though the white newness of the marble is not perfectly agreeable after being accustomed to the milder tint which time bestows on sculpture.   The tombs and statues appeared like shapes and images of new-fallen snow. The most interesting thing which we saw in this church (and, admitting its authenticity, there can scarcely be a more interesting one anywhere) was the table at which the Last Supper was eaten. It is preserved in a corridor, on one side of the tribune or chancel, and is shown by torchlight suspended upon the wall beneath a covering of glass. Only the top of the table is shown, presenting a broad, flat surface of wood, evidently very old, and showing traces of dry-rot in one or two places. There are nails in it, and the attendant said that it had formerly been covered with bronze. As well as I can remember, it may be five or six feet square, and I suppose would accommodate twelve persons, though not if they reclined in the Roman fashion, nor if they sat as they do in Leonardo da Vinci's picture. It would be very delightful to believe in this table.

There are several other sacred relics preserved in the church : for instance, the staircase of Pilate's house up which Jesus went, and the porphyry slab on which the soldiers cast lots for his garments. These, however, we did not see. There are very glowing frescos on portions of the walls ; but, there being much whitewash instead of encrusted marble, it has not the pleasant aspect which one's eye learns to demand in Roman churches. There is a good deal of statuary along the columns of the nave, and in the monuments of the side-aisles.

In reference to the interior splendor of Roman churches, I must say that I think it a pity that painted windows are exclusively a Gothic ornament; for the elaborate ornamentation of these interiors puts the ordinary daylight out of countenance, so that a window with only the white sunshine coming through it, or even with a glimpse of the blue Italian sky, looks like a portion left unfinished, and therefore a blotch in the rich wall. It is like the one spot in Aladdin's palace which he left for the king, his father-in-law, to finish, after his fairy architects had exhausted their magnificence on the rest; and the sun, like the king, fails in the effort. It has what is called a *porta santa*, which we saw walled up, in front of the church, one side of the main entrance. I know not what gives it its sanctity, but it appears to be opened by the pope on a year of jubilee, once every quarter of a century.

After our return . . . I took Rose along the Pincian Hill, and finally, after witnessing what of the Carnival could be seen in the Piazza del Popolo from that safe height, we went down into the Corso, and some little distance along it. Except for the sunshine, the scene was much the same as I have already described; perhaps fewer confetti and more bouquets. Some Americans and English are said to have been brought before the police authorities, and fined for throwing lime.   It is remarkable that the jollity, such as it is, of the Carnival, does not extend an inch beyond the line of the Corso; there it flows along in a narrow stream, while in the nearest street we see nothing but the ordinary Roman gravity.

February 15. — Yesterday was a bright day, but I did not go out till the afternoon, when I took an hour's walk along the Pincian, stopping a good while to look at the old beggar who, for many years past, has occupied one of the platforms of the flight of steps leading from the Piazza di Spagna to the Trinita di Monti. Hillard commemorates him in his book.   He is an unlovely object, moving about on his hands and knees, principally by aid of his hands, which are fortified with a sort of wooden shoes; while his poor, wasted lower shanks stick up in the air behind him, loosely vibrating as he progresses.   He is gray, old, ragged, — a pitiable sight, — but seems very active in his own fashion, and bestirs himself on the approach of his visitors with the alacrity of a spider when a fly touches the remote circumference of his web. While I looked down at him he received alms from three persons, one of whom was a young woman of the lower orders; the other two were gentlemen, probably either English or American. I could not quite make out the principle on which he let some people pass without molestation, while he shuffled from one end of the platform to the other to intercept an occasional individual. He is not persistent in his demands, nor, indeed, is this a usual fault among Italian beggars. A shake of the head will stop him when wriggling towards you from a distance. I fancy he reaps a pretty fair harvest, and no doubt leads as contented and as interesting a life as most people, sitting there all day on those sunny steps, looking at the world, and making his profit out of it. It must be pretty much such an occupation as fishing, in its effect upon the hopes and apprehensions ; and probably he suffers no more from the many refusals he meets with than the angler does, when he sees a fish smell at his bait and swim away. One success pays for a hundred disappointments, and the game is all the better for not being entirely in his own favor.

Walking onward, I found the Pincian thronged with promenaders, as also with carriages, which drove round the verge of the gardens in an unbroken ring.

To-day has been very rainy. I went out in the forenoon, and took a sitting for my bust in one of a suite of rooms formerly occupied by Canova. It was large, high, and dreary from the want of a carpet, furniture, or anything but clay and plaster. A sculptor's studio has not the picturesque charm of that of a painter, where there is color, warmth, and cheerfulness, and where the artist continually turns towards you the glow of some picture, which is resting against the wall. . . . I was asked not to look at the bust at the close of the sitting, and, of course, I obeyed; though I have a vague idea of a heavy-browed physiognomy, something like what I have seen in the glass, but looking strangely in that guise of clay. . . .

It is a singular fascination that Rome exercises upon artists. There is clay elsewhere, and marble enough, and heads to model, and ideas may be made sensible objects at home as well as here. I think it is the peculiar mode of life that attracts, and its freedom from the enthralments of society, more than the artistic advantages which Rome offers; and, no doubt, though the artists care little about one another's works, yet they keep each other warm by the presence of so many of them.

The Carnival still continues, though I hardly see how it can have withstood such a damper as this rainy day. There were several people — three, I think — killed in the Corso on Saturday: some accounts say that they were run over by the horses in the race; others, that they

were ridden down by the dragoons in clearing
the course.

After leaving Canova's studio, I stepped into
the church of San Luigi de Franchesi, in the
Via di Ripetta. It was built, I believe, by Catherine de' Medici, and is under the protection
of the French government, and a most shame-
fully dirty place of worship, the beautiful marble columns looking dingy, for the want of loving and pious care. There are many tombs
and monuments of French people, both of the
past and present, — artists, soldiers, priests, and
others, who have died in Rome. It was so
dusky within the church that I could hardly
distinguish the pictures in the chapels and over
the altar, nor did I know that there were any
worth looking for. Nevertheless, there were
frescos by Domenichino, and oil-paintings by
Guido and others. I found it peculiarly touching to read the records, in Latin or French,
of persons who had died in this foreign land,
though they were not my own country people,
and though I was even less akin to them than
they to Italy. Still, there was a sort of relation-
ship in the fact that neither they nor I belonged
here.

February 17. — Yesterday morning was perfectly sunny, and we went out betimes to see

churches; going first to the Capuchins', close by the Piazza Barberini.

[The Marble Faun takes up this description of the church and of the dead monk, which we really saw, just as recounted, even to the sudden stream of blood which flowed from the nostrils, as we looked at him. — S. H.]

We next went to the Trinita di Monti, which stands at the head of the steps, leading, in several flights, from the Piazza di Spagna. It is now connected with a convent of French nuns, and when we rang at a side door, one of the sisterhood answered the summons, and admitted us into the church. This, like that of the Capuchins, had a vaulted roof over the nave, and no side-aisles, but rows of chapels instead. Unlike the Capuchins', which was filthy, and really disgraceful to behold, this church was most exquisitely neat, as women alone would have thought it worth while to keep it. It is not a very splendid church, not rich in gorgeous marbles, but pleasant to be in, if it were only for the sake of its godly purity. There was only one person in the nave; a young girl, who sat perfectly still, with her face towards the altar, as long as we stayed. Between the nave and the rest of the church, there is a high iron railing, and on the other side of it there were two kneeling figures in black, so motionless that I at first thought them statues; but they proved to be two nuns at their devotions ; and others of the sisterhood came by and by and joined them. Nuns, at least these nuns, who are French and probably ladies of refinement, having the education of young girls in charge, are far pleasanter objects to see and think about than monks ; the odor of sanctity, in the latter, not being an agreeable fragrance. But these holy sisters, with their black crape and white muslin, looked really pure and unspotted from the world.

On the iron railing above mentioned was the representation of a golden heart, pierced with arrows ; for these are nuns of the Sacred Heart. In the various chapels there are several paintings in fresco, some by Daniele da Volterra ; and one of them, The Descent from the Cross, has been pronounced the third greatest picture in the world. I never should have had the slightest suspicion that it was a great picture at all, so worn and faded it looks, and so hard, so difficult to be seen and so undelightful when one does see it.

From the Trinita we went to the Santa Maria del Popolo, a church built on a spot where Nero is said to have been buried, and which was afterwards made horrible by devilish phantoms. It now being past twelve, and all the churches closing from twelve till two, we had not time to pay much attention to the frescos, oil-pictures,

and statues, by Raphael and other famous men,
which are to be seen here.   I remember dimly
the magnificent chapel of the Chigi family, and
little else, for we stayed but a short time ; and
went next to the sculptor's studio, where I had
another sitting for my bust.   After I had been
moulded for about an hour, we turned homeward ; but my wife concluded to hire a balcony
for this last afternoon and evening of the Carnival, and she took possession of it, while I went
home to send to her Miss S——— and the two
elder children.   For my part, I took Rose, and
walked, by way of the Pincian, to the Piazza del
Popolo and thence along the Corso, where by
this time the warfare of bouquets and confetti
raged pretty fiercely.   The sky being blue and
the sun bright, the scene looked much gayer
and brisker than I had before found it ; and I
can conceive of its being rather agreeable than
otherwise, up to the age of twenty.   We got
several volleys of confetti.   Rose received a
bouquet and a sugar-plum, and I a resounding
hit from something that looked more like a cab-
bage than a flower.   Little as I have enjoyed the
Carnival, I think I could make quite a brilliant
sketch of it without very widely departing from
truth.

February 19. — Day before yesterday, pretty
early, we went to St. Peter's, expecting to see

the pope cast ashes on the heads of the cardinals, it being Ash Wednesday. On arriving, however, we found no more than the usual number of visitants and devotional people scattered through the broad interior of St. Peter's; and thence concluded that the ceremonies were to be performed in the Sistine Chapel. Accordingly we went out of the Cathedral, through the door in the left transept, and passed round the exterior, and through the vast courts of the Vatican, seeking for the chapel. We had blundered into the carriage entrance of the palace; there is an entrance from some point near the front of the church, but this we did not find. The papal guards, in the strangest antique and antic costume that was ever seen, — a party-colored dress, striped with blue, red, and yellow, white and black, with a doublet and ruff, and trunk-breeches, and armed with halberds, — were on duty at the gateways, but suffered us to pass without question. Finally we reached a large court, where some cardinals' red equipages and other carriages were drawn up, but were still at a loss as to the whereabouts of the chapel. At last an attendant kindly showed us the proper door and led us up flights of stairs, along passages and galleries, and through halls, till at last we came to a spacious and lofty apartment adorned with frescos; this was the Sala Regia, and the antechamber to the Sistine Chapel.

The attendant, meanwhile, had informed us that my wife could not be admitted to the chapel in her bonnet, and that I myself could not enter at all, for lack of a dress-coat; so my wife took off her bonnet, and, covering her head with her black lace veil, was readily let in, while I remained in the Sala Regia, with several other gentlemen, who found themselves in the same predicament as I was. There was a wonderful variety of costume to be seen and studied among the persons around me, comprising garbs that have been elsewhere laid aside for at least three centuries, — the broad, plaited, double ruff, and black velvet cloak, doublet, trunk-breeches, and sword of Queen Elizabeth's time, — the papal guard, in their striped and party-colored dress as before described, looking not a little like harlequins; other soldiers in helmets and jack-boots; French officers of various uniform; monks and priests; attendants in old-fashioned and gorgeous livery; gentlemen, some in black dress-coats and pantaloons, others in wide-awake hats, and tweed overcoats; and a few ladies in the prescribed costume of black; so that, in any other country, the scene might have been taken for a fancy ball. By and by the cardinals began to arrive, and added their splendid purple robes and red hats to make the picture still more brilliant. They were old men, one or two very aged and infirm, and generally men of bulk and

218

substance, with heavy faces, fleshy about the chin.   Their red hats, trimmed with gold-lace, are a beautiful piece of finery, and are identical in shape with the black, loosely cocked beavers worn by the Catholic ecclesiastics generally. Wolsey's hat, which I saw at the Manchester Exhibition, might have been made on the same block, but apparently was never cocked, as the fashion now is.   The attendants changed the upper portions of their masters' attire, and put a little cap of scarlet cloth on each of their heads, after which the cardinals, one by one, or two by two, as they happened to arrive, went into the chapel, with a page behind each holding up his purple train.   In the meanwhile, in the chapel, we heard singing and chanting; and whenever the voluminous curtains that hung before the entrance were slightly drawn apart, we outsiders glanced through, but could see only a mass of people, and beyond them still another chapel, divided from the hither one by a screen.   When almost everybody had gone in, there was a stir among the guards and attendants, and a door opened, — apparently communicating with the inner apartments of the Vatican.   Through this door came, not the pope, as I had partly expected, but a bulky old lady in black, with a red face, who bowed towards the spectators with an aspect of dignified complaisance as she passed towards the entrance of the chapel.   I took off my hat, unlike certain English gentlemen who stood nearer, and found that I had not done amiss, for it was the Queen of Spain.

There was nothing else to be seen ; so I went back through the antechambers (which are noble halls, richly frescoed on the walls and ceilings), endeavoring to get out through the same passages that had let me in. I had already tried to descend what I now suppose to be the Scala Santa, but had been turned back by a sentinel. After wandering to and fro a good while, I at last found myself in a long, long gallery, on each side of which were innumerable inscriptions, in Greek and Latin, on slabs of marble, built into the walls ; and classic altars and tablets were ranged alone, from end to end. At the extremity was a closed iron grating, from which I was retreating ; but a French gentlemen accosted me, with the information that the custode would admit me, if I chose, and would accompany me through the sculpture department of the Vatican. I acceded, and thus took my first view of those innumerable art treasures, passing from one object to another at an easy pace, pausing hardly a moment anywhere, and dismissing even the Apollo, and the Laocoön, and the Torso of Hercules, in the space of half a dozen breaths. I was well enough content to do so, in order to get a general idea of the contents of the galleries, before settling down upon individual objects.

Most of the world-famous sculptures presented themselves to my eye with a kind of familiarity, through the copies and casts which I had seen ; but I found the originals more different than I anticipated.   The Apollo, for instance, has a face which I have never seen in any cast or copy.   I must confess, however, taking such transient glimpses as I did, I was more impressed with the extent of the Vatican, and the beautiful order in which it is kept, and its great sunny, open courts, with fountains, grass, and shrubs, and the views of Rome and the Campagna from its windows, — more impressed with these, and with certain vastly capacious vases and two great sarcophagi, — than with the statuary.   Thus I went round the whole, and was dismissed through the grated barrier into the gallery of inscriptions again ; and after a little more wandering, I made my way out of the palace. . . .

Yesterday I went out betimes, and strayed through some portion of ancient Rome, to the Column of Trajan, to the Forum, thence along the Appian Way; after which I lost myself among the intricacies of the streets, and finally came out at the bridge of St. Angelo.   The first observation which a stranger is led to make, in the neighborhood of Roman ruins, is that the inhabitants seem to be strangely addicted to the washing of clothes; for all the precincts of Trajan's Forum, and of the Roman Forum, and wherever else an iron railing affords opportunity to hang them, were whitened with sheets, and other linen and cotton, drying in the sun.   It must be that washerwomen burrow among the old temples.   The second observation is not quite so favorable to the cleanly character of the modern Romans; indeed, it is so very unfavorable, that I hardly know how to express it.   But the fact is, that, through the Forum, . . . and anywhere out of the commonest foot-track and roadway, you must look well to your steps. . . . If you tread beneath the triumphal arch of Titus or Constantine, you had better look downward than upward, whatever be the merit of the sculptures aloft. . . .

After a while the visitant finds himself getting accustomed to this horrible state of things; and the associations of moral sublimity and beauty seem to throw a veil over the physical meannesses to which I allude.   Perhaps there is something in the mind of the people of these countries that enables them quite to dissever small ugliness from great sublimity and beauty.   They spit upon the glorious pavement of St. Peter's, and wherever else they like; they place paltry-looking wooden confessionals beneath its sublime arches, and ornament them with cheap little colored prints of the crucifixion; they hang tin hearts and other tinsel and trumpery at the gorgeous shrines of the saints, in chapels that are encrusted with gems, or marbles almost as precious; they put pasteboard statues of saints beneath the dome of the Pantheon ; in short, they let the sublime and the ridiculous come close together, and are not in the least troubled by the proximity. It must be that their sense of the beautiful is stronger than in the Anglo-Saxon mind, and that it observes only what is fit to gratify it.

To-day, which was bright and cool, my wife and I set forth immediately after breakfast, in search of the Baths of Diocletian, and the church of Santa Maria degl' Angeli. We went too far along the Via di Porta Pia, and after passing by two or three convents, and their high garden walls, and the villa Bonaparte on one side, and the villa Torlonia on the other, at last issued through the city gate. Before us, far away, were the Alban hills, the loftiest of which was absolutely silvered with snow and sunshine, and set in the bluest and brightest of skies. We now retraced our steps to the Fountain of the Termini, where is a ponderous heap of stone, representing Moses striking the rock ; a colossal figure, not without a certain enormous might and dignity, though rather too evidently looking his awfullest. This statue was the death of its sculptor, whose heart was broken on account of the ridicule it excited. There are many more absurd aquatic devices in Rome, however, and few better.

We turned into the Piazza di Termini, the entrance of which is at this fountain; and after some inquiry of the French soldiers, a numerous detachment of whom appear to be quartered in the vicinity, we found our way to the portal of Santa Maria degl' Angeli. The exterior of this church has no pretensions to beauty or majesty, or, indeed, to architectural merit of any kind, or to any architecture whatever; for it looks like a confused pile of ruined brickwork, with a façade resembling half the inner curve of a large oven. No one would imagine that there was a church under that enormous heap of ancient rubbish. But the door admits you into a circular vestibule, once an apartment of Diocletian's Baths, but now a portion of the nave of the church, and surrounded with monumental busts; and thence you pass into what was the central hall; now, with little change, except of detail and ornament, transformed into the body of the church. This space is so lofty, broad, and airy, that the soul forthwith swells out and magnifies itself, for the sake of filling it. It was Michel Angelo who contrived this miracle; and I feel even more grateful to him for rescuing such a noble interior from destruction, than if he had originally built it himself. In the ceiling above, you see the metal

fixtures whereon the old Romans hung their
lamps ; and there are eight gigantic pillars of
Egyptian granite, standing as they stood of yore.
There is a grand simplicity about the church,
more satisfactory than elaborate ornament ; but
the present pope has paved and adorned one of
the large chapels of the transept in very beautiful style, and the pavement of the central part is
likewise laid in rich marbles.   In the choir there
are several pictures, one of which was veiled, as
celebrated pictures frequently are in churches.
A person, who seemed to be at his devotions,
withdrew the veil for us, and we saw a Martyrdom of St. Sebastian, by Domenichino, originally, I believe, painted in fresco in St. Peter's,
but since transferred to canvas, and removed
hither.   Its place at St. Peter's is supplied by a
mosaic copy.   I was a good deal impressed by
this picture, — the dying saint, amid the sorrow
of those who loved him, and the fury of his
enemies, looking upward, where a company of
angels, and Jesus with them, are waiting to welcome him and crown him ; and I felt what an
influence pictures might have upon the devotional part of our nature.   The nail-marks in the
hands and feet of Jesus, ineffaceable, even after
he had passed into bliss and glory, touched my
heart with a sense of his love for us.   I think
this really a great picture.   We walked round
the church, looking at other paintings and fres-

cos, but saw no others that greatly interested us. In the vestibule there are monuments to Carlo Maratti and Salvator Rosa, and there is a statue of St. Bruno, by Houdon, which is pronounced to be very fine.   I thought it good, but scarcely worthy of vast admiration.   Houdon was the sculptor of the first statue of Washington, and of the bust, whence, I suppose, all subsequent statues have been, and will be, mainly modelled.

After emerging from the church, I looked back with wonder at the stack of shapeless old brickwork that hid the splendid interior.   I must go there again, and breathe freely in that noble space.

February 20. — This morning, after breakfast, I walked across the city, making a pretty straight course to the Pantheon, and thence to the bridge of St. Angelo, and to St. Peter's. It had been my purpose to go to the Fontana Paolina ; but, finding that the distance was too great, and being weighed down with a Roman lassitude, I concluded to go into St. Peter's. Here I looked at Michel Angelo's Pietà, a representation of the dead Christ, in his mother's lap.   Then I strolled round the great church, and find that it continues to grow upon me both in magnitude and beauty, by comparison with the many interiors of sacred edifices which I have lately seen.   At times, a single,

casual, momentary glimpse of its magnificence
gleams upon my soul, as it were, when I happen to glance at arch opening beyond arch,
and I am surprised into admiration. I have
experienced that a landscape and the sky unfold the deepest beauty in a similar way ; not
when they are gazed at of set purpose, but when
the spectator looks suddenly through a vista,
among a crowd of other thoughts. Passing
near the confessionals for foreigners to-day, I
saw a Spaniard, who had just come out of the
one devoted to his native tongue, taking leave
of his confessor, with an affectionate reverence,
which — as well as the benign dignity of the
good father — it was good to behold. . . .

I returned home early, in order to go with
my wife to the Barberini Palace at two o'clock.
We entered through the gateway, through the
Via delle Quattro Fontane, passing one or two
sentinels ; for there is apparently a regiment of
dragoons quartered on the ground floor of the
palace ; and I stumbled upon a room containing their saddles the other day, when seeking
for Mr. Story's staircase. The entrance to the
picture gallery is by a door on the right hand,
affording us a sight of a beautiful spiral staircase, which goes circling upward from the very
basement to the very summit of the palace, with
a perfectly easy ascent, yet confining its sweep
within a moderate compass. We looked up

through the interior of the spiral, as through a
tube, from the bottom to the top.   The pictures are contained in three contiguous rooms
of the lower piano, and are few in number, comprising barely half a dozen which I should care
to see again, though doubtless all have value
in their way.   One that attracted our attention
was a picture of Christ Disputing with the Doc-
tors, by Albert Dürer, in which was represented
the ugliest, most evil-minded, stubborn, prag-
matical, and contentious old Jew that ever lived
under the law of Moses ; and he and the child
Jesus were arguing, not only with their tongues,
but making hieroglyphics, as it were, by the
motion of their hands and fingers.   It is a very
queer, as well as a very remarkable picture.
But we passed hastily by this, and almost all
others, being eager to see the two which chiefly
make the collection famous, — Raphael's Fornarina, and Guido's portrait of Beatrice Cenci.
These were found in the last of the three
rooms, and, as regards Beatrice Cenci, I might
as well not try to say anything ; for its spell is
indefinable, and the painter has wrought it in a
way more like magic than anything else. . . .

It is the most profoundly wrought picture in
the world ; no artist did it, nor could do it
again. Guido may have held the brush, but he
painted better than he knew. I wish, however,
it were possible for some spectator, of deep

sensibility, to see the picture without knowing anything of its subject or history ; for, no doubt, we bring all our knowledge of the Cenci tragedy to the interpretation of it.

Close beside the Beatrice Cenci hangs the Fornarina. . . .

While we were looking at these works Miss M—— unexpectedly joined us, and we went, all three together, to the Rospigliosi Palace, in the Piazza di Monte Cavallo. A porter, in cocked hat, and with a staff of office, admitted us into a spacious court before the palace, and directed us to a garden on one side, raised as much as twenty feet above the level on which we stood. The gardener opened the gate for us, and we ascended a beautiful stone staircase, with a carved balustrade, bearing many marks of time and weather. Reaching the garden level, we found it laid out in walks, bordered with box and ornamental shrubbery, amid which were lemon-trees, and one large old exotic from some distant clime. In the centre of the garden, surrounded by a stone balustrade, like that of the staircase, was a fish-pond, into which several jets of water were continually spouting ; and on pedestals, that made part of the balusters, stood eight marble statues of Apollo, Cupid, nymphs, and other such sunny and beautiful people of classic mythology. There had been many more of these statues, but the rest had disappeared, and those which remained had suffered grievous damage, here to a nose, there to a hand or foot, and often a fracture of the body, very imperfectly mended. There was a pleasant sunshine in the garden, and a spring-like, or rather a genial, autumnal atmosphere, though elsewhere it was a day of poisonous Roman chill.

At the end of the garden, which was of no great extent, was an edifice, bordering on the piazza, called the Casino — which, I presume, means a garden house. The front is richly ornamented with bas-reliefs, and statues in niches; as if it were a place for pleasure and enjoyment, and therefore ought to be beautiful. As we approached it, the door swung open, and we went into a large room on the ground floor, and, looking up to the ceiling, beheld Guido's Aurora. The picture is as fresh and brilliant as if he had painted it with the morning sunshine which it represents. It could not be more lustrous in its hues, if he had given it the last touch an hour ago. Three or four artists were copying it at that instant, and positively their colors did not look brighter, though a great deal newer than his. The alacrity and movement, briskness and morning stir and glow of the picture are wonderful. It seems impossible to catch its glory in a copy. Several artists, as I said, were making the attempt, and we saw two

other attempted copies leaning against the wall,
but it was easy to detect failure in just essential
points.   My memory, I believe, will be somewhat enlivened by this picture hereafter : not
that I remember it very distinctly even now ;
but bright things leave a sheen and glimmer in
the mind, like Christian's tremulous glimpse of
the Celestial City.

In two other rooms of the Casino we saw pictures by Domenichino, Rubens, and other famous painters, which I do not mean to speak
of, because I cared really little or nothing about
them.   Returning into the garden, the sunny
warmth of which was most grateful after the chill
air and cold pavement of the Casino, we walked
round the laguna, examining the statues, and
looking down at some little fishes that swarmed
at the stone margin of the pool.   There were
two infants of the Rospigliosi family : one, a
young child playing with a maid and head-ser-
vant ; another, the very chubbiest and rosiest
boy in the world, sleeping on its nurse's bosom.
The nurse was a comely woman enough, dressed
in bright colors, which fitly set off the deep hues
of her Italian face.   An old painter very likely
would have beautified and refined the pair into
a Madonna, with the child Jesus ; for an artist
need not go far in Italy to find a picture ready
composed and tinted, needing little more than
to be literally copied.

Miss M—— had gone away before us; but my wife and I, after leaving the Palazzo Rospigliosi, and on our way home, went into the Church of St. Andrea, which belongs to a convent of Jesuits. I have long ago exhausted all my capacity of admiration for splendid interiors of churches, but methinks this little, little temple (it is not more than fifty or sixty feet across) has a more perfect and gem-like beauty than any other. Its shape is oval, with an oval dome, and, above that, another little dome, both of which are magnificently frescoed. Around the base of the larger dome is wreathed a flight of angels, and the smaller and upper one is encircled by a garland of cherubs, — cherub and angel all of pure white marble. The oval centre of the church is walled round with precious and lustrous marble, of a red-veined variety interspersed with columns and pilasters of white; and there are arches opening through this rich wall, forming chapels, which the architect seems to have striven hard to make even more gorgeous than the main body of the church. They contain beautiful pictures, not dark and faded, but glowing, as if just from the painter's hands; and the shrines are adorned with whatever is most rare, and in one of them was the great carbuncle; at any rate, a bright, fiery gem as big as a turkey's egg. The pavement of the church was one star of various-colored marble, and in the centre was a mosaic, covering, I believe, the tomb of the founder.   I have not seen, nor expect to see, anything else so entirely and satisfactorily finished as this small oval church; and I only wish I could pack it in a large box, and send it home.

I must not forget that, on our way from the Barberini Palace, we stopped an instant to look at the house, at the corner of the street of the four fountains, where Milton was a guest while in Rome.   He seems quite a man of our own day, seen so nearly at the hither extremity of the vista through which we look back, from the epoch of railways to that of the oldest Egyptian obelisk.   The house (it was then occupied by the Cardinal Barberini) looks as if it might have been built within the present century; for mediæval houses in Rome do not assume the aspect of antiquity; perhaps because the Italian style of architecture, or something similar, is the one more generally in vogue in most cities.

February 21. — This morning I took my way through the Porta del Popolo, intending to spend the forenoon in the Campagna; but, getting weary of the straight, uninteresting street that runs out of the gate, I turned aside from it, and soon found myself on the shores of the Tiber.   It looked, as usual, like a saturated solution of yellow mud, and eddied hastily along between deep banks of clay, and over a clay bed, in which doubtless are hidden many a richer treasure than we now possess. The French once proposed to draw off the river, for the purpose of recovering all the sunken statues and relics; but the Romans made strenuous objection, on account of the increased virulence of malaria which would probably result. I saw a man on the immediate shore of the river, fifty feet or so beneath the bank on which I stood, sitting patiently, with an angling rod; and I waited to see what he might catch. Two other persons likewise sat down to watch him; but he caught nothing so long as I stayed, and at last seemed to give it up. The banks and vicinity of the river are very bare and uninviting, as I then saw them; no shade, no verdure, — a rough, neglected aspect, and a peculiar shabbiness about the few houses that were visible. Farther down the stream the dome of St. Peter's showed itself on the other side, seeming to stand on the outskirts of the city. I walked along the banks, with some expectation of finding a ferry, by which I might cross the river; but my course was soon interrupted by the wall, and I turned up a lane that led me straight back again to the Porta del Popolo. I stopped a moment, however, to see some young men pitching quoits, which they appeared to do with a good deal of skill.

I went along the Via di Ripetta, and through other streets, stepping into two or three churches, one of which was the Pantheon. . . .

There are, I think, seven deep, pillared recesses around the circumference of it, each of which becomes a sufficiently capacious chapel; and alternately with these chapels there is a marble structure, like the architecture of a doorway, beneath which is the shrine of a saint; so that the whole circle of the Pantheon is filled up with the seven chapels and seven shrines. A number of persons were sitting or kneeling around; others came in while I was there, dipping their fingers in the holy water, and bending the knee, as they passed the shrines and chapels, until they reached the one which, apparently, they had selected as the particular altar for their devotions. Everybody seemed so devout, and in a frame of mind so suited to the day and place, that it really made me feel a little awkward not to be able to kneel down along with them. Unlike the worshippers in our own churches, each individual here seems to do his own individual acts of devotion, and I cannot but think it better so than to make an effort for united prayer as we do. It is my opinion that a great deal of devout and reverential feeling is kept alive in people's hearts by the Catholic mode of worship.

Soon leaving the Pantheon, a few minutes'

walk towards the Corso brought me to the Church of St. Ignazio, which belongs to the College of the Jesuits. It is spacious and of beautiful architecture, but not strikingly distinguished, in the latter particular, from many others; a wide and lofty nave, supported upon marble columns, between which arches open into the side-aisles, and at the junction of the nave and transept a dome, resting on four great arches. The church seemed to be purposely somewhat darkened, so that I could not well see the details of the ornamentation, except the frescos on the ceiling of the nave, which were very brilliant, and done in so effectual a style, that I really could not satisfy myself that some of the figures did not actually protrude from the ceiling, — in short, that they were not colored bas-reliefs, instead of frescos. No words can express the beautiful effect, in an upholstery point of view, of this kind of decoration. Here, as at the Pantheon, there were many persons sitting silent, kneeling, or passing from shrine to shrine.

I reached home at about twelve, and at one set out again, with my wife, towards St. Peter's, where we meant to stay till after Vespers. We walked across the city, and through the Piazza de Navona, where we stopped to look at one of Bernini's absurd fountains, of which the water makes but the smallest part, — a little squirt or

two amid a prodigious fuss of gods and mon-
sters.   Thence we passed by the poor, battered-
down torso of Pasquin, and came, by devious
ways, to the bridge of St. Angelo; the streets
bearing pretty much their week-day aspect, many
of the shops open, the market-stalls doing their
usual business, and the people brisk and gay,
though not indecorously so.   I suppose there
was hardly a man or woman who had not heard
mass, confessed, and said their prayers; a thing
which — the prayers, I mean, — it would be
absurd to predicate of London, New York, or
any Protestant city.   In however adulterated a
guise, the Catholics do get a draught of devotion to slake the thirst of their souls, and methinks it must needs do them good, even if not
quite so pure as if it came from better cisterns,
or from the original fountain head.

Arriving at St. Peter's shortly after two, we
walked round the whole church, looking at all
the pictures and most of the monuments, . . .
and paused longest before Guido's Archangel
Michael overcoming Lucifer.   This is surely
one of the most beautiful things in the world,
one of the human conceptions that are imbued
most deeply with the celestial. . . .

We then sat down in one of the aisles and
awaited the beginning of Vespers, which we
supposed would take place at half past three.
Four o'clock came, however, and no Vespers;

and as our dinner hour is five, . . . we at last came away without hearing the vesper hymn.

February 23. — Yesterday, at noon, we set out for the Capitol, and after going up the acclivity (not from the Forum, but from the opposite direction), stopped to look at the statues of Castor and Pollux, which, with other sculptures, look down the ascent. Castor and his brother seem to me to have heads disproportionately large, and are not so striking, in any respect, as such great images ought to be. But we heartily admired the equestrian statue of Marcus Aurelius Antoninus, . . . and looked at a fountain, principally composed, I think, of figures representing the Nile and the Tiber, who loll upon their elbows and preside over the gushing water; and between them, against the façade of the Senator's Palace, there is a statue of Minerva, with a petticoat of red porphyry. Having taken note of these objects, we went to the Museum, in an edifice on our left, entering the piazza, and here, in the vestibule, we found various old statues and relics. Ascending the stairs, we passed through a long gallery, and, turning to our left, examined somewhat more carefully a suite of rooms running parallel with it. The first of these contained busts of the Cæsars and their kindred, from the epoch of the mightiest Julius downward; eighty-three,

I believe, in all.   I had seen a bust of Julius
Cæsar in the British Museum, and was surprised at its thin and withered aspect ; but this
head is of a very ugly old man indeed, — wrin-
kled, puckered, shrunken, lacking breadth and
substance ; careworn, grim, as if he had fought
hard with life, and had suffered in the conflict ;
a man of schemes, and of eager effort to bring
his schemes to pass.   His profile is by no means
good, advancing from the top of his forehead
to the tip of his nose, and retreating, at about
the same angle, from the latter point to the bottom of his chin, which seems to be thrust forci-
bly down into his meagre neck, — not that he
pokes his head forward, however, for it is particularly erect.

The head of Augustus is very beautiful, and
appears to be that of a meditative, philosophic
man, saddened with the sense that it is not very
much worth while to be at the summit of human greatness after all.   It is a sorrowful thing
to trace the decay of civilization through this
series of busts, and to observe how the artistic
skill, so requisite at first, went on declining
through the dreary dynasty of the Cæsars, till
at length the master of the world could not get
his head carved in better style than the figure-
head of a ship.

In the next room there were better statues
than we had yet seen ; but in the last room of

the range we found The Dying Gladiator, of which I had already caught a glimpse in passing by the open door. It had made all the other treasures of the gallery tedious in my eagerness to come to that. I do not believe that so much pathos is wrought into any other block of stone. Like all works of the highest excellence, however, it makes great demands upon the spectator. He must make a generous gift of his sympathies to the sculptor, and help out his skill with all his heart, or else he will see little more than a skilfully wrought surface. It suggests far more than it shows. I looked long at this statue, and little at anything else, though, among other famous works, a statue of Antinoüs was in the same room.

I was glad when we left the Museum, which, by the bye, was piercingly chill, as if the multitude of statues radiated cold out of their marble substance. We might have gone to see the pictures in the Palace of the Conservatori, and Sophia, whose receptivity is unlimited and forever fresh, would willingly have done so; but I objected, and we went towards the Forum. I had noticed, two or three times, an inscription over a mean-looking door in this neighborhood, stating that here was the entrance to the prison of the holy Apostles Peter and Paul; and we soon found the spot, not far from the Forum, with two wretched frescos of the apostles above

the inscription. We knocked at the door without effect; but a lame beggar, who sat at another door of the same house (which looked
exceedingly like a liquor shop), desired us to
follow him, and began to ascend to the Capitol,
by the causeway leading from the Forum.   A
little way upward we met a woman, to whom
the beggar delivered us over, and she led us into
a church or chapel door, and pointed to a long
flight of steps, which descended through twilight into utter darkness.   She called to somebody in the lower regions, and then went away,
leaving us to get down this mysterious staircase
by ourselves.   Down we went, farther and farther from the daylight, and found ourselves,
anon, in a dark chamber or cell, the shape or
boundaries of which we could not make out,
though it seemed to be of stone, and black and
dungeon-like. Indistinctly, and from a still farther depth in the earth, we heard voices, — one
voice, at least, — apparently not addressing ourselves, but some other persons; and soon, directly beneath our feet, we saw a glimmering of
light through a round, iron-grated hole in the
bottom of the dungeon. In a few moments the
glimmer and the voice came up through this
hole, and the light disappeared, and it and the
voice came glimmering and babbling up a flight
of stone stairs, of which we had not hitherto
been aware. It was the custode, with a party of

visitors, to whom he had been showing St. Peter's dungeon. Each visitor was provided with a wax taper, and the custode gave one to each of us, bidding us wait a moment while he conducted the other party to the upper air. During his absence we examined the cell, as well as our dim lights would permit, and soon found an indentation in the wall, with an iron grate put over it for protection, and an inscription above informing us that the Apostle Peter had here left the imprint of his visage; and, in truth, there is a profile there, — forehead, nose, mouth, and chin, — plainly to be seen, an intaglio in the solid rock. We touched it with the tips of our fingers, as well as saw it with our eyes.

The custode soon returned, and led us down the darksome steps, chattering in Italian all the time. It is not a very long descent to the lower cell, the roof of which is so low that I believe I could have reached it with my hand. We were now in the deepest and ugliest part of the old Mamertine Prison, one of the few remains of the kingly period of Rome, and which served the Romans as a state prison for hundreds of years before the Christian era. A multitude of criminals or innocent persons, no doubt, have languished here in misery, and perished in darkness. Here Jugurtha starved; here Catiline's adherents were strangled; and, methinks, there cannot be in the world another such an evil den, so haunted with black memories and indistinct surmises of guilt and suffering. In old Rome, I suppose, the citizens never spoke of this dungeon above their breath. It looks just as bad as it is; round, only seven paces across, yet so obscure that our tapers could not illuminate it from side to side, — the stones of which it is constructed being as black as midnight. The custode showed us a stone post, at the side of the cell, with the hole in the top of it, into which, he said, St. Peter's chain had been fastened; and he uncovered a spring of water, in the middle of the stone floor, which he told us had miraculously gushed up to enable the saint to baptize his jailer. The miracle was perhaps the more easily wrought, inasmuch as Jugurtha had found the floor of the dungeon oozy with wet. However, it is best to be as simple and childlike as we can in these matters; and whether St. Peter stamped his visage into the stone, and wrought this other miracle or no, and whether or no he ever was in the prison at all, still the belief of a thousand years and more gives a sort of reality and substance to such traditions. The custode dipped an iron ladle into the miraculous water, and we each of us drank a sip; and, what is very remarkable, to me it seemed hard water and almost brackish, while many persons think it the sweetest in Rome. I suspect that St. Peter still dabbles in this water, and tempers its qualities according to the faith of those who drink it.

The staircase descending into the lower dungeon is comparatively modern, there having been no entrance of old, except through the small circular opening in the roof. In the upper cell the custode showed us an ancient flight of stairs, now built into the wall, which used to lead from the Capitol. The whole precincts are now consecrated, and I believe the upper portion, perhaps both upper and lower, are a shrine or a chapel.

I now left Sophia in the Forum, and went to call on Mr. J. P. K—— at the Hôtel d'Europe. I found him just returned from a drive, — a gentleman of about sixty or more, with gray hair, a pleasant, intellectual face, and penetrating, but not unkindly eyes. He moved infirmly, being on the recovery from an illness. We went up to his saloon together, and had a talk, — or, rather, he had it nearly all to himself, — and particularly sensible talk, too, and full of the results of learning and experience. In the first place, he settled the whole Kansas difficulty ; then he made havoc of St. Peter, who came very shabbily out of his hands, as regarded his early character in the Church, and his claims to the position he now holds in it. Mr. K—— also gave a curious illustration, from something that happened to himself, of the little

dependence that can be placed on tradition purporting to be ancient, and I capped his story by
telling him how the site of my town pump, so
plainly indicated in the sketch itself, has already
been mistaken in the city council and in the public prints.

February 24. — Yesterday I crossed the Ponte
Sisto, and took a short ramble on the other side
of the river; and it rather surprised me to discover, pretty nearly opposite the Capitoline
Hill, a quay, at which several schooners and
barks, of two or three hundred tons' burden,
were moored. There was also a steamer, armed
with a large gun and two brass swivels on her
forecastle, and I know not what artillery besides. Probably she may have been a revenue
cutter.

Returning I crossed the river by way of the
island of St. Bartholomew over two bridges.
The island is densely covered with buildings,
and is a separate small fragment of the city. It
was a tradition of the ancient Romans that it
was formed by the aggregation of soil and rubbish brought down by the river, and accumulating round the nucleus of some sunken baskets.

On reaching the hither side of the river, I
soon struck upon the ruins of the theatre of
Marcellus, which are very picturesque, and the
more so from being closely linked in, indeed

identified with the shops, habitations, and swarming life of modern Rome.   The most striking
portion was a circular edifice, which seemed to
have been composed of a row of Ionic columns,
standing upon a lower row of Doric, many of
the antique pillars being yet perfect; but the
intervening arches built up with brickwork, and
the whole once magnificent structure now ten-
anted by poor and squalid people, as thick as
mites within the round of an old cheese. From
this point I cannot very clearly trace out my
course ; but I passed, I think, between the Circus Maximus and the Palace of the Cæsars,
and near the Baths of Caracalla, and went into
the cloisters of the Church of San Gregorio.
All along I saw massive ruins, not particularly
picturesque or beautiful, but huge, mountainous piles, chiefly of brickwork, somewhat weed-
grown here and there, but oftener bare and
dreary. . . . All the successive ages since Rome
began to decay have done their best to ruin the
very ruins by taking away the marble and the
hewn stone for their own structures, and leaving only the inner filling up of brickwork, which
the ancient architects never designed to be seen.
The consequence of all this is, that, except for
the lofty and poetical associations connected
with it, and except, too, for the immense difference in magnitude, a Roman ruin may be in itself not more picturesque than I have seen an

old cellar, with a shattered brick chimney half crumbling down into it, in New England.

By this time I knew not whither I was going, and turned aside from a broad, paved road (it was the Appian Way) into the Via Latina, which I supposed would lead to one of the city gates. It was a lonely path : on my right hand extensive piles of ruin, in strange shapes or shapelessness, built of the broad and thin old Roman bricks, such as may be traced everywhere, when the stucco has fallen away from a modern Roman house ; for I imagine there has not been a new brick made here for a thousand years. On my left, I think, was a high wall, and before me, grazing in the road . . . [the buffalo calf of The Marble Faun. — S. H.]. The road went boldly on, with a well-worn track up to the very walls of the city ; but there it abruptly terminated at an ancient, closed-up gateway. From a notice posted against a door, which appeared to be the entrance to the ruins on my left, I found that these were the remains of Columbaria, where the dead used to be put away in pigeon-holes. Reaching the paved road again, I kept on my course, passing the tomb of the Scipios, and soon came to the gate of San Sebastiano, through which I entered the Campagna. Indeed, the scene around was so rural, that I had fancied myself already beyond the walls. As the afternoon was getting advanced, I did not proceed any farther towards the blue hills which I saw in the distance, but turned to my left, following a road that runs round the exterior of the city wall. It was very dreary and solitary, — not a house on the whole track, with the broad and shaggy Campagna on one side, and the high, bare wall, looking down over my head, on the other. It is not, any more than the other objects of the scene, a very picturesque wall, but is little more than a brick garden-fence seen through a magnifying-glass, with now and then a tower, however, and frequent buttresses, to keep its height of fifty feet from toppling over. The top was ragged, and fringed with a few weeds ; there had been embrasures for guns and eyelet-holes for musketry, but these were plastered up with brick or stone. I passed one or two walled-up gateways (by the bye, the Porta Latina was the gate through which Belisarius first entered Rome), and one of these had two high, round towers, and looked more Gothic and venerable with antique strength than any other portion of the wall. Immediately after this I came to the gate of San Giovanni, just within which is the Basilica of St. John Lateran, and there I was glad to rest myself upon a bench before proceeding homeward.

There was a French sentinel at this gateway, as at all the others ; for the Gauls have always

been a pest to Rome, and now gall her worse
than ever.   I observed, too, that an official, in
citizen's dress, stood there also, and appeared
to exercise a supervision over some carts with
country produce, that were entering just then.

February 25. — We went this forenoon to
the Palazzo Borghese, which is situated on a
street that runs at right angles with the Corso,
and very near the latter.   Most of the palaces
in Rome, and the Borghese among them, were
built somewhere about the sixteenth century;
this in 1590, I believe.   It is an immense edifice standing round the four sides of a quadrangle; and though the suite of rooms comprising the picture-gallery forms an almost
interminable vista, they occupy only a part of
the ground floor of one side.   We enter from
the street into a large court, surrounded with a
corridor, the arches of which support a second
series of arches above.   The picture rooms
open from one into another, and have many
points of magnificence, being large and lofty,
with vaulted ceilings and beautiful frescos, generally of mythological subjects, in the flat central part of the vault.   The cornices are gilded;
the deep embrasures of the windows are panelled with woodwork; the doorways are of
polished and variegated marble, or covered with
a composition as hard, and seemingly as dur-

able. The whole has a kind of splendid shabbiness thrown over it, like a slight coating of rust; the furniture, at least the damask chairs, being a good deal worn, though there are marble and mosaic tables, which may serve to adorn another palace when this one crumbles away with age. One beautiful hall, with a ceiling more richly gilded than the rest, is panelled all round with large looking-glasses, on which are painted pictures, both landscapes and human figures, in oils; so that the effect is somewhat as if you saw these objects represented in the mirrors. These glasses must be of old date, perhaps coeval with the first building of the palace; for they are so much dimmed, that one's own figure appears indistinct in them, and more difficult to be traced than the pictures which cover them half over. It was very comfortless, — indeed, I suppose nobody ever thought of being comfortable there, since the house was built, — but especially uncomfortable on a chill, damp day like this. My fingers were quite numb before I got halfway through the suite of apartments, in spite of a brazier of charcoal which was smouldering into ashes in two or three of the rooms. There was not, so far as I remember, a single fireplace in the suite. A considerable number of visitors — not many, however — were there; and a good many artists; and three or four ladies among them were making copies of the more celebrated pictures, and in all or in most cases missing the especial points that made their celebrity and value. The Prince Borghese certainly demeans himself like a kind and liberal gentleman, in throwing open this invaluable collection to the public to see, and for artists to carry away with them, and diffuse all over the world, so far as their own power and skill will permit. It is open every day of the week, except Saturday and Sunday, without any irksome restriction or supervision; and the fee, which custom requires the visitor to pay to the custode, has the good effect of making us feel that we are not intruders, nor received in an exactly eleemosynary way. The thing could not be better managed.

The collection is one of the most celebrated in the world, and contains between eight and nine hundred pictures, many of which are esteemed masterpieces. I think I was not in a frame for admiration to-day, nor could achieve that free and generous surrender of myself which I have already said is essential to the proper estimate of anything excellent. Besides, how is it possible to give one's soul, or any considerable part of it, to a single picture, seen for the first time, among a thousand others, all of which set forth their own claims in an equally good light? Furthermore, there is an external weariness, and sense of a thousand-fold sameness to be overcome, before we can begin to enjoy a gallery of the old Italian masters. . . . I remember but one painter, Francia, who seems really to have approached this awful class of subjects (Christs and Madonnas) in a fitting spirit; his pictures are very singular and awkward, if you look at them with merely an external eye, but they are full of the beauty of holiness, and evidently wrought out as acts of devotion, with the deepest sincerity; and are veritable prayers upon canvas. . . .

I was glad, in the very last of the twelve rooms, to come upon some Dutch and Flemish pictures, very few, but very welcome; Rubens, Rembrandt, Vandyke, Paul Potter, Teniers, and others, — men of flesh and blood and warm fists and human hearts. As compared with them, these mighty Italian masters seem men of polished steel; not human, nor addressing themselves so much to human sympathies as to a formed, intellectual taste.

March 1. — To-day began very unfavorably; but we ventured out at about eleven o'clock, intending to visit the gallery of the Colonna Palace. Finding it closed, however, on account of the illness of the custode, we determined to go to the picture-gallery of the Capitol; and on our way thither, we stepped into St. Gesù, the grand and rich church of the Jesuits, where we found a priest in white, preaching a sermon, with vast earnestness of action and variety of tones, insomuch that I fancied sometimes that two priests were in the agony of sermonizing at once. He had a pretty large and seemingly attentive audience clustered round him from the entrance of the church, halfway down the nave ; while in the chapels of the transepts and in the remoter distances were persons occupied with their own individual devotion. We sat down near the chapel of St. Ignazio, which is adorned with a picture over the altar, and with marble sculptures of the Trinity aloft, and of angels fluttering at the sides. What I particularly noted (for the angels were not very real personages, being neither earthly nor celestial) was the great ball of lapis lazuli, the biggest in the world, at the feet of the First Person in the Trinity. The church is a splendid one, lined with a great variety of precious marbles, . . . but partly, perhaps owing to the dusky light, as well as to the want of cleanliness, there was a dingy effect upon the whole. We made but a very short stay, our New England breeding causing us to feel shy of moving about the church in sermon time.

It rained when we reached the Capitol, and, as the museum was not yet open, we went into the Palace of the Conservators, on the opposite side of the piazza. Around the inner court of the ground floor, partly under two opposite arcades, and partly under the sky, are several statues and other ancient sculptures; among them a statue of Julius Cæsar, said to be the only authentic one, and certainly giving an impression of him more in accordance with his character than the withered old face in the museum; also, a statue of Augustus in middle age, still retaining a resemblance to the bust of him in youth; some gigantic heads and hands and feet in marble and bronze; a stone lion and horse, which lay long at the bottom of a river, broken and corroded, and were repaired by Michel Angelo; and other things which it were wearisome to set down. We inquired of two or three French soldiers the way into the picture-gallery; but it is our experience that French soldiers in Rome never know anything of what is around them, not even the name of the palace or public place over which they stand guard; and though invariably civil, you might as well put a question to a statue of an old Roman as to one of them. While we stood under the loggia, however, looking at the rain plashing into the court, a soldier of the Papal Guard kindly directed us up the staircase, and even took pains to go with us to the very entrance of the picture rooms. Thank Heaven, there are but two of them, and not many pictures which one cares to look at very long.

Italian galleries are at a disadvantage as compared with English ones, inasmuch as the pictures are not nearly such splendid articles of upholstery; though, very likely, having undergone less cleaning and varnishing, they may retain more perfectly the finer touches of the masters. Nevertheless, I miss the mellow glow, the rich and mild external lustre, and even the brilliant frames of the pictures I have seen in England. You feel that they have had loving care taken of them; even if spoiled, it is because they have been valued so much. But these pictures in Italian galleries look rusty and lustreless, as far as the exterior is concerned; and, really, the splendor of the painting, as a production of intellect and feeling, has a good deal of difficulty in shining through such clouds.

There is a picture at the Capitol, The Rape of Europa, by Paul Veronese, that would glow with wonderful brilliancy if it were set in a magnificent frame and covered with a sunshine of varnish; and it is a kind of picture that would not be desecrated, as some deeper and holier ones might be, by any splendor of external adornment that could be bestowed on it. It is deplorable and disheartening to see it in faded and shabby plight,—this joyous, exuberant, warm, voluptuous work. There is the head of a cow thrust into the picture, and staring with wild, ludicrous wonder at the godlike bull, so as to introduce quite a new sentiment.

Here, and at the Borghese Palace, there were some pictures by Garofalo, an artist of whom I never heard before, but who seemed to have been a man of power. A picture by Marie Sublegras — a miniature copy from one by her husband, of the woman anointing the feet of Christ — is most delicately and beautifully finished, and would be an ornament to a drawing-room; a thing that could not truly be said of one in a hundred of these grim masterpieces. When they were painted life was not what it is now, and the artists had not the same ends in view. . . . It depresses the spirits to go from picture to picture, leaving a portion of your vital sympathy at every one, so that you come, with a kind of half-torpid desperation, to the end. On our way down the staircase we saw several noteworthy bas-reliefs, and among them a very ancient one of Curtius plunging on horseback into the chasm in the Forum. It seems to me, however, that old sculpture affects the spirits even more dolefully than old painting; it strikes colder to the heart, and lies heavier upon it, being marble, than if it were merely canvas.

My wife went to revisit the museum, which we had already seen, on the other side of the piazza; but, being cold, I left her there, and went out to ramble in the sun; for it was now brightly, though fitfully, shining again.   I walked through the Forum (where a thorn thrust itself out and tore the sleeve of my talma), and under the Arch of Titus, towards the Coliseum. About a score of French drummers were beating a long, loud roll-call, at the base of the Coliseum and under its arches; and a score of trumpeters responded to these, from the rising ground opposite the Arch of Constantine ; and the echoes of the old Roman ruins, especially those of the Palace of the Cæsars, responded to this martial uproar of the barbarians.   There seemed to be no cause for it; but the drummers beat, and the trumpeters blew, as long as I was within hearing.

I walked along the Appian Way as far as the Baths of Caracalla.   The Palace of the Cæsars, which I have never yet explored, appears to be crowned by the walls of a convent, built, no doubt, out of some of the fragments that would suffice to build a city; and I think there is another convent among the baths.   The Catholics have taken a peculiar pleasure in planting themselves in the very citadels of paganism, whether temples or palaces.   There has been a good deal of enjoyment in the destruction of old Rome. I often think so when I see the elaborate pains that have been taken to smash and demolish some beautiful column, for no purpose whatever, except the mere delight of annihilating a noble piece of work. There is something in the impulse with which one sympathizes; though I am afraid the destroyers were not sufficiently aware of the mischief they did to enjoy it fully. Probably, too, the early Christians were impelled by religious zeal to destroy the pagan temples, before the happy thought occurred of converting them into churches.

March 3. — This morning was Una's birthday, and we celebrated it by taking a barouche, and driving (the whole family) out on the Appian Way as far as the tomb of Cecilia Metella. For the first time since we came to Rome, the weather was really warm, — a kind of heat producing languor and disinclination to active movement, though still a little breeze which was stirring threw an' occasional coolness over us, and made us distrust the almost sultry atmosphere. I cannot think the Roman climate healthy in any of its moods that I have experienced.

Close on the other side of the road are the ruins of a Gothic chapel, little more than a few bare walls and painted windows, and some other fragmentary structures which we did not particularly examine. Una and I clambered through a gap in the wall, extending from the basement of the tomb, and thus, getting into the field beyond, went quite round the mausoleum and the remains of the castle connected with it. The latter, though still high and stalwart, showed few or no architectural features of interest, being built, I think, principally of large bricks, and not to be compared to English ruins as a beautiful or venerable object.

A little way beyond Cecilia Metella's tomb, the road still shows a specimen of the ancient Roman pavement, composed of broad, flat flagstones, a good deal cracked and worn, but sound enough, probably, to outlast the little cubes which make the other portions of the road so uncomfortable. We turned back from this point, and soon reëntered the gate of St. Sebastian, which is flanked by two small towers, and just within which is the old triumphal arch of Drusus, — a sturdy construction, much dilapidated as regards its architectural beauty, but rendered far more picturesque than it could have been in its best days by a crown of verdure on its head. Probably so much of the dust of the highway has risen in clouds and settled there, that sufficient soil for shrubbery to root itself has thus been collected, by small annual contributions, in the course of two thousand years. A little farther towards the city we turned aside from the Appian Way, and came to the site of some ancient Columbaria, close by what seemed to partake of the character of a villa and a farmhouse. A man came out of the house and unlocked a door in a low building, apparently quite modern ; but on entering we found ourselves looking into a large, square chamber, sunk entirely beneath the surface of the ground. A very narrow and steep staircase of stone, and evidently ancient, descended into this chamber ; and, going down, we found the walls hollowed on all sides into little semicircular niches, of which, I believe, there were nine rows, one above another, and nine niches in each row. Thus they looked somewhat like the little entrances to a pigeon house, and hence the name of Columbarium. Each semicircular niche was about a foot in its semidiameter. In the centre of this subterranean chamber was a solid square column, or pier, rising to the roof, and containing other niches of the same pattern, besides one that was high and deep, rising to the height of a man from the floor on each of the four sides. In every one of the semicircular niches were two round holes covered with an earthen plate, and in each hole were ashes and little fragments of bones, — the ashes and bones of the dead, whose names were inscribed in Roman capitals on marble slabs inlaid into the wall over each individual niche. Very likely the great ones in the central pier had contained statues, or busts, or large urns ; indeed, I remember that some such things were there, as well as bas-reliefs in the walls ; but hardly more than the general aspect of this strange place remains in my mind. It was the Columbarium of the connections or dependants of the Cæsars; and the impression left on me was, that this mode of disposing of the dead was infinitely preferable to any which has been adopted since that day. The handful or two of dry dust and bits of dry bones in each of the small round holes had nothing disgusting in them, and they are no drier now than they were when first deposited there. I would rather have my ashes scattered over the soil to help the growth of the grass and daisies; but still I should not murmur much at having them decently pigeonholed in a Roman tomb.

After ascending out of this chamber of the dead, we looked down into another similar one, containing the ashes of Pompey's household, which was discovered only a very few years ago. Its arrangement was the same as that first described, except that it had no central pier with a passage round it, as the former had.

While we were down in the first chamber the proprietor of the spot — a half-gentlemanly and very affable kind of person — came to us, and explained the arrangements of the Columbarium, though, indeed we understood them better by their own aspect than by his explanation. The whole soil around his dwelling is elevated much above the level of the road, and it is prob-

able that, if he chose to excavate, he might bring
to light many more sepulchral chambers, and
find his profits in them too, by disposing of the
urns and busts.   What struck me as much as
anything was the neatness of these subterranean
apartments, which were quite as fit to sleep in
as most of those occupied by living Romans;
and, having undergone no wear and tear, they
were in as good condition as on the day they
were built.

In this Columbarium, measuring about twenty
feet square, I roughly estimate that there have
been deposited together the remains of at least
seven or eight hundred persons, reckoning two
little heaps of bones and ashes in each pigeon-
hole, nine pigeonholes in each row, and nine
rows on each side, besides those on the middle
pier.   All difficulty in finding space for the dead
would be obviated by returning to the ancient
fashion of reducing them to ashes, — the only
objection, though a very serious one, being the
quantity of fuel that it would require.   But perhaps future chemists may discover some better
means of consuming or dissolving this trouble-
some mortality of ours.

We got into the carriage again, and, driving
farther towards the city, came to the tomb of
the Scipios, of the exterior of which I retain no
very definite idea.   It was close upon the Appian Way, however, though separated from it

by a high fence, and accessible through a gateway, leading into a court.   I think the tomb is
wholly subterranean, and that the ground above
it is covered with the buildings of a farmhouse ;
but of this I cannot be certain, as we were led
immediately into a dark, underground passage,
by an elderly peasant, of a cheerful and affable
demeanor.   As soon as he had brought us into
the twilight of the tomb, he lighted a long wax
taper for each of us, and led us groping into
blacker and blacker darkness.   Even little Rose
followed courageously in the procession, which
looked very picturesque, as we glanced backward or forward, and beheld a twinkling line of
seven lights, glimmering faintly on our faces,
and showing nothing beyond.   The passages
and niches of the tomb seem to have been hewn
and hollowed out of the rock, not built by any
art of masonry ; but the walls were very dark,
almost black, and our tapers so dim that I could
not gain a sufficient breadth of view to ascertain
what kind of place it was.   It was very dark,
indeed ; the Mammoth Cave of Kentucky could
not be darker.   The rough-hewn roof was within
touch, and sometimes we had to stoop, to avoid
hitting our heads ; it was covered with damps,
which collected and fell upon us in occasional
drops.   The passages, besides being narrow,
were so irregular and crooked, that, after going
a little way, it would have been impossible to

return upon our steps without the help of the guide; and we appeared to be taking quite an extensive ramble underground, though in reality I suppose the tomb includes no great space. At several turns of our dismal way, the guide pointed to inscriptions in Roman capitals, commemorating various members of the Scipio family who were buried here; among them, a son of Scipio Africanus, who himself had his death and burial in a foreign land. All these inscriptions, however, are copies, — the originals, which were really found here, having been removed to the Vatican. Whether any bones and ashes have been left, or whether any were found, I do not know. It is not, at all events, a particularly interesting spot, being such shapeless blackness, and a mere dark hole, requiring a stronger illumination than that of our tapers to distinguish it from any other cellar. I did, at one place, see a sort of frieze, rather roughly sculptured; and, as we returned towards the twilight of the entrance passage, I discerned a large spider, who fled hastily away from our tapers — the solitary living inhabitant of the tomb of the Scipios.

One visit that we made, and I think it was before entering the city gates, I forgot to mention. It was to an old edifice, formerly called the Temple of Bacchus, but now supposed to have been the Temple of Virtue and Honor. The interior consists of a vaulted hall, which was converted from its pagan consecration into a church or chapel, by the early Christians; and the ancient marble pillars of the temple may still be seen, built in with the brick and stucco of the later occupants. There is an altar, and other tokens of a Catholic church, and, high towards the ceiling, there are some frescos of saints or angels, very curious specimens of mediæval, and earlier than mediæval art. Nevertheless, the place impressed me as still rather pagan than Christian. What is most remarkable about this spot or this vicinity lies in the fact that the Fountain of Egeria was formerly supposed to be close at hand; indeed, the custode of the chapel still claims the spot as the identical one consecrated by the legend. There is a dark grove of trees, not far from the door of the temple; but Murray, a highly essential nuisance on such excursions as this, throws such overwhelming doubt, or rather incredulity, upon the site, that I seized upon it as a pretext for not going thither. In fact, my small capacity for sight-seeing was already more than satisfied.

On account of —— I am sorry that we did not see the grotto, for her enthusiasm is as fresh as the waters of Egeria's well can be, and she has poetical faith enough to light her cheerfully through all these mists of incredulity.

Our visits to sepulchral places ended with

Scipio's tomb, whence we returned to our dwelling, and Miss M—— came to dine with us.

March 10. — On Saturday last, a very rainy day, we went to the Sciarra Palace, and took Una with us. It is on the Corso, nearly opposite to the Piazza Colonna. It has (Heaven be praised !) but four rooms of pictures, among which, however, are several very celebrated ones. Only a few of these remain in my memory, — Raphael's Violin Player, which I am willing to accept as a good picture ; and Leonardo da Vinci's Vanity and Modesty, which also I can bring up before my mind's eye, and find it very beautiful, although one of the faces has an affected smile, which I have since seen on another picture by the same artist, Joanna of Arragon. The most striking picture in the collection, I think, is Titian's Bella Donna, — the only one of Titian's works that I have yet seen which makes an impression on me corresponding with his fame. It is a very splendid and very scornful lady, as beautiful and as scornful as Gainsborough's Lady Lyndoch, though of an entirely different type. There were two Madonnas by Guido, of which I liked the least celebrated one best; and several pictures by Garofalo, who always produces something noteworthy. All the pictures lacked the charm (no doubt I am a barbarian to think it one) of being in brilliant frames, and looked as if it were

Titian's Bella Donna

a long, long while since they were cleaned or
varnished. The light was so scanty, too, on
that heavily clouded day, and in those gloomy
old rooms of the palace, that scarcely anything
could be fairly made out.

[I cannot refrain from observing here, that
Mr. Hawthorne's inexorable demand for perfection in all things leads him to complain of
grimy pictures and tarnished frames and faded
frescos, distressing beyond measure to eyes that
never failed to see everything before him with
the keenest apprehension. The usual careless
observation of people both of the good and the
imperfect is much more comfortable in this imperfect world. But the insight which Mr. Hawthorne possessed was only equalled by his out-
sight, and he suffered, in a way not to be readily
conceived, from any failure in beauty, physical,
moral, or intellectual. It is not, therefore, mere
love of upholstery that impels him to ask for perfect settings to priceless gems of art ; but a native idiosyncrasy, which always made me feel that
"the New Jerusalem," "even like a jasper stone,
clear as crystal," "where shall in no wise enter
anything that defileth, neither what worketh
abomination nor maketh a lie," would alone
satisfy him, or rather alone not give him actual pain. It may give an idea of this exquisite nicety of feeling to mention, that one day
he took in his fingers a half-bloomed rose,

without blemish, and, smiling with an infinite joy, remarked, " This is perfect. On earth a flower only can be perfect."— S. H.]

The palace is about two hundred and fifty years old, and looks as if it had never been a very cheerful place ; most shabbily and scantily furnished, moreover, and as chill as any cellar. There is a small balcony, looking down on the Corso, which probably has often been filled with a merry little family party, in the carnivals of days long past. It has faded frescos, and tarnished gilding, and green blinds, and a few damask chairs still remain in it.

On Monday we all went to the sculpture-gallery of the Vatican, and saw as much of the sculpture as we could in the three hours during which the public are admissible. There were a few things which I really enjoyed, and a few moments during which I really seemed to see them; but it is in vain to attempt giving the impression produced by masterpieces of art, and most in vain when we see them best. They are a language in themselves, and if they could be expressed as well any way except by themselves, there would have been no need of expressing those particular ideas and sentiments by sculpture. I saw the Apollo Belvidere as something ethereal and godlike ; only for a flitting moment, however, and as if he had alighted from heaven, or shone suddenly out of the sun-

light, and then had withdrawn himself again.
I felt the Laocoön very powerfully, though
very quietly ; an immortal agony, with a strange
calmness diffused through it, so that it resembles the vast rage of the sea, calm on account
of its immensity ; or the tumult of Niagara,
which does not seem to be tumult, because it
keeps pouring on forever and ever. I have not
had so good a day as this (among works of art)
since we came to Rome ; and I impute it partly
to the magnificence of the arrangements of the
Vatican, — its long vistas and beautiful courts,
and the aspect of immortality which marble
statues acquire by being kept free from dust.
A very hungry boy, seeing in one of the cabinets a vast porphyry vase, forty-four feet in
circumference, wished that he had it full of
soup.

Yesterday, we went to the Pamfili Doria
Palace, which, I believe, is the most splendid
in Rome. The entrance is from the Corso into
a court, surrounded by a colonnade, and having
a space of luxuriant verdure and ornamental
shrubbery in the centre. The apartments containing pictures and sculptures are fifteen in
number, and run quite round the court in the
first piano, — all the rooms, halls, and galleries of beautiful proportion, with vaulted roofs,
some of which glow with frescos ; and all are
colder and more comfortless than can possibly

be imagined without having been in them. The pictures, most of them, interested me very little. I am of opinion that good pictures are quite as rare as good poets; and I do not see why we should pique ourselves on admiring any but the very best. One in a thousand, perhaps, ought to live in the applause of men, from generation to generation, till its colors fade or blacken out of sight, and its canvas rots away; the rest should be put in garrets, or painted over by newer artists, just as tolerable poets are shelved when their little day is over. Nevertheless, there was one long gallery containing many pictures that I should be glad to see again under more favorable circumstances, that is, separately, and where I might contemplate them quite undisturbed, reclining in an easy chair. At one end of the long vista of this gallery is a bust of the present Prince Doria, a smooth, sharp-nosed, rather handsome young man, and at the other end his princess, an English lady of the Talbot family, apparently a blonde, with a simple and sweet expression. There is a noble and striking portrait of the old Venetian admiral, Andrea Doria, by Sebastian del Piombo, and some other portraits and busts of the family.

In the whole immense range of rooms I saw but a single fireplace, and that so deep in the wall that no amount of blaze would raise the

atmosphere of the room ten degrees.   If the
builder of the palace, or any of his successors,
have committed crimes worthy of Tophet, it
would be a still worse punishment for him to
wander perpetually through this suite of rooms
on the cold floors of polished brick tiles or
marble or mosaic, growing a little chiller and
chiller through every moment of eternity, — or,
at least, till the palace crumbles down upon
him.

Neither would it assuage his torment in the
least to be compelled to gaze up at the dark
old pictures, — the ugly ghosts of what may
once have been beautiful.   I am not going to
try any more to receive pleasure from a faded,
tarnished, lustreless picture, especially if it be a
landscape.   There were two or three landscapes
of Claude in this palace, which I doubt not
would have been exquisite if they were in the
condition of those in the British National Gallery ; but here they looked most forlorn, and
even their sunshine was sunless.   The merits
of historical painting may be quite independent
of the attributes that give pleasure, and a su-
perficial ugliness may even heighten the effect ;
but not so of landscapes.

Via Porta, Palazzo Larazani, March 11. —
To-day we called at Mr. Thompson's studio,
and . . . he had on the easel a little picture of

St. Peter released from prison by the angel, which I saw once before. It is very beautiful indeed, and deeply and spiritually conceived, and I wish I could afford to have it finished for myself. I looked again, too, at his Georgian Slave, and admired it as much as at first view; so very warm and rich it is, so sensuously beautiful, and with an expression of higher life and feeling within. I do not think there is a better painter than Mr. Thompson living, — among Americans at least; not one so earnest, faithful, and religious in his worship of art. I had rather look at his pictures than at any except the very finest of the old masters, and, taking into consideration only the comparative pleasure to be derived, I would not except more than one or two of those. In painting, as in literature, I suspect there is something in the productions of the day that takes the fancy more than the works of any past age, — not greater merit, nor nearly so great, but better suited to this very present time. . . .

After leaving him, we went to the Piazza di Termini, near the Baths of Diocletian, and found our way with some difficulty to Crawford's studio. It occupies several great rooms, connected with the offices of the Villa Negroni; and all these rooms were full of plaster casts and a few works in marble, — principally portions of his huge Washington Monument,

which he left unfinished at his death.   Close
by the door at which we entered stood a gigantic figure of Mason, in bag-wig, and the coat,
waistcoat, breeches, and knee and shoe buckles
of the last century, — the enlargement of these
unheroic matters to far more than heroic size
having a very odd effect.   There was a figure
of Jefferson on the same scale ; another of
Patrick Henry, besides a horse's head, and
other portions of the equestrian group which is
to cover the summit of the monument. In one
of the rooms was a model of the monument
itself, on a scale, I should think, of about an
inch to a foot.   It did not impress me as having grown out of any great and genuine idea in
the artist's mind, but as being merely an ingen-
ious contrivance enough.   There were also casts
of statues that seemed to be intended for some
other monument referring to Revolutionary
times and personages ; and with these were intermixed some ideal statues or groups, — a
naked boy playing marbles, very beautiful ; a
girl with flowers ; the cast of his Orpheus, of
which I long ago saw the marble statue ; Adam
and Eve ; Flora, — all with a good deal of
merit, no doubt, but not a single one that jus-
tifies Crawford's reputation, or that satisfies me
of his genius. They are but commonplaces in
marble and plaster, such as we should not tolerate on a printed page.   He seems to have

been a respectable man, highly respectable, but no more, although those who knew him seem to have rated him much higher. It is said that he exclaimed, not very long before his death, that he had fifteen years of good work still in him; and he appears to have considered all his life and labor, heretofore, as only preparatory to the great things that he was to achieve hereafter. I should say, on the contrary, that he was a man who had done his best, and had done it early; for his Orpheus is quite as good as anything else we saw in his studio.

People were at work chiselling several statues in marble from the plaster models, — a very interesting process, and what I should think a doubtful and hazardous one; but the artists say that there is no risk of mischief, and that the model is sure to be accurately repeated in the marble. These persons, who do what is considered the mechanical part of the business, are often themselves sculptors, and of higher reputation than those who employ them.

It is rather sad to think that Crawford died before he could see his ideas in the marble, where they gleam with so pure and celestial a light as compared with the plaster. There is almost as much difference as between flesh and spirit.

The floor of one of the rooms was burdened with immense packages, containing parts of the

Washington Monument, ready to be forwarded
to its destination.   When finished, and set up,
it will probably make a very splendid appearance, by its height, its mass, its skilful execution; and will produce a moral effect through
its images of illustrious men, and the associations that connect it with our Revolutionary
history; but I do not think it will owe much
to artistic force of thought or depth of feeling.
It is certainly, in one sense, a very foolish and
illogical piece of work, — Washington, mounted
on an uneasy steed, on a very narrow space,
aloft in the air, whence a single step of the
horse backward, forward, or on either side, must
precipitate him; and several of his contempo-
raries standing beneath him, not looking up to
wonder at his predicament, but each intent on
manifesting his own personality to the world
around.   They have nothing to do with one
another, nor with Washington, nor with any
great purpose which all are to work out together.

March 14. — On Friday evening I dined at
Mr. T. B. Read's, the poet and artist, with a
party composed of painters and sculptors, —
the only exceptions being the American banker
and an American tourist who has given Mr.
Read a commission.   Next to me at table sat
Mr. Gibson, the English sculptor, who, I sup-

pose, stands foremost in his profession at this day. He must be quite an old man now, for it was whispered about the table that he is known to have been in Rome forty-two years ago, and he himself spoke to me of spending thirty-seven years here, before he once returned home. I should hardly take him to be sixty, however, his hair being more dark than gray, his forehead unwrinkled, his features unwithered, his eye undimmed, though his beard is somewhat venerable. . . .

He has a quiet, self-contained aspect, and, being a bachelor, has doubtless spent a calm life among his clay and marble, meddling little with the world, and entangling himself with no cares beyond his studio. He did not talk a great deal; but enough to show that he is still an Englishman in many sturdy traits, though his accent has something foreign about it. His conversation was chiefly about India, and other topics of the day, together with a few reminiscences of people in Liverpool, where he once resided. There was a kind of simplicity both in his manner and matter, and nothing very remarkable in the latter. . . .

The gist of what he said (upon art) was condemnatory of the Pre-Raphaelite modern school of painters, of whom he seemed to spare none, and of their works nothing; though he allowed that the old Pre-Raphaelites had some exqui-

site merits, which the moderns entirely omit in
their imitations.   In his own art, he said the
aim should be to find out the principles on which
the Greek sculptors wrought, and to do the work
of this day on those principles and in their spirit;
a fair doctrine enough, I should think, but which
Mr. Gibson can scarcely be said to practise.
. . . The difference between the Pre-Raphaelites and himself is deep and genuine, they being
literalists and realists, in a certain sense, and he
a pagan idealist.   Methinks they have hold of
the best end of the matter.

March 18. — To-day, it being very bright
and mild, we set out, at noon, for an expedition
to the Temple of Vesta, though I did not feel
much inclined for walking, having been ill and
feverish for two or three days past with a cold,
which keeps renewing itself faster than I can get
rid of it.   We kept along on this side of the
Corso, and crossed the Forum, skirting along
the Capitoline Hill, and thence towards the Circus Maximus.   On our way, looking down a
cross street, we saw a heavy arch, and, on examination, made it out to be the Arch of Janus
Quadrifrons, standing in the Forum Boarium.
Its base is now considerably below the level of
the surrounding soil, and there is a church or
basilica close by, and some mean edifices looking down upon it.   There is something satis-

factory in this arch, from the immense solidity
of its structure. It gives the idea, in the first
place, of a solid mass constructed of huge blocks
of marble, which time can never wear away, nor
earthquakes shake down ; and then this solid
mass is penetrated by two arched passages, meeting in the centre. There are empty niches, three
in a row, and, I think, two rows on each face ;
but there seems to have been very little effort
to make it a beautiful object. On the top is
some brickwork, the remains of a mediæval fortress built by the Frangipanis, looking very frail
and temporary being brought thus in contact
with the antique strength of the arch.

A few yards off across the street, and close
beside the basilica, is what appears to be an ancient portal, with carved bas-reliefs, and an inscription which I could not make out. Some
Romans were lying dormant in the sun, on the
steps of the basilica ; indeed, now that the sun
is getting warmer, they seem to take advantage
of every quiet nook to bask in, and perhaps to
go to sleep.

We had gone but a little way from the arch,
and across the Circus Maximus, when we saw
the Temple of Vesta before us, on the bank of
the Tiber, which, however, we could not see behind it. It is a most perfectly preserved Roman
ruin, and very beautiful, though so small that,
in a suitable locality, one would take it rather

for a garden-house than an ancient temple. A
circle of white marble pillars, much time-worn
and a little battered, though but one of them
broken, surround the solid structure of the
temple, leaving a circular walk between it and
the pillars, the whole covered by a modern roof
which looks like wood, and disgraces and de-
forms the elegant little building. This roof resembles, as much as anything else, the round
wicker cover of a basket, and gives a very squat
aspect to the temple. The pillars are of the
Corinthian order, and when they were new, and
the marble snow-white, and sharply carved and
cut, there could not have been a prettier object
in all Rome; but so small an edifice does not
appear well as a ruin.

Within view of it, and, indeed, a very little
way off, is the Temple of Fortuna Virilis, which
likewise retains its antique form in better preservation than we generally find a Roman ruin,
although the Ionic pillars are now built up with
blocks of stone and patches of brickwork, the
whole constituting a church which is fixed against
the side of a tall edifice, the nature of which I
do not know.

I forgot to say that we gained admittance into
the Temple of Vesta, and found the interior a
plain cylinder of marble, about ten paces across,
and fitted up as a chapel, where the Virgin takes
the place of Vesta.

In very close vicinity we came upon the Ponte
Rotto, the old Pons Emilius, which was broken
down long ago, and has recently been pieced
out by connecting a suspension bridge with the
old piers. We crossed by this bridge, paying
a toll of a baioccho each, and stopped in the
midst of the river to look at the Temple of Vesta,
which shows well, right on the brink of the
Tiber. We fancied, too, that we could discern,
a little farther down the river, the ruined and
almost submerged piers of the Sublician bridge,
which Horatius Cocles defended. The Tiber
here whirls rapidly along, and Horatius must
have had a perilous swim for his life, and the enemy a fair mark at his head with their arrows. I
think this is the most picturesque part of the
Tiber in its passage through Rome.

After crossing the bridge, we kept along the
right bank of the river, through the dirty and
hard-hearted streets of Trastevere (which have
in no respect the advantage over those of hither
Rome), till we reached St. Peter's. We saw a
family sitting before their door on the pavement
in the narrow and sunny street, engaged in their
domestic avocations,— the old woman spinning
with a wheel. I suppose the people now begin
to live out of doors. We entered beneath the
colonnade of St. Peter's, and immediately became
sensible of an evil odor,— the bad odor of our

fallen nature, which there is no escaping in any nook of Rome. . . .

Between the pillars of the colonnade, however, we had the pleasant spectacle of the two fountains, sending up their lily-shaped gush, with rainbows shining in their falling spray.   Parties of French soldiers, as usual, were undergoing their drill in the piazza.   When we entered the church, the long, dusty sunbeams were falling aslantwise through the dome and through the chancel behind it. . . .

March 23. — On the 21st we all went to the Coliseum, and enjoyed ourselves there in the bright, warm sun, — so bright and warm that we were glad to get into the shadow of the walls and under the arches, though, after all, there was the freshness of March in the breeze that stirred now and then.   Julian and baby found some beautiful flowers growing round about the Coliseum ; and far up towards the top of the walls we saw tufts of yellow wall-flowers and a great deal of green grass growing along the ridges between the arches.   The general aspect of the place, however, is somewhat bare, and does not compare favorably with an English ruin, both on account of the lack of ivy and because the material is chiefly brick, the stone and marble having been stolen away by popes and cardinals to build their palaces. While we sat within the circle, many people, of both sexes, passed through, kissing the iron cross which stands in the centre, thereby gaining an indulgence of seven years, I believe. In front of several churches I have seen an inscription in Latin, " Indulgentia plenaria et perpetua pro cunctis mortuis et vivis " ; than which, it seems to me, nothing more could be asked or desired. The terms of this great boon are not mentioned.

Leaving the Coliseum, we went and sat down in the vicinity of the Arch of Constantine, and Julian and Rose went in quest of lizards. Julian soon caught a large one with two tails ; one, a sort of afterthought, or appendix, or corollary, to the original tail, and growing out from it instead of from the body of the lizard. These reptiles are very abundant, and Julian has already brought home several, which make their escape and appear occasionally darting to and fro on the carpet. Since we have been here, Julian has taken up various pursuits in turn. First he devoted himself to gathering snail shells, of which there are many sorts ; afterwards he had a fever for marbles, pieces of which he found on the banks of the Tiber, just on the edge of its muddy waters, and in the Palace of the Cæsars, the Baths of Caracalla, and indeed wherever else his fancy led him ;

verde antique, rosso antico, porphyry, giallo antico, serpentine, sometimes fragments of bas-
reliefs and mouldings, bits of mosaic, still firmly
stuck together, on which the foot of a Cæsar had
perhaps once trodden ; pieces of Roman glass,
with the iridescence glowing on them ; and all
such things, of which the soil of Rome is full. It
would not be difficult, from the spoil of his boy-
ish rambles, to furnish what would be looked
upon as a curious and valuable museum in
America.

Yesterday we went to the sculpture galleries
of the Vatican. I think I enjoy these noble
galleries and their contents and beautiful arrangement better than anything else in the way of
art, and often I seem to have a deep feeling of
something wonderful in what I look at. The
Laocoön on this visit impressed me not less
than before ; it is such a type of human beings,
struggling with an inextricable trouble, and en-
tangled in a complication which they cannot
free themselves from by their own efforts, and
out of which Heaven alone can help them. It
was a most powerful mind, and one capable of
reducing a complex idea to unity, that imagined
this group. I looked at Canova's Perseus, and
thought it exceedingly beautiful, but found myself less and less contented after a moment or
two, though I could not tell why. Afterwards,
looking at the Apollo, the recollection of the

Perseus disgusted me, and yet really I cannot explain how one is better than the other.

I was interested in looking at the busts of the Triumvirs, Antony, Augustus, and Lepidus. The first two are men of intellect evidently, though they do not recommend themselves to one's affections by their physiognomy; but Lepidus has the strangest, most commonplace countenance that can be imagined, — small-featured, weak, such a face as you meet anywhere in a man of no mark, but are amazed to find in one of the three foremost men of the world. I suppose that it is these weak and shallow men, when chance raises them above their proper sphere, who commit enormous crimes without any such restraint as stronger men would feel, and without any retribution in the depth of their conscience. These old Roman busts, of which there are so many in the Vatican, have often a most lifelike aspect, a striking individuality. One recognizes them as faithful portraits, just as certainly as if the living originals were standing beside them. The arrangement of the hair and beard too, in many cases, is just what we see now, the fashions of two thousand years ago having come round again.

March 25. — On Tuesday we went to breakfast at William Story's in the Palazzo Barberini. We had a very pleasant time. He is one of the most agreeable men I know in society. He showed us a note from Thackeray, an invitation to dinner, written in hieroglyphics, with great fun and pictorial merit. He spoke of an expansion of the story of Blue Beard, which he himself had either written or thought of writing, in which the contents of the several chambers which Fatima opened, before arriving at the fatal one, were to be described. This idea has haunted my mind ever since, and if it had but been my own I am pretty sure that it would develop itself into something very rich. I mean to press William Story to work it out. The chamber of Blue Beard, too (and this was a part of his suggestion), might be so handled as to become powerfully interesting. Were I to take up the story, I would create an interest by suggesting a secret in the first chamber, which would develop itself more and more in every successive hall of the great palace, and lead the wife irresistibly to the chamber of horrors.

After breakfast, we went to the Barberini Library, passing through the vast hall, which occupies the central part of the palace. It is the most splendid domestic hall I have seen, eighty feet in length at least, and of proportionate breadth and height; and the vaulted ceiling is entirely covered, to its utmost edge and remotest corners, with a brilliant painting in fresco, looking like a whole heaven of angelic people descending towards the floor. The effect is indescribably gorgeous. On one side stands a Baldacchino, or canopy of state, draped with scarlet cloth, and fringed with gold embroidery; the scarlet indicating that the palace is inhabited by a cardinal. Green would be appropriate to a prince. In point of fact, the Palazzo Barberini is inhabited by a cardinal, a prince, and a duke, all belonging to the Barberini family, and each having his separate portion of the palace, while their servants have a common territory and meeting-ground in this noble hall.

After admiring it for a few minutes, we made our exit by a door on the opposite side, and went up the spiral staircase of marble to the library, where we were received by an ecclesiastic, who belongs to the Barberini household, and I believe was born in it. He is a gentle, refined, quiet-looking man, as well he may be, having spent all his life among these books, where few people intrude, and few cares can come. He showed us a very old Bible in parchment, a specimen of the earliest printing, beautifully ornamented with pictures, and some monkish illuminations of indescribable delicacy and elaboration. No artist could afford to produce such work, if the life that he thus lavished on one sheet of parchment had any value to him, either for what could be done or enjoyed in it. There are about eight thousand volumes in this

library, and, judging by their outward aspect, the
collection must be curious and valuable ; but
having another engagement, we could spend
only a little time here. We had a hasty glance,
however, of some poems of Tasso, in his own
autograph.

We then went to the Palazzo Galitzin, where
dwell the Misses Weston,with whom we lunched,
and where we met a French abbé, an agreeable
man, and an antiquarian, under whose auspices
two of the ladies and ourselves took carriage
for the Castle of St. Angelo.   Being admitted
within the external gateway, we found ourselves
in the court of guard, as I presume it is called,
where the French soldiers were playing with very
dirty cards, or lounging about, in military idle-
ness.   They were well behaved and courteous,
and when we had intimated our wish to see the
interior of the castle, a soldier soon appeared,
with a large unlighted torch in his hand, ready
to guide us.   There is an outer wall, surrounding the solid structure of Hadrian's tomb ; to
which there is access by one or two drawbridges ;
the entrance to the tomb, or castle, not being at
the base, but near its central height.   The ancient entrance, by which Hadrian's ashes, and
those of other imperial personages, were probably brought into this tomb, has been walled up,
— perhaps ever since the last emperor was buried
here.   We were now in a vaulted passage, both

lofty and broad, which circles round the whole interior of the tomb, from the base to the summit. During many hundred years, the passage was filled with earth and rubbish, and forgotten, and it is but partly excavated, even now; although we found it a long, long, and gloomy descent by torchlight to the base of the vast mausoleum. The passage was once lined and vaulted with precious marbles (which are now entirely gone), and paved with fine mosaics, portions of which still remain; and our guide lowered his flaming torch to show them to us, here and there, amid the earthy dampness over which we trod. It is strange to think what splendor and costly adornment were here wasted on the dead.

After we had descended to the bottom of this passage, and again retraced our steps to the highest part, the guide took a large cannon-ball, and sent it, with his whole force, rolling down the hollow, arched way, rumbling, and reverberating, and bellowing forth long thunderous echoes, and winding up with a loud, distant crash, that seemed to come from the very bowels of the earth.

We saw the place, near the centre of the mausoleum, and lighted from above, through an immense thickness of stone and brick, where the ashes of the emperor and his fellow slumberers were found. It is as much as twelve cen-

turies, very likely, since they were scattered to
the winds, for the tomb has been nearly or quite
that space of time a fortress. The tomb itself is
merely the base and foundation of the castle,
and, being so massively built, it serves just as
well for the purpose as if it were a solid granite rock. The mediæval fortress, with its antiquity of more than a thousand years, and having dark and deep dungeons of its own, is but
a modern excrescence on the top of Hadrian's
tomb.

We now ascended towards the upper region,
and were led into the vaults which used to serve
as a prison, but which, if I mistake not, are situated above the ancient structure, although they
seem as damp and subterranean as if they were
fifty feet under the earth. We crept down to
them through narrow and ugly passages, which
the torchlight would not illuminate, and, stooping under a low, square entrance, we followed
the guide into a small vaulted room, — not a
room, but an artificial cavern, remote from light
or air, where Beatrice Cenci was confined before
her execution. According to the abbé, she spent
a whole year in this dreadful pit, her trial having dragged on through that length of time.
How ghostlike she must have looked when she
came forth ! Guido never painted that beautiful picture from her blanched face, as it appeared
after this confinement. And how rejoiced she

must have been to die at last, having already been in a sepulchre so long !

Adjacent to Beatrice's prison, but not communicating with it, was that of her stepmother ; and next to the latter was one that interested me almost as much as Beatrice's, — that of Benvenuto Cellini, who was confined here, I believe, for an assassination. All these prison vaults are more horrible than can be imagined without seeing them ; but there are worse places here, for the guide lifted a trap-door in one of the passages, and held his torch down into an inscrutable pit beneath our feet. It was an oubliette, a dungeon where the prisoner might be buried alive, and never come forth again, alive or dead. Groping about among these sad precincts, we saw various other things that looked very dismal ; but at last emerged into the sunshine, and ascended from one platform and battlement to another, till we found ourselves right at the feet of the Archangel Michael. He has stood there in bronze for I know not how many hundred years, in the act of sheathing a (now) rusty sword, such being the attitude in which he appeared to one of the popes in a vision, in token that a pestilence which was then desolating Rome was to be stayed.

There is a fine view from the lofty station over Rome and the whole adjacent country, and the abbé pointed out the site of Ardea, of Corioli, of Veii, and other places renowned in story. We were ushered, too, into the French commandant's quarters in the castle. There is a large hall, ornamented with frescos, and accessible from this a drawing-room, comfortably fitted up, and where we saw modern furniture, and a chessboard, and a fire burning clear, and other symptoms that the place had perhaps just been vacated by civilized and kindly people. But in one corner of the ceiling the abbé pointed out a ring, by which, in the times of mediæval anarchy, when popes, cardinals, and barons were all by the ears together, a cardinal was hanged. It was not an assassination, but a legal punishment, and he was executed in the best apartment of the castle as an act of grace.

The fortress is a straight-lined structure on the summit of the immense round tower of Hadrian's tomb ; and to make out the idea of it we must throw in drawbridges, esplanades, piles of ancient marble balls for cannon ; battlements and embrasures, lying high in the breeze and sunshine, and opening views round the whole horizon ; accommodation for the soldiers ; and many small beds in a large room.

How much mistaken was the emperor in his expectation of a stately, solemn repose for his ashes through all the coming centuries, as long as the world should endure ! Perhaps his ghost glides up and down disconsolate, in that spiral passage which goes from top to bottom of the tomb, while the barbarous Gauls plant themselves in his very mausoleum to keep the imperial city in awe.

Leaving the Castle of St. Angelo, we drove, still on the same side of the Tiber, to the Villa Pamfili, which lies a short distance beyond the walls. As we passed through one of the gates (I think it was that of San Pancrazio) the abbé pointed out the spot where the Constable de Bourbon was killed while attempting to scale the walls. If we are to believe Benvenuto Cellini, it was he who shot the constable. The road to the villa is not very interesting, lying (as the roads in the vicinity of Rome often do) between very high walls, admitting not a glimpse of the surrounding country; the road itself white and dusty, with no verdant margin of grass or border of shrubbery. At the portal of the villa we found many carriages in waiting, for the Prince Doria throws open the grounds to all comers, and on a pleasant day like this they are probably sure to be thronged. We left our carriage just within the entrance, and rambled among these beautiful groves, admiring the live-oak trees, and the stone pines, which latter are truly a majestic tree, with tall columnar stems, supporting a cloud-like density of boughs far aloft, and not a straggling branch between them and the ground. They stand in straight rows, but

are now so ancient and venerable as to have lost
the formal look of a plantation, and seem like
a wood that might have arranged itself almost
of its own will.   Beneath them is a flower-strewn
turf, quite free of underbrush.   We found open
fields and lawns, moreover, all abloom with
anemones, white and rose-colored and purple
and golden, and far larger than could be found
out of Italy, except in hothouses.   Violets, too,
were abundant and exceedingly fragrant.   When
we consider that all this floral exuberance occurs
in the midst of March, there does not appear
much ground for complaining of the Roman
climate ; and so long ago as the first week of
February I found daisies among the grass, on
the sunny side of the Basilica of St. John Lateran.   At this very moment I suppose the
country within twenty miles of Boston may be
two feet deep with snow, and the streams solid
with ice.

We wandered about the grounds, and found
them very beautiful indeed ; nature having done
much for them by an undulating variety of
surface, and art having added a good many
charms, which have all the better effect now that
decay and neglect have thrown a natural grace
over them likewise.   There is an artificial ruin,
so picturesque that it betrays itself ; weather-
beaten statues, and pieces of sculpture, scattered
here and there ; an artificial lake, with upgush-

293

ing fountains ; cascades, and broad-bosomed coves, and long, canal-like reaches, with swans taking their delight upon them. I never saw such a glorious and resplendent lustre of white as shone between the wings of two of these swans. It was really a sight to see, and not to be imagined beforehand. Angels, no doubt, have just such lustrous wings as those. English swans partake of the dinginess of the atmosphere, and their plumage has nothing at all to be compared to this ; in fact, there is nothing like it in the world, unless it be the illuminated portion of a fleecy, summer cloud.

While we were sauntering along beside this piece of water, we were surprised to see Una on the other side. She had come hither with Edith Story and her two little brothers, and with our Rose, the whole under the charge of Mrs. Story's nursery-maids. Una and Edith crossed, not over, but beneath the water, through a grotto, and exchanged greetings with us. Then, as it was getting towards sunset and cool, we took our departure ; the abbé, as we left the grounds, taking me aside to give me a glimpse of a Columbarium, which descends into the earth to about the depth to which an ordinary house might rise above it. These grounds, it is said, formed the country residence of the Emperor Galba, and he was buried here after his assassination. It is a sad thought that so much natural beauty and long refinement of picturesque culture is thrown away, the villa being uninhabitable during all the most delightful season of the year on account of malaria. There is truly a curse on Rome and all its neighborhood.

On our way home we passed by the great Paolina fountain, and were assailed by many beggars during the short time we stopped to look at it. It is a very copious fountain, but not so beautiful as the Trevi, taking into view merely the water-gush of the latter.

March 26. — Yesterday, between twelve and one, our whole family went to the Villa Ludovisi, the entrance to which is at the termination of a street which passes out of the Piazza Barberini, and it is no very great distance from our own street, Via Porta Pinciana. The grounds, though very extensive, are wholly within the walls of the city, which skirt them, and comprise a part of what were formerly the gardens of Sallust. The villa is now the property of Prince Piombini, a ticket from whom procured us admission. A little within the gateway, to the right, is a casino, containing two large rooms filled with sculpture, much of which is very valuable. A colossal head of Juno, I believe, is considered the greatest treasure of the collection, but I did not myself feel it to be so, nor indeed did I receive any strong impression of its excellence.   I admired nothing so much, I think, as the face of Penelope (if it be her face) in the group supposed also to represent Electra and Orestes.   The sitting statue of Mars is very fine; so is the Aria and Pætus; so are many other busts and figures.

By and by we left the casino and wandered among the grounds, threading interminable alleys of cypress, through the long vistas of which we could see here and there a statue, an urn, a pillar, a temple, or garden house, or a bas-relief against the wall.   It seems as if there must have been a time, — and not so very long ago, — when it was worth while to spend money and thought upon the ornamentation of grounds in the neighborhood of Rome.   That time is past, however, and the result is very melancholy; for great beauty has been produced, but it can be enjoyed in its perfection only at the peril of one's life. . . .   For my part, and judging from my own experience, I suspect that the Roman atmosphere, never wholesome, is always more or less poisonous.

We came to another and larger casino remote from the gateway, in which the Prince resides during two months of the year.   It was now under repair, but we gained admission, as did several other visitors, and saw in the entrance hall the Aurora of Guercino, painted in fresco on the ceiling.   There is beauty in the design;

but the painter certainly was most unhappy in his black shadows, and in the work before us they give the impression of a cloudy and lowering morning, which is likely enough to turn to rain by and by. After viewing the fresco we mounted by a spiral staircase to a lofty terrace, and found Rome at our feet, and, far off, the Sabine and Alban mountains, some of them still capped with snow. In another direction there was a vast plain, on the horizon of which, could our eyes have reached to its verge, we might perhaps have seen the Mediterranean Sea. After enjoying the view and the warm sunshine we descended, and went in quest of the gardens of Sallust, but found no satisfactory remains of them.

One of the most striking objects in the first casino was a group by Bernini, — Pluto, an outrageously masculine and strenuous figure, heavily bearded, ravishing away a little, tender Proserpine, whom he holds aloft, while his forcible gripe impresses itself into her soft virgin flesh. It is very disagreeable, but it makes one feel that Bernini was a man of great ability. There are some works in literature that bear an analogy to his works in sculpture, where great power is lavished a little outside of nature, and therefore proves to be only a fashion, and not permanently adapted to the tastes of mankind.

March 27. — Yesterday forenoon my wife and I went to St. Peter's to see the pope pray at the chapel of the Holy Sacrament. We found a good many people in the church, but not an inconvenient number; indeed, not so many as to make any remarkable show in the great nave, nor even in front of the chapel. A detachment of the Swiss Guard, in their strange, picturesque, harlequin-like costume, were on duty before the chapel, in which the wax tapers were all lighted, and a *prie-dieu* was arranged near the shrine, and covered with scarlet velvet. On each side, along the breadth of the side-aisle, were placed seats, covered with rich tapestry or carpeting; and some gentlemen and ladies — English, probably, or American — had comfortably deposited themselves here, but were compelled to move by the guards before the pope's entrance. His holiness should have appeared precisely at twelve, but we waited nearly half an hour beyond that time; and it seemed to me particularly ill mannered in the pope, who owes the courtesy of being punctual to the people, if not to St. Peter. By and by, however, there was a stir; the guard motioned to us to stand away from the benches, against the backs of which we had been leaning; the spectators in the nave looked towards the door, as if they beheld something approaching; and first, there appeared some cardinals, in scarlet skull-caps and purple

298

robes, intermixed with some of the Noble Guard
and other attendants.   It was not a very formal
and stately procession, but rather straggled onward, with ragged edges, the spectators standing
aside to let it pass, and merely bowing, or perhaps slightly bending the knee, as good Catholics are accustomed to do when passing before
the shrines of saints.   Then, in the midst of
the purple cardinals, all of whom were gray-
haired men, appeared a stout old man, with a
white skull-cap, a scarlet, gold-embroidered cape
falling over his shoulders, and a white silk robe,
the train of which was borne up by an attendant. He walked slowly, with a sort of dignified
movement, stepping out broadly, and planting
his feet (on which were red shoes) flat upon the
pavement, as if he were not much accustomed
to locomotion, and perhaps had known a twinge
of the gout.   His face was kindly and venerable, but not particulariy impressive.   Arriving
at the scarlet-covered *prie-dieu*, he kneeled down
and took off his white skull-cap ; the cardinals
also kneeled behind and on either side of him,
taking off their scarlet skull-caps ; while the
Noble Guard remained standing, six on one side
of his holiness and six on the other.   The pope
bent his head upon the *prie-dieu*, and seemed to
spend three or four minutes in prayer ; then
rose, and all the purple cardinals, and bishops,
and priests, of whatever degree, rose behind and

beside him.   Next, he went to kiss St. Peter's toe; at least I believe he kissed it, but I was not near enough to be certain; and lastly, he knelt down, and directed his devotions towards the high altar. This completed the ceremonies, and his holiness left the church by a side door, making a short passage into the Vatican.

I am very glad I have seen the pope, because now he may be crossed out of the list of sights to be seen. His proximity impressed me kindly and favorably towards him, and I did not see one face among all his cardinals (in whose number, doubtless, is his successor) which I would so soon trust as that of Pio Nono.

This morning I walked as far as the gate of San Paolo, and, on approaching it, I saw the gray sharp pyramid of Caius Cestius pointing upward close to the two dark-brown, battlemented Gothic towers of the gateway, each of these very different pieces of architecture looking the more picturesque for the contrast of the other. Before approaching the gateway and pyramid, I walked onward, and soon came in sight of Monte Testaccio, the artificial hill made of potsherds. There is a gate admitting into the grounds around the hill, and a road encircling its base. At a distance, the hill looks greener than any other part of the landscape, and has all the curved outlines of a natural hill,

resembling in shape a headless sphinx, or Saddle-
back Mountain, as I used to see it from Lenox.
It is of very considerable height, — two or three
hundred feet, at least, I should say, — and well
entitled, both by its elevation and the space it
covers, to be reckoned among the hills of Rome.
Its base is almost entirely surrounded with small
structures, which seem to be used as farm buildings.   On the summit is a large iron cross, the
Church having thought it expedient to redeem
these shattered pipkins from the power of paganism, as it has so many other Roman ruins.
There was a pathway up the hill, but I did not
choose to ascend it under the hot sun, so steeply
did it clamber up.   There appears to be a good
depth of soil on most parts of Monte Testaccio,
but on some of the sides you observe precipices,
bristling with fragments of red or brown earthenware, or pieces of vases of white unglazed clay ;
and it is evident that this immense pile is entirely composed of broken crockery, which I
should hardly have thought would have aggre-
gated to such a heap had it all been thrown
here, — urns, teacups, porcelain, or earthen, —
since the beginning of the world.

I walked quite round the hill, and saw, at no
great distance from it, the enclosure of the Protestant burial-ground, which lies so close to the
pyramid of Caius Cestius that the latter may
serve as a general monument to the dead.   De-

ferring, for the present, a visit to the cemetery, or to the interior of the pyramid, I returned to the gateway of San Paolo, and, passing through it, took a view of it from the outside of the city wall. It is itself a portion of the wall, having been built into it by the Emperor Aurelian, so that about half of it lies within and half without. The brick or red stone material of the wall being so unlike the marble of the pyramid, the latter is as distinct, and seems as insulated, as if it stood alone in the centre of a plain; and really I do not think there is a more striking architectural object in Rome. It is in perfect condition, just as little ruined or decayed as on the day when the builder put the last peak on the summit; and it ascends steeply from its base, with a point so sharp that it looks as if it would hardly afford foothold to a bird. The marble was once white, but is now covered with a gray coating like that which has gathered upon the statues of Castor and Pollux on Monte Cavallo. Not one of the great blocks is displaced, nor seems likely to be through all time to come. They rest one upon another, in straight and even lines, and present a vast smooth triangle, ascending from a base of a hundred feet, and narrowing to an apex at the height of a hundred and twenty-five, the junctures of the marble slabs being so close that, in all these twenty centuries, only a few little tufts of grass and a trailing plant or two have succeeded in rooting themselves into the interstices.

It is good and satisfactory to see anything which, being built for an enduring monument, has endured so faithfully, and has a prospect of such an interminable futurity before it.   Once, indeed, it seemed likely to be buried; for three hundred years ago it had become covered to the depth of sixteen feet, but the soil has since been dug away from its base, which is now lower than that of the road which passes through the neighboring gate of San Paolo.   Midway up the pyramid, cut in the marble, is an inscription in large Roman letters, still almost as legible as when first wrought.

I did not return through the Paolo gateway, but kept onward, round the exterior of the wall, till I came to the gate of San Sebastiano. It was a hot and not a very interesting walk, with only a high bare wall of brick, broken by frequent square towers, on one side of the road, and a bank and hedge or a garden wall on the other.   Roman roads are most inhospitable, offering no shade, and no seat, and no pleasant views of rustic domiciles; nothing but the wheel track of white dust, without a footpath running by its side, and seldom any grassy margin to refresh the wayfarer's feet.

April 3. — A few days ago we visited the

studio of Mr. ——, an American, who seems
to have a good deal of vogue as a sculptor. We
found a figure of Pocahontas, which he has repeated several times; another, which he calls
The Wept of the Wish-ton-Wish, a figure of
a smiling girl playing with a cat and dog, and
a schoolboy mending a pen. These two last
were the only ones that gave me any pleasure,
or that really had any merit; for his cleverness
and ingenuity appear in homely subjects, but
are quite lost in attempts at a higher ideality.
Nevertheless, he has a group of the Prodigal
Son, possessing more merit than I should have
expected from Mr. ——, the son reclining his
head on his father's breast, with an expression
of utter weariness, at length finding perfect rest,
while the father bends his benign countenance
over him, and seems to receive him calmly into
himself. This group (the plaster cast standing
beside it) is now taking shape out of an immense
block of marble, and will be as indestructible as
the Laocoön; an idea at once awful and ludicrous, when we consider that it is at best but a
respectable production. I have since been told
that Mr.—— had stolen, adopted, we will rather
say, the attitude and idea of the group from one
executed by a student of the French Academy,
and to be seen there in plaster.[1]

Mr. —— has now been ten years in Italy,

[1] We afterwards saw it in the Medici Casino.

and, after all this time, he is still entirely American in everything but the most external surface
of his manners ; scarcely Europeanized, or much
modified even in that.　He is a native of ——,
but had his early breeding in New York, and
might, for any polish or refinement that I can
discern in him, still be a country shopkeeper
in the interior of New York State or New England.　How strange !　For one expects to find
the polish, the close grain and white purity of
marble, in the artist who works in that noble
material ;　but, after all, he handles *clay*, and,
judging by the specimens I have seen here, is
apt to *be* clay, not of the finest, himself.　Mr.
—— is sensible, shrewd, keen, clever ;　an ingen-
ious workman, no doubt ;　with tact enough, and
not destitute of taste ;　very agreeable and lively
in his conversation, talking as fast and as naturally as a brook runs, without the slightest
affectation.　His naturalness is, in fact, a rather
striking characteristic, in view of his lack of culture, while yet his life has been concerned with
idealities and a beautiful art.　What degree of
taste he pretends to, he seems really to possess,
nor did I hear a single idea from him that struck
me as otherwise than sensible.

He called to see us last evening, and talked
for about two hours in a very amusing and interesting style, his topics being taken from his
own personal experience, and shrewdly treated.

He spoke much of Greenough, whom he described as an excellent critic of art, but possessed of not the slightest inventive genius. His statue of Washington, at the Capitol, is taken precisely from the Phidian Jupiter; his Chanting Cherubs are copied in marble from two figures in a picture by Raphael. He did nothing that was original with himself. . . . To-day we took Rose, and went to see Miss ——, and as her studio seems to be mixed up with Gibson's, we had an opportunity of glancing at some of his beautiful works. We saw a Venus and a Cupid, both of them tinted; and, side by side with them, other statues identical with these except that the marble was left in its pure whiteness.

We found Miss —— in a little upper room. She has a small, brisk, wide-awake figure, not ungraceful; frank, simple, straightforward, and downright. She had on a robe, I think, but I did not look so low, my attention being chiefly drawn to a sort of man's sack of purple or plum-colored broadcloth, into the side-pockets of which her hands were thrust as she came forward to greet us. She withdrew one hand, however, and presented it cordially to my wife (whom she already knew) and to myself, without waiting for an introduction. She had on a shirt-front, collar, and cravat like a man's, with a brooch of Etruscan gold, and on her curly head was a picturesque little cap of black velvet, and her face was as bright and merry, and as small of feature, as a child's. It looked in one aspect youthful, and yet there was something worn in it too. There never was anything so jaunty as her movement and action ; she was very peculiar, but she seemed to be her actual self, and nothing affected or made up ; so that, for my part, I gave her full leave to wear what may suit her best, and to behave as her inner woman prompts. I don't quite see, however, what she is to do when she grows older, for the decorum of age will not be consistent with a costume that looks pretty and excusable enough in a young woman.

Miss —— led us into a part of the extensive studio, or collection of studios, where some of her own works were to be seen : Beatrice Cenci, which did not very greatly impress me ; and a monumental design, a female figure, — wholly draped even to the stockings and shoes, — in a quiet sleep. I liked this last. There was also a Puck, doubtless full of fun ; but I had hardly time to glance at it. Miss —— evidently has good gifts in her profession, and doubtless she derives great advantage from her close association with a consummate artist like Gibson ; nor yet does his influence seem to interfere with the originality of her own conceptions. In one way, at least, she can hardly fail to profit, — that is, by the opportunity of showing her works to the throngs of people who go to see Gibson's own ;

and these are just such people as an artist would most desire to meet, and might never see in a lifetime, if left to himself. I shook hands with this frank and pleasant little person, and took leave, not without purpose of seeing her again.

Within a few days there have been many pilgrims in Rome, who come hither to attend the ceremonies of Holy Week, and to perform their vows, and undergo their penances. I saw two of them near the Forum yesterday, with their pilgrim staves, in the fashion of a thousand years ago. . . . I sat down on a bench near one of the chapels, and a woman immediately came up to me to beg. I at first refused; but she knelt down by my side, instead of praying to the saint prayed to me; and, being thus treated as a canonized personage, I thought it incumbent on me to be gracious to the extent of half a paul. My wife, some time ago, came in contact with a pickpocket at the entrance of a church; and, failing in his enterprise upon her purse, he passed in, dipped his thieving fingers in the holy water, and paid his devotions at a shrine. Missing the purse, he said his prayers, in the hope, perhaps, that the saint would send him better luck another time.

April 10. — I have made no entries in my journal recently, being exceedingly lazy, partly from indisposition, as well as from an atmo-

sphere that takes the vivacity out of everybody.
Not much has happened or been effected.   Last
Sunday, which was Easter Sunday, I went with
Julian to St. Peter's, where we arrived at about
nine o'clock, and found a multitude of people
already assembled in the church.   The interior
was arrayed in festal guise, there being a covering of scarlet damask over the pilasters of the
nave, from base to capital, giving an effect of
splendor, yet with a loss as to the apparent di-
mensions of the interior.   A guard of soldiers
occupied the nave, keeping open a wide space
for the passage of a procession that was mo-
mently expected, and soon arrived.   The crowd
was too great to allow of my seeing it in detail;
but I could perceive that there were priests, cardinals, Swiss guards, some of them with corse-
lets on, and by and by the pope himself was
borne up the nave, high over the heads of all,
sitting under a canopy crowned with his tiara.
He floated slowly along, and was set down in
the neighborhood of the high altar; and the
procession being broken up, some of its scattered
members might be seen here and there, about
the church, — officials, in antique Spanish
dresses ; Swiss guards, in polished steel breast-
plates ; serving men, in richly embroidered liveries ; officers, in scarlet coats and military boots ;
priests, and divers other shapes of men ; for the
papal ceremonies seem to forego little or nothing

that belongs to times past, while it includes
everything appertaining to the present.   I ought
to have waited to witness the papal benediction
from the balcony in front of the church ; or, at
least, to hear the famous silver trumpets, sound-
ing from the dome; but Julian grew weary
(to say the truth, so did I), and we went on a
long walk, out of the nearest city gate, and back
through the Janiculum, and, finally, homeward
over the Ponte Rotto.   Standing on the bridge,
I saw the arch of the Cloaca Maxima, close by
the Temple of Vesta, with the water rising within
two or three feet of its keystone.

The same evening we went to Monte Cavallo,
where, from the gateway of the Pontifical Palace, we saw the illumination of St. Peter's.   Mr.
Akers, the sculptor, had recommended this position to us, and accompanied us thither, as the
best point from which the illumination could be
witnessed at a distance, without the incommodity
of such a crowd as would be assembled at the
Pincian.   The first illumination, the silver one,
as it is called, was very grand and delicate, de-
scribing the outline of the great edifice and crown-
ing dome in light; while the day was not yet
wholly departed.   As —— finally remarked, it
seemed like the glorified spirit of the Church,
made visible, or, as I will add, it looked as this
famous and never-to-be-forgotten structure will
look to the imaginations of men, through the

waste and gloom of future ages, after it shall have gone quite to decay and ruin: the brilliant, though scarcely distinct gleam of a statelier dome than ever was seen, shining on the background of the night of Time. This simile looked prettier in my fancy than I have made it look on paper.

After we had enjoyed the silver illumination a good while, and when all the daylight had given place to the constellated night, the distant outline of St. Peter's burst forth, in the twinkling of an eye, into a starry blaze, being quite the finest effect that I ever witnessed. I stayed to see it, however, only a few minutes; for I was quite ill and feverish with a cold, — which, indeed, I have seldom been free from, since my first breathing of the genial atmosphere of Rome. This pestilence kept me within doors all the next day, and prevented me from seeing the beautiful fireworks that were exhibited in the evening from the platform on the Pincian, above the Piazza del Popolo.

On Thursday, I paid another visit to the sculpture gallery of the Capitol, where I was particularly struck with a bust of Cato the Censor, who must have been the most disagreeable, stubborn, ugly-tempered, pig-headed, narrow-minded, strong-willed old Roman that ever lived. The collection of busts here and at the Vatican are most interesting, many of the individual heads being full of character, and commending themselves by intrinsic evidence as faithful portraits of the originals. These stone people have stood face to face with Cæsar, and all the other emperors, and with statesmen, soldiers, philosophers, and poets of the antique world, and have been to them like their reflections in a mirror. It is the next thing to seeing the men themselves.

We went afterwards into the Palace of the Conservatori, and saw, among various other interesting things, the bronze wolf suckling Romulus and Remus, who sit beneath her dugs, with open mouths to receive the milk.

On Friday, we all went to see the Pope's Palace on the Quirinal. There was a vast hall, and an interminable suite of rooms, cased with marble, floored with marble or mosaics or inlaid wood, adorned with frescos on the vaulted ceilings, and many of them lined with Gobelin tapestry ; not woefully faded, like almost all that I have hitherto seen, but brilliant as pictures. Indeed, some of them so closely resembled paintings, that I could hardly believe they were not so ; and the effect was even richer than that of oil paintings. In every room there was a crucifix ; but I did not see a single nook or corner where anybody could have dreamed of being comfortable. Nevertheless, as a stately and solemn residence for his holiness, it is quite a satisfactory affair. Afterwards, we went into the Pontifical Gardens, connected with the palace. They are very extensive, and laid out in straight avenues, bordered with walls of box, as impervious as if of stone, — not less than twenty feet high, and pierced with lofty archways, cut in the living wall. Some of the avenues were overshadowed with trees, the tops of which bent over and joined one another from either side, so as to resemble a side-aisle of a Gothic cathedral. Marble sculptures, much weather-stained, and generally broken-nosed, stood along these stately walks ; there were many fountains gushing up into the sunshine; we likewise found a rich flower-garden, containing rare specimens of exotic flowers, and gigantic cactuses, and also an aviary, with vultures, doves, and singing birds. We did not see half the garden, but, stiff and formal as its general arrangement is, it is a beautiful place, — a delightful, sunny, and serene seclusion. Whatever it may be to the pope, two young lovers might find the Garden of Eden here, and never desire to stray out of its precincts. They might fancy angels standing in the long, glimmering vistas of the avenues.

It would suit me well enough to have my daily walk along such straight paths, for I think them favorable to thought, which is apt to be disturbed by variety and unexpectedness.

April 12. — We all, except Rose, went to-day to the Vatican, where we found our way to the Stanze of Raphael, these being four rooms, or halls, painted with frescos.   No doubt they were once very brilliant and beautiful ; but they have encountered hard treatment since Raphael's time, especially when the soldiers of the Constable de Bourbon occupied these apartments, and made fires on the mosaic floors.   The entire walls and ceilings are covered with pictures ; but the handiwork or designs of Raphael consist of paintings on the four sides of each room, and include several works of art.   The School of Athens is perhaps the most celebrated ; and the longest side of the largest hall is occupied by a battle-piece, of which the Emperor Constantine is the hero, and which covers almost space enough for a real battlefield.   There was a wonderful light in one of the pictures, — that of St. Peter awakened in his prison, by the angel ; it really seemed to throw a radiance into the hall below.   I shall not pretend, however, to have been sensible of any particular rapture at the sight of these frescos ; so faded as they are, so battered by the mischances of years, insomuch that, through all the power and glory of Raphael's designs, the spectator cannot but be continually sensible that the groundwork of them is an old plaster wall. They have been scrubbed, I suppose, — brushed, at least, — a thousand times over, till the surface, brilliant or soft, as Raphael left it, must have been quite rubbed off, and with it all the consummate finish, and everything that made them originally delightful. The sterner features remain, the skeleton of thought, but not the beauty that once clothed it. In truth, the frescos, excepting a few figures, never had the real touch of Raphael's own hand upon them, having been merely designed by him, and finished by his scholars, or by other artists.

The halls themselves are specimens of antique magnificence, paved with elaborate mosaics ; and wherever there is any woodwork, it is richly carved with foliage and figures. In their newness, and probably for a hundred years afterwards, there could not have been so brilliant a suite of rooms in the world.

Connected with them — at any rate, not far distant — is the little Chapel of San Lorenzo, the very site of which, among the thousands of apartments of the Vatican, was long forgotten, and its existence only known by tradition. After it had been walled up, however, beyond the memory of man, there was still a rumor of some beautiful frescos by Fra Angelico, in an old Chapel of Pope Nicholas V., that had strangely disappeared out of the palace, and, search at length being made, it was discovered, and entered through a window. It is a small, lofty room, quite covered over with frescos of sacred subjects, both on the walls and ceiling, a good deal faded, yet pretty distinctly preserved. It would have been no misfortune to me, if the little old chapel had remained still hidden.

We next issued into the Loggie, which consist of a long gallery, or arcade or colonnade, the whole extent of which was once beautifully adorned by Raphael. These pictures are almost worn away, and so defaced as to be untraceable and unintelligible, along the side wall of the gallery; although traceries of Arabesque, and compartments where there seem to have been rich paintings, but now only an indistinguishable waste of dull color, are still to be seen. In the coved ceiling, however, there are still some bright frescos, in better preservation than any others; not particularly beautiful, nevertheless. I remember to have seen (indeed, we ourselves possess them) a series of very spirited and energetic engravings, old and coarse, of these frescos, the subject being the Creation and the early Scripture history; and I really think that their translation of the pictures is better than the original. On reference to Murray, I find that little more than the designs is attributed to

Raphael, the execution being by Giulio Romano and other artists.

Escaping from these forlorn splendors, we went into the sculpture gallery, where I was able to enjoy, in some small degree, two or three wonderful works of art ; and had a perception that there were a thousand other wonders around me. It is as if the statues kept, for the most part, a veil about them, which they sometimes withdraw, and let their beauty gleam upon my sight ; only a glimpse, or two or three glimpses, or a little space of calm enjoyment, and then I see nothing but a discolored marble image again. The Minerva Medica revealed herself to-day. I wonder whether other people are more fortunate than myself, and can invariably find their way to the inner soul of a work of art. I doubt it ; they look at these things for just a minute, and pass on, without any pang of remorse, such as I feel, for quitting them so soon and so willingly. I am partly sensible that some unwritten rules of taste are making their way into my mind ; that all this Greek beauty has done something towards refining me, though I am still, however, a very sturdy Goth. . . .

April 15. — Yesterday I went with Julian to the Forum, and descended into the excavations at the base of the Capitol, and on the site of the

Basilica of Julia.   The essential elements of old Rome are there : columns, single, or in groups of two or three, still erect, but battered and bruised at some forgotten time with infinite pains and labor ; fragments of other columns lying prostrate, together with rich capitals and friezes ; the bust of a colossal female statue, showing the bosom and upper part of the arms, but headless ; a long, winding space of pavement, forming part of the ancient ascent to the Capitol, still as firm and solid as ever ; the foundation of the Capitol itself wonderfully massive, built of immense square blocks of stone, doubtless three thousand years old, and durable for whatever may be the lifetime of the world ; the Arch of Septimius Severus, with bas-reliefs of Eastern wars ; the Column of Phocas, with the rude series of steps ascending on four sides to its pedestal ; the floor of beautiful and precious marbles in the Basilica of Julia, the slabs cracked across, — the greater part of them torn up and removed, the grass and weeds growing up through the chinks of what remain ; heaps of bricks, shapeless bits of granite, and other ancient rubbish, among which old men are lazily rummaging for specimens that a stranger may be induced to buy, — this being an employment that suits the indolence of a modern Roman.   The level of these excavations is about fifteen feet, I should judge, below the present street which passes through the Forum, and only

a very small part of this alien surface has been
removed, though there can be no doubt that it
hides numerous treasures of art and monuments
of history.   Yet these remains do not make that
impression of antiquity upon me, which Gothic
ruins do.   Perhaps it is so because they belong
to quite another system of society and epoch of
time, and in view of them, we forget all that has
intervened betwixt them and us ; being morally
unlike and disconnected with them, and not belonging to the same train of thought ; so that
we look across a gulf to the Roman ages, and
do not realize how wide the gulf is.   Yet in
that intervening valley lie Christianity, the Dark
Ages, the feudal system, chivalry and romance,
and a deeper life of the human race than Rome
brought to the verge of the gulf.

   To-day we went to the Colonna Palace, where
we saw some fine pictures, but, I think, no masterpieces.   They did not depress and dishearten
me so much as the pictures in Roman palaces
usually do ; for they were in remarkably good
order as regards frames and varnish ; indeed, I
rather suspect some of them had been injured
by the means adopted to preserve their beauty.
The palace is now occupied by the French Ambassador, who probably looks upon the pictures
as articles of furniture and household adornment,
and does not choose to have squares of black and
forlorn canvas upon his walls.   There were a

few noble portraits by Vandyke ; a very striking
one by Holbein, one or two by Titian, also by
Guercino, and some pictures by Rubens, and
other *forestieri* painters, which refreshed my
weary eyes.   But what chiefly interested me was
the magnificent and stately hall of the palace ;
fifty-five of my paces in length, besides a large
apartment at either end, opening into it through
a pillared space, as wide as the gateway of a city.
The pillars are of giallo antico, and there are pilasters of the same all the way up and down the
walls, forming a perspective of the richest aspect,
especially as the broad cornice flames with gilding, and the spaces between the pilasters are
emblazoned with heraldic achievements and em-
blems in gold, and there are Venetian looking-
glasses, richly decorated over the surface with
beautiful pictures of flowers and cupids, through
which you catch the gleam of the mirror ; and
two rows of splendid chandeliers extend from end
to end of the hall, which, when lighted up, if
ever it be lighted up now-a-nights, must be the
most brilliant interior that ever mortal eye beheld.   The ceiling glows with pictures in fresco,
representing scenes connected with the history
of the Colonna family ; and the floor is paved
with beautiful marbles, polished and arranged in
square and circular compartments ; and each of
the many windows is set in a great architectural
frame of precious marble, as large as the portal

of a door.   The apartment at the farther end of
the hall is elevated above it, and is attained by
several marble steps, whence it must have been
glorious in former days to have looked down
upon a gorgeous throng of princes, cardinals,
warriors, and ladies, in such rich attire as might
be worn when the palace was built.   It is singular how much freshness and brightness it still
retains ; and the only objects to mar the effect
were some ancient statues and busts, not very
good in themselves, and now made dreary of
aspect by their corroded surfaces, — the result
of long burial under ground.

In the room at the entrance of the hall are two
cabinets, each a wonder in its way, — one being
adorned with precious stones ; the other with
ivory carvings of Michel Angelo's Last Judgment, and of the frescos of Raphael's Loggie.
The world has ceased to be so magnificent as it
once was.   Men make no such marvels nowadays.   The only defect that I remember in this
hall was in the marble steps that ascend to the
elevated apartment at the end of it ; a large piece
had been broken out of one of them, leaving a
rough irregular gap in the polished marble stair.
It is not easy to conceive what violence can have
done this, without also doing mischief to all the
other splendor around it.

April 16. — We went this morning to the

Academy of St. Luke (the Fine Arts Academy
at Rome) in the Via Bonella, close by the Forum.   We rang the bell at the house door ; and
after a few moments it was unlocked or unbolted
by some unseen agency from above, no one making his appearance to admit us.   We ascended
two or three flights of stairs, and entered a hall,
where was a young man, the custode, and two
or three artists engaged in copying some of the
pictures.   The collection not being vastly large,
and the pictures being in more presentable condition than usual, I enjoyed them more than I
generally do ; particularly a Virgin and Child by
Vandyke, where two angels are singing and playing, one on a lute and the other on a violin, to
remind the holy infant of the strains he used to
hear in heaven.   It is one of the few pictures
that there is really any pleasure in looking at.
There were several paintings by Titian, mostly
of a voluptuous character, but not very charm-
ing ; also two or more by Guido, one of which,
representing Fortune, is celebrated.   They did
not impress me much, nor do I find myself
strongly drawn towards Guido, though there is
no other painter who seems to achieve things so
magically and inscrutably as he sometimes does.
Perhaps it requires a finer taste than mine to appreciate him ; and yet I do appreciate him so far
as to see that his Michael, for instance, is perfectly beautiful. . . . In the gallery there are

whole rows of portraits of members of the Academy of St. Luke, most of whom, judging by
their physiognomies, were very commonplace
people ; a fact which makes itself visible in a portrait, however much the painter may try to flat-
ter his sitter.   Several of the pictures by Titian,
Paul Veronese, and other artists, now exhibited
in the gallery, were formerly kept in a secret cab-
inet in the Capitol, being considered of a too voluptuous character for the public eye.   I did not
think them noticeably indecorous, as compared
with a hundred other pictures that are shown and
looked at without scruple, — Calypso and her
Nymphs, a knot of nude women by Titian, is
perhaps as objectionable as any.   But even Titian's flesh tints cannot keep, and have not kept,
their warmth through all these centuries.   The
illusion and lifelikeness effervesces and exhales
out of a picture as it grows old ; and we go on
talking of a charm that has forever vanished.

From St. Luke's we went to San Pietro in
Vincoli, occupying a fine position on or near
the summit of the Esquiline mount.   A little
abortion of a man (and, by the bye, there are
more diminutive and ill-shapen men and women
in Rome than I ever saw elsewhere, a phenome-
non to be accounted for, perhaps, by their custom of wrapping the new-born infant in swad-
dling-clothes), this two-foot abortion hastened
before us, as we drew nigh, to summon the

sacristan to open the church door. It was a needless service, for which we rewarded him with two baiocchi. San Pietro is a simple and noble church, consisting of a nave divided from the side-aisles by rows of columns, that once adorned some ancient temple ; and its wide, un-encumbered interior affords better breathing space than most churches in Rome. The statue of Moses occupies a niche in one of the side-aisles on the right, not far from the high altar. I found it grand and sublime, with a beard flow-ing down like a cataract ; a truly majestic figure, but not so benign as it were desirable that such strength should be. The horns, about which so much has been said, are not a very promi-nent feature of the statue, being merely two diminutive tips rising straight up over his fore-head, neither adding to the grandeur of the head, nor detracting sensibly from it. The whole force of this statue is not to be felt in one brief visit, but I agree with an English gentleman who, with a large party, entered the church while we were there, in thinking that Moses has " very fine features," — a compliment for which the colossal Hebrew ought to have made the Englishman a bow.

Besides the Moses, the church contains some attractions of a pictorial kind, which are repos-ited in the sacristy, into which we passed through a side door. The most remarkable of these pic-

Michel Angelo's Moses

tures is a face and bust of Hope, by Guido,
with beautiful eyes lifted upwards ; it has a
grace which artists are continually trying to get
into their innumerable copies, but always without success ; for, indeed, though nothing is more
true than the existence of this charm in the picture, yet if you try to analyze it, or even look
too intently at it, it vanishes, till you look again
with more trusting simplicity.

Leaving the church, we wandered to the Coliseum, and to the public grounds contiguous
to them, where a score and more of French drummers were beating each man his drum, without
reference to any rub-a-dub but his own.   This
seems to be a daily or periodical practice and
point of duty with them.   After resting ourselves
on one of the marble benches, we came slowly
home, through the Basilica of Constantine, and
along the shady sides of the streets and piazzas,
sometimes, perforce, striking boldly through the
white sunshine, which, however, was not so hot
as to shrivel us up bodily.   It has been a most
beautiful and perfect day as regards weather,
clear and bright, very warm in the sunshine, yet
freshened throughout by a quiet stir in the air.
Still there is something in this air malevolent,
or, at least, not friendly.   The Romans lie down
and fall asleep in it, in any vacant part of the
streets, and wherever they can find any spot sufficiently clean, and among the ruins of temples.

I would not sleep in the open air for whatever my life may be worth.

On our way home, sitting in one of the narrow streets, we saw an old woman spinning with a distaff; a far more ancient implement than the spinning-wheel, which the housewives of other nations have long since laid aside.

April 18. — Yesterday, at noon, the whole family of us set out on a visit to the Villa Borghese and its grounds, the entrance to which is just outside of the Porta del Popolo. After getting within the grounds, however, there is a long walk before reaching the casino, and we found the sun rather uncomfortably hot, and the road dusty and white in the sunshine; nevertheless, a footpath ran alongside of it most of the way through the grass and among the young trees. It seems to me that the trees do not put forth their leaves with nearly the same magical rapidity in this southern land at the approach of summer, as they do in more northerly countries. In these latter, having a much shorter time to develop themselves, they feel the necessity of making the most of it. But the grass, in the lawns and enclosures along which we passed, looked already fit to be mowed, and it was interspersed with many flowers.

Saturday being, I believe, the only day of the week on which visitors are admitted to the

casino, there were many parties in carriages, artists on foot, gentlemen on horseback, and miscellaneous people, to whom the door was opened
by a custode on ringing a bell.   The whole of
the basement floor of the casino, comprising a
suite of beautiful rooms, is filled with statuary.
The entrance hall is a very splendid apartment,
brightly frescoed, and paved with ancient mosaics, representing the combats with beasts and
gladiators in the Coliseum, curious, though very
rudely and awkwardly designed, apparently after
the arts had begun to decline.   Many of the
specimens of sculpture displayed in these rooms
are fine, but none of them, I think, possess the
highest merit.   An Apollo is beautiful ; a group
of a fighting Amazon, and her enemies trampled
under her horse's feet, is very impressive ; a
Faun, copied from that of Praxiteles, and another who seems to be dancing, were exceedingly pleasant to look at.   I like these strange,
sweet, playful, rustic creatures, . . . linked so
prettily, without monstrosity, to the lower
tribes. . . .   Their character has never, that I
know of, been wrought out in literature ; and
something quite good, funny, and philosophi-
cal, as well as poetic, might very likely be educed
from them. . . .   The faun is a natural and delightful link betwixt human and brute life, with
something of a divine character intermingled.

The gallery, as it is called, on the basement

floor of the casino, is sixty feet in length, by perhaps a third as much in breadth, and is (after all I have seen at the Colonna Palace and elsewhere) a more magnificent hall than I imagined to be in existence. It is floored with rich marble in beautifully arranged compartments, and the walls are almost entirely cased with marble of various sorts, the prevailing kind being giallo antico, intermixed with verde antique, and I know not what else ; but the splendor of the giallo antico gives the character to the room, and the large and deep niches along the walls appear to be lined with the same material. Without coming to Italy, one can have no idea of what beauty and magnificence are produced by these fittings-up of polished marble. Marble to an American means nothing but white limestone.

This hall, moreover, is adorned with pillars of Oriental alabaster, and wherever is a space vacant of precious and richly colored marble it is frescoed with arabesque ornaments ; and over the whole is a coved and vaulted ceiling, glowing with picture. There never can be anything richer than the whole effect. As to the sculpture here it was not very fine, so far as I can remember, consisting chiefly of busts of the emperors in porphyry ; but they served a good purpose in the upholstery way. There were also magnificent tables, each composed of one great slab of porphyry ; and also vases of nero antico, and other rarest substance. It remains to be mentioned that, on this almost summer day, I was quite chilled in passing through these glorious halls ; no fireplace anywhere ; no possibility of comfort ; and in the hot season, when their coolness might be agreeable, it would be death to inhabit them.

Ascending a long winding staircase, we arrived at another suite of rooms, containing a good many not very remarkable pictures, and a few more pieces of statuary. Among the latter is Canova's statue of Pauline, the sister of Bonaparte, who is represented with but little drapery, and in the character of Venus holding the apple in her hand. It is admirably done, and, I have no doubt, a perfect likeness ; very beautiful too ; but it is wonderful to see how the artificial elegance of the woman of this world makes itself perceptible in spite of whatever simplicity she could find in almost utter nakedness. The statue does not afford pleasure in the contemplation.

In one of these upper rooms are some works of Bernini ; two of them, Æneas and Anchises, and David on the point of slinging a stone at Goliath, have great merit, and do not tear and rend themselves quite out of the laws and limits of marble, like his later sculpture. Here is also his Apollo overtaking Daphne, whose feet take root, whose finger-tips sprout into twigs, and whose tender body roughens round about with bark, as he embraces her. It did not seem very wonderful to me ; not so good as Hillard's description of it made me expect ; and one does not enjoy these freaks in marble.

We were glad to emerge from the casino into the warm sunshine ; and, for my part, I made the best of my way to a large fountain, surrounded by a circular stone seat of wide sweep, and sat down in a sunny segment of the circle. Around grew a solemn company of old trees, — ilexes, I believe, — with huge, contorted trunks and evergreen branche͏̃ .. deep groves, sunny openings, the air͏̃ gush of fountains, marble statues, dimly ͏̃sible in recesses of foliage, great urns and ͏̃ses, terminal figures, temples, — all these ͏̃orks of art looking as if they had stood there long enough to feel at home, and to be on friendly and familiar terms with the grass and trees. It is a most beautiful place, . . . and the Malaria is its true master and inhabitant !

April 22. — We have been recently to the studio of Mr. Brown,[1] the American landscape-painter, and were altogether surprised and delighted with his pictures. He is a plain, homely Yankee, quite unpolished by his many years' residence in Italy ; he talks ungrammati-

[1] Now dead.

cally and in Yankee idioms; walks with a
strange, awkward gait and stooping shoulders; is
altogether unpicturesque, but wins one's confidence by his very lack of grace. It is not often
that we see an artist so entirely free from affectation in his aspect and deportment. His pictures were views of Swiss and Italian scenery,
and were most beautiful and true. One of
them, a moonlight picture, was really magical,
— the moon shining so brightly that it seemed
to throw a light even beyond the limits of the
picture, — and yet his sunrises and sunsets, and
noontides too, were nowise inferior to this,
although their excellence required somewhat
longer study, to be fully appreciated. I seemed
to receive more pleasure from Mr. Brown's
pictures than from any of the landscapes by the
old masters; and the fact serves to strengthen
me in the belief that the most delicate if not the
highest charm of a picture is evanescent, and that
we continue to admire pictures prescriptively
and by tradition, after the qualities that first won
them their fame have vanished. I suppose
Claude was a greater landscape-painter than
Brown; but for my own pleasure I would prefer one of the latter artist's pictures, — those of
the former being quite changed from what he
intended them to be by the effect of time on
his pigments. Mr. Brown showed us some
drawings from nature, done with incredible care

and minuteness of detail, as studies for his paintings. We complimented him on his patience; but he said, " O, it 's not patience, — it 's love !"   In fact, it was a patient and most successful wooing of a beloved object, which at last rewarded him by yielding itself wholly.

We have likewise been to Mr. B——'s [1] studio, where we saw several pretty statues and busts, and among them an Eve, with her wreath of fig-leaves lying across her poor nudity; comely in some points, but with a frightful volume of thighs and calves.   I do not altogether see the necessity of ever sculpturing another nakedness.   Man is no longer a naked animal; his clothes are as natural to him as his skin, and sculptors have no more right to undress him than to flay him.

Also, we have seen again William Story's Cleopatra, — a work of genuine thought and energy, representing a terribly dangerous woman; quiet enough for the moment, but very likely to spring upon you like a tigress.   It is delightful to escape to his creations from this universal prettiness, which seems to be the highest conception of the crowd of modern sculptors, and which they almost invariably attain.

Miss Bremer called on us the other day. We find her very little changed from what she was when she came to take tea and spend an even-

[1] Now dead.

ing at our little red cottage, among the Berkshire hills, and went away so dissatisfied with my conversational performances, and so laudatory of my brow and eyes, while so severely criticising my poor mouth and chin. She is the funniest little old fairy in person whom one can imagine, with a huge nose, to which all the rest of her is but an insufficient appendage ; but you feel at once that she is most gentle, kind, womanly, sympathetic, and true. She talks English fluently, in a low quiet voice, but with such an accent that it is impossible to understand her without the closest attention. This was the real cause of the failure of our Berkshire interview ; for I could not guess, half the time, what she was saying, and, of course, had to take an uncertain aim with my responses. A more intrepid talker than myself would have shouted his ideas across the gulf ; but, for me, there must first be a close and unembarrassed contiguity with my companion, or I cannot say one real word. I doubt whether I have ever really talked with half a dozen persons in my life, either men or women.

To-day my wife and I have been at the picture and sculpture galleries of the Capitol. I rather enjoyed looking at several of the pictures, though at this moment I particularly remember only a beautiful face of a man, one of two heads on the same canvas, by Vandyke.

Yes; I did look with new admiration at Paul Veronese's Rape of Europa. It must have been, in its day, the most brilliant and rejoicing picture, the most voluptuous, the most exuberant, that ever put the sunshine to shame. The bull has all Jupiter in him, so tender and gentle, yet so passionate, that you feel it indecorous to look at him; and Europa, under her thick, rich stuffs and embroideries, is all a woman. What a pity that such a picture should fade, and perplex the beholder with such splendor, shining through such forlornness!

We afterwards went into the sculpture gallery, where I looked at the Faun of Praxiteles, and was sensible of a peculiar charm in it; a sylvan beauty and homeliness, friendly and wild at once. The lengthened, but not preposterous ears, and the little tail, which we infer, have an exquisite effect, and make the spectator smile in his very heart. This race of fauns was the most delightful of all that antiquity imagined. It seems to me that a story, with all sorts of fun and pathos in it, might be contrived on the idea of their species having become intermingled with the human race; a family with the faun blood in them having prolonged itself from the classic era till our own days. The tail might have disappeared, by dint of constant intermarriages with ordinary mortals; but the pretty hairy ears should occasionally reappear in members of the family ; and the moral instincts and intellectual characteristics of the faun might be most picturesquely brought out, without detriment to the human interest of the story. Fancy this combination in the person of a young lady !

I have spoken of Mr. Gibson's colored statues. It seems (at least Mr. Nichols tells me) that he stains them with tobacco juice. . . . Were he to send a Cupid to America, he need not trouble himself to stain it beforehand.

April 25. — Night before last, my wife and I took a moonlight ramble through Rome, it being a very beautiful night, warm enough for comfort, and with no perceptible dew or dampness. We set out at about nine o'clock, and, our general direction being towards the Coliseum, we soon came to the Fountain of Trevi, full on the front of which the moonlight fell, making Bernini's sculptures look stately and beautiful, though the semicircular gush and fall of the cascade, and the many jets of the water, pouring and bubbling into the great marble basin, are of far more account than Neptune and his steeds, and the rest of the figures. . . .

We ascended the Capitoline Hill, and I felt a satisfaction in placing my hand on those immense blocks of stone, the remains of the ancient Capitol, which form the foundation of the present edifice, and will make a sure basis for as many edifices as posterity may choose to rear upon it, till the end of the world. It is wonderful, the solidity with which those old Romans built; one would suppose they contemplated the whole course of Time as the only limit of their individual life. This is not so strange in the days of the Republic, when, probably, they believed in the permanence of their institutions; but they still seemed to build for eternity in the reigns of the emperors, when neither rulers nor people had any faith or moral substance, or laid any earnest grasp on life.

Reaching the top of the Capitoline Hill, we ascended the steps of the portal of the Palace of the Senator, and looked down into the piazza, with the equestrian statue of Marcus Aurelius in the centre of it. The architecture that surrounds the piazza is very ineffective; and so, in my opinion, are all the other architectural works of Michel Angelo, including St. Peter's itself, of which he has made as little as could possibly be made of such a vast pile of material. He balances everything in such a way that it seems but half of itself.

We soon descended into the piazza, and walked round and round the statue of Marcus Aurelius, contemplating it from every point and admiring it in all. . . . On these beautiful moonlight nights, Rome appears to keep awake and stirring, though in a quiet and decorous

way. It is, in fact, the pleasantest time for
promenades, and we both felt less wearied than
by any promenade in the daytime, of similar
extent, since our residence in Rome. In future
I mean to walk often after nightfall.

Yesterday, we set out betimes, and ascended
the dome of St. Peter's. The best view of the
interior of the church, I think, is from the first
gallery beneath the dome. The whole inside
of the dome is set with mosaic work, the separate pieces being, so far as I could see, about
half an inch square. Emerging on the roof we
had a fine view of all the surrounding Rome,
including the Mediterranean Sea in the remote
distance. Above us still rose the whole mountain of the great dome, and it made an impression on me of greater height and size than I
had yet been able to receive. The copper ball
at the summit looked hardly bigger than a man
could lift; and yet, a little while afterwards,
Una, Julian, and I stood all together in that
ball, which could have contained a dozen more
along with us. The esplanade of the roof is,
of course, very extensive ; and along the front
of it are ranged the statues which we see from
below, and which, on nearer examination, prove
to be roughly hewn giants. There is a small
house on the roof, where, probably, the custodes
of this part of the edifice reside ; and there is
a fountain gushing abundantly into a stone

trough, that looked like an old sarcophagus. It is strange where the water comes from at such a height. The children tasted it, and pronounced it very warm and disagreeable. After taking in the prospect on all sides we rang a bell, which summoned a man, who directed us towards a door in the side of the dome, where a custode was waiting to admit us. Hitherto the ascent had been easy, along a slope without stairs, up which, I believe, people sometimes ride on donkeys. The rest of the way we mounted steep and narrow staircases, winding round within the wall, or between the two walls of the dome, and growing narrower and steeper, till, finally, there is but a perpendicular iron ladder, by means of which to climb into the copper ball. Except through small windows and peep-holes, there is no external prospect of a higher point than the roof of the church. Just beneath the ball there is a circular room capable of containing a large company, and a door which ought to give access to a gallery on the outside; but the custode informed us that this door is never opened. As I have said, Una, Julian, and I clambered into the copper ball, which we found as hot as an oven ; and, after putting our hands on its top, and on the summit of St. Peter's, were glad to clamber down again. I have made some mistake, after all, in my narration. There certainly is a circular balcony at the top of the dome, for I remember walking round it, and looking, not only across the country, but downwards along the ribs of the dome; to which are attached the iron contrivances for illuminating it on Easter Sunday. . . .

Before leaving the church we went to look at the mosaic copy of The Transfiguration, because we were going to see the original in the Vatican, and wished to compare the two. Going round to the entrance of the Vatican, we went first to the manufactory of mosaics, to which we had a ticket of admission. We found it a long series of rooms, in which the mosaic artists were at work, chiefly in making some medallions of the heads of saints for the new church of St. Paul's. It was rather coarse work, and it seemed to me that the mosaic copy was somewhat stiffer and more wooden than the original, the bits of stone not flowing into color quite so freely as paint from a brush. There was no large picture now in process of being copied; but two or three artists were employed on small and delicate subjects. One had a Holy Family of Raphael in hand; and the Sibyls of Guercino and Domenichino were hanging on the wall, apparently ready to be put into mosaic. Wherever great skill and delicacy, on the artists' part, were necessary, they seemed quite adequate to the occasion; but, after all, a mosaic of any celebrated picture is but a copy of a copy. The substance employed is a stone-paste, of innumerable different hues, and in bits of various sizes, quantities of which were seen in cases along the whole series of rooms.

We next ascended an amazing height of staircases, and walked along I know not what extent of passages, . . . till we reached the picture gallery of the Vatican, into which I had never been before. There are but three rooms, all lined with red velvet, on which hang about fifty pictures, each one of them, no doubt, worthy to be considered a masterpiece. In the first room were three Murillos, all so beautiful that I could have spent the day happily in looking at either of them; for, methinks, of all painters he is the tenderest and truest. I could not enjoy these pictures now, however, because in the next room, and visible through the open door, hung The Transfiguration. Approaching it, I felt that the picture was worthy of its fame, and was far better than I could at once appreciate; admirably preserved, too, though I fully believe it must have possessed a charm when it left Raphael's hand that has now vanished forever. As church furniture and an external adornment, the mosaic copy is preferable to the original, but no copy could ever reproduce all the life and expression which we see here. Opposite to it hangs The Communion of St. Jerome, the aged, dying saint, half torpid with death already, partaking of the sacrament, and a sunny garland of cherubs in the upper part of the picture, looking down upon him, and quite comforting the spectator with the idea that the old man needs only to be quite dead in order to flit away with them. As for the other pictures I did but glance at, and have forgotten them.

The Transfiguration is finished with great minuteness and detail, the weeds and blades of grass in the foreground being as distinct as if they were growing in a natural soil. A partly decayed stick of wood with the bark is likewise given in close imitation of nature. The reflection of a foot of one of the apostles is seen in a pool of water at the verge of the picture. One or two heads and arms seem almost to project from the canvas. There is great lifelikeness and reality, as well as higher qualities. The face of Jesus, being so high aloft and so small in the distance, I could not well see; but I am impressed with the idea that it looks too much like human flesh and blood to be in keeping with the celestial aspect of the figure, or with the probabilities of the scene, when the divinity and immortality of the Saviour beamed from within him through the earthly features that ordinarily shaded him. As regards the composition of the picture, I am not convinced of the propriety of its being in two so distinctly separate parts, — the upper portion not thinking of the lower, and the lower portion not being aware of the higher. It symbolizes, however, the spiritual shortsightedness of mankind that, amid the trouble and grief of the lower picture, not a single individual, either of those who seek help or those who would willingly afford it, lifts his eyes to that region, one glimpse of which would set everything right. One or two of the disciples point upward, but without really knowing what abundance of help is to be had there.

April 27. — To-day we have all been with Mr. Akers to some studios of painters ; first to that of Mr. Wilde, an artist originally from Boston. His pictures are principally of scenes from Venice, and are miracles of color, being as bright as if the light were transmitted through rubies and sapphires. And yet, after contemplating them awhile, we became convinced that the painter had not gone in the least beyond nature, but, on the contrary, had fallen short of brilliancies which no palette, or skill, or boldness in using color, could attain. I do not quite know whether it is best to attempt these things. They may be found in nature, no doubt, but always so tempered by what surrounds them, so put out of sight even while they seem full before our eyes, that we question the accuracy of a faithful reproduction of them on canvas.   There was a picture of sunset, the whole sky of which would have outshone any gilded frame that could have been put around it.   There was a most gorgeous sketch of a handful of weeds and leaves, such as may be seen strewing acres of forest ground in an American autumn.   I doubt whether any other man has ever ventured to paint a picture like either of these two, the Italian sunset or the American autumnal foliage.   Mr. Wilde, who is still young, talked with genuine feeling and enthusiasm of his art, and is certainly a man of genius.

We next went to the studio of an elderly Swiss artist, named Müller, I believe, where we looked at a great many water-color and crayon drawings of scenes in Italy, Greece, and Switzerland.   The artist was a quiet, respectable, somewhat heavy-looking old gentleman, from whose aspect one would expect a plodding pertinacity of character rather than quickness of sensibility. He must have united both these qualities, however, to produce such pictures as these, such faithful transcripts of whatever Nature has most beautiful to show, and which she shows only to those who love her deeply and patiently.   They are wonderful pictures, compressing plains, seas, and mountains, with miles and miles of distance, into the space of a foot or two without crowding anything or leaving out a feature, and diffusing the free, blue atmosphere throughout. The works of the English water-color artists which I saw at the Manchester Exhibition seemed to me nowise equal to these. Now, here are three artists, Mr. Brown, Mr. Wilde, and Mr. Müller, who have smitten me with vast admiration within these few days past, while I am continually turning away disappointed from the landscapes of the most famous among the old masters, unable to find any charm or illusion in them. Yet I suppose Claude, Poussin, and Salvator Rosa must have won their renown by real achievements. But the glory of a picture fades like that of a flower.

Contiguous to Mr. Müller's studio was that of a young German artist, not long resident in Rome, and Mr. Akers proposed that we should go in there, as a matter of kindness to the young man, who is scarcely known at all, and seldom has a visitor to look at his pictures. His studio comprised his whole establishment; for there was his little bed, with its white drapery, in a corner of the small room, and his dressing-table, with its brushes and combs, while the easel and the few sketches of Italian scenes and figures occupied the foreground. I did not like his pictures very well, but would gladly have bought them all if I could have afforded it, the artist looked so cheerful, patient, and quiet, doubtless amidst huge discouragement.

He is probably stubborn of purpose, and is the
sort of man who will improve with every year
of his life.   We could not speak his language,
and were therefore spared the difficulty of paying him any compliments ; but Miss Shepard
said a few kind words to him in German, and
seemed quite to win his heart, insomuch that he
followed her with bows and smiles a long way
down the staircase.   It is a terrible business,
this looking at pictures, whether good or bad,
in the presence of the artists who paint them ;
it is as great a bore as to hear a poet read his
own verses.   It takes away all my pleasure in
seeing the pictures, and even makes me question
the genuineness of the impressions which I receive from them.

After this latter visit Mr. Akers conducted
us to the shop of the jeweller Castellani, who is
a great reproducer of ornaments in the old Roman and Etruscan fashion.   These antique styles
are very fashionable just now, and some of the
specimens he showed us were certainly very
beautiful, though I doubt whether their quaint-
ness and old-time curiousness, as patterns of
gewgaws dug out of immemorial tombs, be not
their greatest charm.   We saw the toilet-case
of an Etruscan lady, — that is to say, a modern
imitation of it, — with her rings for summer
and winter, and for every day of the week, and
for thumb and fingers ; her ivory comb ; her

bracelets; and more knickknacks than I can half remember. Splendid things of our own time were likewise shown us; a necklace of diamonds worth eighteen thousand scudi, together with emeralds and opals and great pearls. Finally we came away, and my wife and Miss Shepard were taken up by the Misses Weston, who drove with them to visit the Villa Albani. During their drive my wife happened to raise her arm, and Miss Shepard espied a little Greek cross of gold which had attached itself to the lace of her sleeve. . . . Pray Heaven the jeweller may not discover his loss before we have time to restore the spoil! He is apparently so free and careless in displaying his precious wares,— putting inestimable gems and brooches great and small into the hands of strangers like ourselves, and leaving scores of them strewn on the top of his counter,— that it would seem easy enough to take a diamond or two; but I suspect there must needs be a sharp eye somewhere. Before we left the shop he requested me to honor him with my autograph in a large book that was full of the names of his visitors. This is probably a measure of precaution.

April 30. — I went yesterday to the sculpture gallery of the Capitol, and looked pretty thoroughly through the busts of the illustrious men, and less particularly at those of the emperors and their relatives. I likewise took particular note of the Faun of Praxiteles, because the idea keeps recurring to me of writing a little romance about it, and for that reason I shall endeavor to set down a somewhat minutely itemized detail of the statue and its surroundings. . . .

We have had beautiful weather for two or three days, very warm in the sun, yet always freshened by the gentle life of a breeze, and quite cool enough the moment you pass within the limit of the shade. . . .

In the morning there are few people there (on the Pincian) except the gardeners, lazily trimming the borders, or filling their watering-pots out of the marble-brimmed basin of the fountain; French soldiers, in their long mixed-blue surtouts, and wide scarlet pantaloons, chatting with here and there a nursery-maid, and playing with the child in her care; and perhaps a few smokers, . . . choosing each a marble seat or wooden bench in sunshine or shade as best suits him. In the afternoon, especially within an hour or two of sunset, the gardens are much more populous, and the seats, except when the sun falls full upon them, are hard to come by. Ladies arrive in carriages, splendidly dressed; children are abundant, much impeded in their frolics, and rendered stiff and stately by the finery which they wear; English gentlemen,

and Americans with their wives and families ;
the flower of the Roman population, too, both
male and female, mostly dressed with great
nicety ; but a large intermixture of artists, shabbily picturesque ; and other persons, not of the
first stamp. A French band, comprising a great
many brass instruments, by and by begins to
play ; and what with music, sunshine, a delightful atmosphere, flowers, grass, well-kept path-
ways, bordered with box-hedges, pines, cy-
presses, horse-chestnuts, flowering shrubs, and
all manner of cultivated beauty, the scene is a
very lively and agreeable one. The fine equipages that drive round and round through the
carriage-paths are another noticeable item. The
Roman aristocracy are magnificent in their aspect, driving abroad with beautiful horses, and
footmen in rich liveries, sometimes as many as
three behind and one sitting by the coachman.

May 1. — This morning, I wandered for the
thousandth time through some of the narrow
intricacies of Rome, stepping here and there
into a church. I do not know the name of the
first one, nor had it anything that in Rome could
be called remarkable, though, till I came here,
I was not aware that any such churches existed,
— a marble pavement in variegated compartments, a series of shrines and chapels round the
whole floor, each with its own adornment of

also lemons and oranges ; stalls of fish, mostly about the size of smelts, taken from the Tiber ; cigars of various qualities, the best at a baioccho and a half apiece ; bread in loaves or in small rings, a great many of which are strung together on a long stick, and thus carried round for sale. Women and men sit with these things for sale, or carry them about in trays, or on boards on their heads, crying them with shrill and hard voices.   There is a shabby crowd and much babble ; very little picturesqueness of costume or figure, however, the chief exceptions being, here and there, an old white-bearded beggar. A few of the men have the peasant costume, — a short jacket and breeches of light blue cloth and white stockings, — the ugliest dress I ever saw.   The women go bareheaded, and seem fond of scarlet and other bright colors, but are homely and clumsy in form.   The piazza is dingy in its general aspect, and very dirty, being strewn with straw, vegetable tops, and the rubbish of a week's marketing ; but there is more life in it than one sees elsewhere in Rome.

On one side of the piazza is the Church of St. Agnes, traditionally said to stand on the site of the house where that holy maiden was exposed to infamy by the Roman soldiers, and where her modesty and innocence were saved by miracle.   I went into the church, and found it very splendid, with rich marble columns, all

as brilliant as if just built ; a frescoed dome
above ; beneath, a range of chapels all round
the church, ornamented not with pictures but
bas-reliefs, the figures of which almost step and
struggle out of the marble. They did not seem
very admirable as works of art, none of them
explaining themselves or attracting me long
enough to study out their meaning ; but, as part
of the architecture of the church, they had a
good effect. Out of the busy square two or
three persons had stepped into this bright and
calm seclusion to pray and be devout for a little
while ; and, between sunrise and sunset of the
bustling market-day, many doubtless snatch a
moment to refresh their souls.

In the Pantheon (to-day) it was pleasant looking up to the circular opening, to see the clouds
flitting across it, sometimes covering it quite over,
then permitting a glimpse of sky, then showing
all the circle of sunny blue. Then would come
the ragged edge of a cloud, brightened throughout with sunshine, passing and changing quickly,
— not that the divine smile was not always the
same, but continually variable through the medium of earthly influences. The great slanting
beam of sunshine was visible all the way down to
the pavement, falling upon motes of dust or a thin
smoke of incense imperceptible in the shadow.
Insects were playing to and fro in the beam,
high up toward the opening. There is a won-

derful charm in the naturalness of all this ; and one might fancy a swarm of cherubs coming down through the opening and sporting in the broad ray, to gladden the faith of worshippers on the pavement beneath ; or angels bearing prayers upward, or bringing down responses to them, visible with dim brightness as they pass through the pathway of heaven's radiance, even the many hues of their wings discernible by a trusting eye ; though, as they pass into the shadow, they vanish like the motes. So the sunbeam would represent those rays of divine intelligence which enable us to see wonders and to know that they are natural things.

Consider the effect of light and shade in a church where the windows are opened and darkened with curtains that are occasionally lifted by a breeze, letting in the sunshine, which whitens a carved tombstone on the pavement of the church, disclosing, perhaps, the letters of the name and inscription, a death's head, a crosier, or other emblem ; then the curtain falls and the bright spot vanishes.

May 8. — This morning my wife and I went to breakfast with Mrs. William Story at the Barberini Palace, expecting to meet Mrs. Jameson, who has been in Rome for a month or two. We had a very pleasant breakfast, but Mrs. Jameson was not present on account of indis-

position, and the only other guests were Mrs.
A—— and Mrs. H——, two sensible Ameri-
can ladies. Mrs. Story, however, received a note
from Mrs. Jameson, asking her to bring us to
see her at her lodgings ; so in the course of the
afternoon she called for us, and took us thither
in her carriage. Mrs. Jameson lives on the first
piano of an old palazzo on the Via di Ripetta,
nearly opposite the ferry-way across the Tiber,
and affording a pleasant view of the yellow river
and the green bank and fields on the other
side. I had expected to see an elderly lady,
but not quite so venerable a one as Mrs. Jameson proved to be ; a rather short, round, and
massive personage, of benign and agreeable aspect, with a sort of black skullcap on her head,
beneath which appeared her hair, which seemed
once to have been fair, and was now almost
white. I should take her to be about seventy
years old. She began to talk to us with affectionate familiarity, and was particularly kind in
her manifestations towards myself, who, on my
part, was equally gracious towards her. In
truth, I have found great pleasure and profit
in her works, and was glad to hear her say that
she liked mine. We talked about art, and she
showed us a picture leaning up against the wall
of the room ; a quaint old Byzantine painting,
with a gilded background, and two stiff figures
(our Saviour and St. Catherine) standing shyly

at a sacred distance from one another, and going through the marriage ceremony. There was a great deal of expression in their faces and figures ; and the spectator feels, moreover, that the artist must have been a devout man, — an impression which we seldom receive from modern pictures, however awfully holy the subject, or however consecrated the place they hang in. Mrs. Jameson seems to be familiar with Italy, its people and life, as well as with its picture galleries. She is said to be rather irascible in her temper ; but nothing could be sweeter than her voice, her look, and all her manifestation to-day. When we were coming away she clasped my hand in both of hers, and again expressed the pleasure of having seen me, and her gratitude to me for calling on her ; nor did I refrain from responding Amen to these effusions. . . .

Taking leave of Mrs. Jameson, we drove through the city, and out of the Lateran Gate ; first, however, waiting a long while at Monaldini's bookstore in the Piazza di Spagna for Mr. Story, whom we finally took up in the street, after losing nearly an hour.

Just two miles beyond the gate is a space on the green Campagna where, for some time past, excavations have been in progress, which thus far have resulted in the discovery of several tombs, and the old, buried, and almost forgotten church or basilica of San Stefano. It

is a beautiful spot, that of the excavations, with
the Alban hills in the distance, and some heavy,
sunlighted clouds hanging above, or recumbent
at length upon them, and, behind, the city and
its mighty dome. The excavations are an object of great interest both to the Romans and to
strangers, and there were many carriages and a
great many visitors viewing the progress of the
works, which are carried forward with greater
energy than anything else I have seen attempted
at Rome. A short time ago the ground in the
vicinity was a green surface, level, except here
and there a little hillock, or scarcely perceptible
swell; the tomb of Cecilia Metella showing itself a mile or two distant, and other rugged
ruins of great tombs rising on the plain. Now
the whole site of the basilica is uncovered, and
they have dug into the depths of several tombs,
bringing to light precious marbles, pillars, a
statue, and elaborately wrought sarcophagi; and
if they were to dig into almost every other
inequality that frets the surface of the Campagna, I suppose the result might be the same.
You cannot dig six feet downward anywhere
into the soil, deep enough to hollow out a grave,
without finding some precious relic of the past;
only they lose somewhat of their value when
you think that you can almost spurn them out
of the ground with your foot. It is a very wonderful arrangement of Providence that these

marble cluste
other round tl
The work was
gave it his las
to be placed ir
admired by co
ble should en
with better sk
to be shut up
This seems t
world, the mo
If they had bi
could underst
no sooner hac
furnished the
of art, than t
ness.   It was
the physical a
was no good

We went (
by, the walls
medallions in
numerous ser
the hand in
could not ha
utes) while tl
being mould
of the fertili
pidity and a
given substa

things should have been preserved for a long series of coming generations by that accumulation of dust and soil and grass and trees and houses over them, which will keep them safe, and cause their reappearance above ground to be gradual, so that the rest of the world's lifetime may have for one of its enjoyments the uncovering of old Rome.

The tombs were accessible by long flights of steps, going steeply downward, and they were thronged with so many visitors that we had to wait some little time for our own turn.   In the first into which we descended we found two tombs side by side, with only a partition wall between ; the outer tomb being, as is supposed, a ' urial-place constructed by the early Christians, while the adjoined and minor one was a work of pagan Rome about the second century after Christ.   The former was much less interesting than the latter.   It contained some large sarcophagi, with sculpture upon them of rather heathenish aspect ; and in the centre of the front of each sarcophagus was a bust in basrelief, the features of which had never been wrought, but were left almost blank, with only the faintest indications of a nose, for instance. It is supposed that sarcophagi were kept on hand by the sculptors, and were bought ready made, and that it was customary to work out the portrait of the deceased upon the blank face in the

cer
de:
pr

in
R
we
lit
tin
th
wi
in
th
be
ve
id
th
fr
T
fu
ar
si
co
a
in
o
se
sa
w
b

too — all of them such adornments as would
have suited a festal hall — were made to be
buried forthwith in eternal darkness. I saw and
handled in this tomb a great thigh-bone, and
measured it with my own ; it was one of many
such relics of the guests who were laid to sleep
in these rich chambers. The sarcophagi that
served them for coffins could not now be put to
a more appropriate use than as wine coolers in
a modern dining-room ; and it would heighten
the enjoyment of a festival to look at them.

We would gladly have stayed much longer;
but it was drawing towards sunset, and the evening, though bright, was unusually cool, so we
drove home ; and on the way, Mr. Story told
us of the horrible practices of the modern
Romans with their dead, — how they place
them in the church, where, at midnight, they are
stripped of their last rag of funeral attire, put
into the rudest wooden coffins, and thrown into
a trench, — a half-mile, for instance, of promis-
cuous corpses. This is the fate of all, except
those whose friends choose to pay an exorbitant
sum to have them buried under the pavement
of a church. The Italians have an excessive
dread of corpses, and never meddle with those of
their nearest and dearest relatives. They have a
horror of death, too, especially of sudden death,
and most particularly of apoplexy ; and no wonder, as it gives no time for the last rites of the

Church, and so exposes them to a fearful risk
of perdition forever. On the whole, the ancient
practice was, perhaps, the preferable one ; but
Nature has made it very difficult for us to do
anything pleasant and satisfactory with a dead
body. God knows best ; but I wish He had so
ordered it that our mortal bodies, when we have
done with them might vanish out of sight and
sense, like bubbles. A person of delicacy hates
to think of leaving such a burden as his decay-
ing mortality to the disposal of his friends ; but,
I say again, how delightful it would be, and how
helpful towards our faith in a blessed futurity,
if the dying could disappear like vanishing bubbles, leaving, perhaps, a sweet fragrance diffused
for a minute or two throughout the death-cham-
ber. This would be the odor of sanctity ! And
if sometimes the evaporation of a sinful soul
should leave an odor not so delightful, a breeze
through the open windows would soon waft it
quite away.

Apropos of the various methods of disposing
of dead bodies, William Story recalled a newspaper paragraph respecting a ring, with a stone
of a new species in it, which a widower was observed to wear upon his finger. Being ques-
tioned as to what the gem was, he answered, " It
is my wife." He had procured her body to be
chemically resolved into this stone. I think I
could make a story on this idea : the ring should

going in, we saw a cast from Michel Angelo's
statue of the Saviour ; and not far from the
threshold of the church, yet perhaps in the centre of the edifice, which is extremely small, a circular stone is placed, a little raised above the
pavement, and surrounded by a low wooden
railing.   Pointing to this stone, Mrs. Jameson
showed me the prints of two feet side by side,
impressed into its surface, as if a person had
stopped short while pursuing his way to Rome.
These, she informed me, were supposed to be
the miraculous prints of the Saviour's feet ; but
on looking into Murray, I am mortified to find
that they are merely facsimiles of the original
impressions, which are treasured up among the
relics of the neighboring Basilica of San Sebastiano.   The marks of sculpture seemed to me, indeed, very evident in these prints, nor did they
indicate such beautiful feet as should have belonged to the bearer of the best of glad tidings.

Hence we drove on a little way farther, and
came to the Basilica of San Sebastiano, where
also we alighted, and, leaning on my arm, Mrs.
Jameson went in.   It is a stately and noble interior, with a spacious unencumbered nave, and
a flat ceiling frescoed and gilded.   In a chapel
at the left of the entrance is the tomb of St. Sebastian, — a sarcophagus containing his remains,
raised on high before the altar, and beneath it a
recumbent statue of the saint pierced with gilded

arrows.   The sculpture is of the school of Bernini, — done after the design of Bernini himself, Mrs. Jameson said, and is more agreeable
and in better taste than most of his works.   We
walked round the basilica, glancing at the pictures in the various chapels, none of which
seemed to be of remarkable merit, although
Mrs. Jameson pronounced rather a favorable
verdict on one of St. Francis.   She says that
she can read a picture like the page of a book ;
in fact, without perhaps assuming more taste
and judgment than really belong to her, it was
impossible not to perceive that she gave her
companion no credit for knowing one single simplest thing about art.   Nor, on the whole, do I
think she underrated me ; the only mystery is,
how she came to be so well aware of my ignorance on artistical points.

In the basilica the Franciscan monks were
arranging benches on the floor of the nave, and
some peasant children and grown people besides
were assembling, probably to undergo an examination in the catechism, and we hastened to depart, lest our presence should interfere with their
arrangements.   At the door a monk met us, and
asked for a contribution in aid of his church
or some other religious purpose.   Boys, as we
drove on, ran stoutly along by the side of the
chaise, begging as often as they could find
breath, but were constrained finally to give up

as Nature makes us sensible of the fact when
men and women are graceful, beautiful, and noble, through whatever costume they wear, so it
ought to be the test of the sculptor's genius
that he should do the same. Mrs. Jameson de-
cidedly objected to buttons, breeches, and all
other items of modern costume; and, indeed,
they do degrade the marble, and make high
sculpture utterly impossible. Then let the art
perish as one that the world has done with, as it
has done with many other beautiful things that
belonged to an earlier time.

It was long past the hour of Mrs. Jameson's
dinner engagement when we drove up to her
door in the Via Ripetta. I bade her farewell
with much good feeling on my own side, and,
I hope, on hers, excusing myself, however, from
keeping the previous engagement to spend the
evening with her, for, in point of fact, we had
mutually had enough of one another for the
time being. I am glad to record that she expressed a very favorable opinion of our friend
Mr. Thompson's pictures.

May 12. — To-day we have been to the Villa
Albani, to which we had a ticket of admission
through the agency of Mr. Cass (the American
Minister). We set out between ten and eleven
o'clock, and walked through the Via Felice, the
Piazza Barberini, and a long, heavy, dusty range

of streets beyond, to the Porta Salara, whence
th road extends, white and sunny, between two
hi ;h blank walls to the gate of the villa, which
is at no great distance. We were admitted by a
{ rl, and went first to the casino, along an aisle
/f overshadowing trees, the branches of which
net above our heads. In the portico of the casino, which extends along its whole front, there
are many busts and statues, and, among them,
one of Julius Cæsar, representing him at an earlier period of life than others which I have seen.
His aspect is not particularly impressive ; there
is lack of chin, though not so much as in the
older statues and busts. Within the edifice there
is a large hall, not so brilliant, perhaps, with
frescos and gilding as those at the Villa Borghese, but lined with the most beautiful variety
of marbles. But, in fact, each new splendor of
this sort outshines the last, and unless we could
pass from one to another all in the same suite,
we cannot remember them well enough to compare the Borghese with the Albani, the effect
being more on the fancy than on the intellect.
I do not recall any of the sculpture, except a
colossal bas-relief of Antinoüs, crowned with
flowers, and holding flowers in his hand, which
was found in the ruins of Hadrian's Villa. This
is said to be the finest relic of antiquity next to
the Apollo and the Laocoön ; but I could not
feel it to be so, partly, I suppose, because the

and olives ; and there are shrubberies and tangled wildernesses of palm, cactus, rhododendron, and I know not what ; and a profusion of roses that bloom and wither with nobody to pluck and few to look at them.   They climb about the sculpture of fountains, rear themselves against pillars and porticos, run brimming over the walls, and strew the paths with their falling leaves.   We stole a few, and feel that we have wronged our consciences in not stealing more. In one part of the grounds we saw a field actually ablaze with scarlet poppies.   There are great lagunas ; fountains presided over by naiads, who squirt their little jets into basins ; sunny lawns ; a temple, so artificially ruined that we half believed it a veritable antique ; and at its base a reservoir of water, in which stone swans seemed positively to float ; groves of cypress ; balustrades and broad flights of stone stairs, descending to lower levels of the garden ; beauty, peace, sunshine, and antique repose on every side ; and far in the distance the blue hills that encircle the Campagna of Rome.   The day was very fine for our purpose ; cheerful, but not too bright, and tempered by a breeze that seemed even a little too cool when we sat long in the shade. We enjoyed it till three o'clock. . . .

At the Capitol there is a sarcophagus with a most beautiful bas-relief of the discovery of Achilles by Ulysses, in which there is even an expression of mirth on the faces of many of the spectators. And to-day at the Albani a sarcophagus was ornamented with the nuptials of Peleus and Thetis.

Death strides behind every man, to be sure, at more or less distance, and, sooner or later, enters upon any event of his life; so that, in this point of view, they might each and all serve for bas-reliefs on a sarcophagus; but the Romans seem to have treated Death as lightly and playfully as they could, and tried to cover his dart with flowers, because they hated it so much.

May 15. — My wife and I went yesterday to the Sistine Chapel, it being my first visit. It is a room of noble proportions, lofty and long, though divided in the midst by a screen or partition of white marble, which rises high enough to break the effect of spacious unity. There are six arched windows on each side of the chapel, throwing down their light from the height of the walls, with as much as twenty feet of space (more I should think) between them and the floor. The entire walls and ceiling of this stately chapel are covered with paintings in fresco, except the space about ten feet in height from the floor, and that portion was intended to be adorned by tapestries from pictures by Raphael, but, the design being prevented by his in all future days, when we see ourselves as we are — man's only inexorable judge will be himself, and the punishment of his sins will be the perception of them.

In the lower corner of this great picture, at the right hand of the spectator, is a hideous figure of a damned person, girdled about with a serpent, the folds of which are carefully knotted between his thighs, so as, at all events, to give no offence to decency. This figure represents a man who suggested to Pope Paul III. that the nudities of The Last Judgment ought to be draped, for which offence Michel Angelo at once consigned him to hell. It shows what a debtor's prison and dungeon of private torment men would make of hell if they had the control of it. As to the nudities, if they were ever more nude than now, I should suppose, in their fresh brilliancy, they might well have startled a not very squeamish eye. The effect, such as it is, of this picture, is much injured by the high altar and its canopy, which stands close against the wall, and intercepts a considerable portion of the sprawl of nakedness with which Michel Angelo has filled his sky. However, I am not unwilling to believe, with faith beyond what I can actually see, that the greatest pictorial miracles ever yet achieved have been wrought upon the walls and ceiling of the Sistine Chapel.

In the afternoon I went with Mr. Thompson

to see what bargain could be made with vettu-
rinos for taking myself and family to Florence.
We talked with three or four, and found them
asking prices of various enormity, from a hundred and fifty scudi down to little more than
ninety; but Mr. Thompson says that they always begin in this way; and will probably come
down to somewhere about seventy-five. Mr.
Thompson took me into the Via Portoghese,
and showed me an old palace, above which rose
— not a very customary feature of the architecture of Rome — a tall, battlemented tower. At
one angle of the tower we saw a shrine of the
Virgin, with a lamp, and all the appendages of
those numerous shrines which we see at the
street corners and in hundreds of places about
the city. Three or four centuries ago this palace was inhabited by a nobleman who had an
only son, and a large, pet monkey, and one day
the monkey caught the infant up and clambered
to this lofty turret, and sat there with him in
his arms grinning and chattering like the Devil
himself. The father was in despair, but was
afraid to pursue the monkey lest he should fling
down the child from the height of the tower
and make his escape. At last he vowed that if
the boy were safely restored to him he would
build a shrine at the summit of the tower, and
cause it to be kept as a sacred place forever.
By and by the monkey came down and de-

377

posited the child on the ground ; the father ful-
filled his vow, built the shrine, and made it ob-
ligatory on all future possessors of the palace
to keep the lamp burning before it.   Centuries
have passed, the property has changed hands ;
but still there is the shrine on the giddy top of
the tower, far aloft over the street, on the very
spot where the monkey sat, and there burns the
lamp, in memory of the father's vow.   This
being the tenure by which the estate is held, the
extinguishment of that flame might yet turn the
present owner out of the palace.

May 21. — Mamma and I went, yesterday
forenoon, to the Spada Palace, which we found
among the intricacies of Central Rome ; a dark
and massive old edifice, built around a court,
the fronts giving on which are adorned with
statues in niches and sculptured ornaments.   A
woman led us up a staircase, and ushered us
into a great, gloomy hall, square and lofty, and
wearing a very gray and ancient aspect, its walls
being painted in chiaro-oscuro, apparently a
great many years ago.   The hall was lighted
by small windows, high upward from the floors,
and admitting only a dusky light.   The only
furniture or ornament, so far as I recollect, was
the colossal statue of Pompey, which stands on
its pedestal at one side, certainly the sternest
and severest of figures, and producing the most

awful impression on the spectator. Much of the effect, no doubt, is due to the sombre obscurity of the hall, and to the loneliness in which the great naked statue stands. It is entirely nude, except for a cloak that hangs down from the left shoulder; in the left hand it holds a globe; the right arm is extended. The whole expression is such as the statue might have assumed, if, during the tumult of Cæsar's murder, it had stretched forth its marble hand, and motioned the conspirators to give over the attack, or to be quiet, now that their victim had fallen at its feet. On the left leg, about midway above the ankle, there is a dull, red stain, said to be Cæsar's blood; but, of course, it is just such a red stain in the marble as may be seen on the statue of Antinoüs at the Capitol. I could not see any resemblance in the face of the statue to that of the bust of Pompey, shown as such at the Capitol, in which there is not the slightest moral dignity or sign of intellectual eminence. I am glad to have seen this statue, and glad to remember it in that gray, dim, lofty hall; glad that there were no bright frescos on the walls, and that the ceiling was wrought with massive beams, and the floor paved with ancient brick.

From this anteroom we passed through several saloons containing pictures, some of which were by eminent artists; the Judith of Guido, a copy of which used to weary me to death, year

pays a larger share of the profits which people of a different system of trade morality would take equally from the poor man. The effect on the conscience of the vetturino, however, and of tradesmen of all kinds, cannot be good; their only intent being, not to do justice between man and man, but to go as deep as they can into all pockets, and to the very bottom of some.

We had nearly concluded a bargain, a day or two ago, with a vetturino to take or send us to Florence, *via* Perugia, in eight days, for a hundred scudi; but he now drew back, under pretence of having misunderstood the terms, though, in reality, no doubt, he was in hopes of getting a better bargain from somebody else. We made an agreement with another man, whom Mr. Thompson knows and highly recommends, and immediately made it sure and legally binding, by exchanging a formal written contract, in which everything is set down, even to milk, butter, bread, eggs, and coffee, which we are to have for breakfast; the vetturino being to pay every expense for himself, his horses, and his passengers, and include it within ninety-five scudi, and five crowns in addition for *buonmano*. . . .

May 22. — Yesterday, while we were at dinner, Mr. Bryant called. I never saw him but

once before, and that was at the door of our
little red cottage in Lenox; he sitting in a
wagon with one or two of the Sedgwicks, merely
exchanging a greeting with me from under the
brim of his straw hat, and driving on.   He presented himself now with a long white beard,
such as a palmer might have worn as the growth
of his long pilgrimages, a brow almost entirely
bald, and what hair he has quite hoary; a forehead impending, yet not massive; dark, bushy
eyebrows and keen eyes, without much softness
in them; a dark and sallow complexion; a
slender figure, bent a little with age; but at
once alert and infirm.   It surprised me to see
him so venerable; for, as poets are Apollo's
kinsmen, we are inclined to attribute to them
his enviable quality of never growing old. There
was a weary look in his face, as if he were tired
of seeing things and doing things, though with
certainly enough still to see and do, if need
were.   My family gathered about him, and he
conversed with great readiness and simplicity
about his travels, and whatever other subject
came up; telling us that he had been abroad
five times, and was now getting a little home-
sick, and had no more eagerness for sights,
though his "gals" (as he called his daughter and
another young lady) dragged him out to see the
wonders of Rome again.   His manners and
whole aspect are very particularly plain, though

not affectedly so; but it seems as if in the decline of life, and the security of his position, he had put off whatever artificial polish he may have heretofore had, and resumed the simpler habits and deportment of his early New England breeding. Not but what you discover, nevertheless, that he is a man of refinement, who has seen the world, and is well aware of his own place in it. He spoke with great pleasure of his recent visit to Spain. I introduced the subject of Kansas, and methought his face forthwith assumed something of the bitter keenness of the editor of a political newspaper, while speaking of the triumph of the administration over the free-soil opposition. I inquired whether he had seen Sumner, and he gave a very sad account of him as he appeared at their last meeting, which was in Paris. Sumner, he thought, had suffered terribly, and would never again be the man he was; he was getting fat; he talked continually of himself, and of trifles concerning himself, and seemed to have no interest for other matters; and Mr. Bryant feared that the shock upon his nerves had extended to his intellect, and was irremediable. He said that Sumner ought to retire from public life, but had no friend true enough to tell him so. This is about as sad as anything can be. I hate to have Sumner undergo the fate of a martyr, because he was not naturally of the stuff that martyrs are made of, and it is altogether by mistake that he has thrust himself into the position of one. He was merely, though with excellent abilities, one of the best of fellows, and ought to have lived and died in good fellowship with all the world.

Mr. Bryant was not in the least degree excited about this or any other subject. He uttered neither passion nor poetry, but excellent good sense, and accurate information on whatever subject transpired ; a very pleasant man to associate with, but rather cold, I should imagine, if one should seek to touch his heart with one's own. He shook hands kindly all round, but not with any warmth of gripe ; although the ease of his deportment had put us all on sociable terms with him.

At seven o'clock we went by invitation to take tea with Miss Bremer. After much search, and lumbering painfully up two or three staircases in vain, and at last going about in a strange circuity, we found her in a small chamber of a large old building, situated a little way from the brow of the Tarpeian Rock. It was the tiniest and humblest domicile that I have seen in Rome, just large enough to hold her narrow bed, her tea table and a table covered with books, — photographs of Roman ruins, and some pages written by herself. I wonder whether she be poor. Probably so ; for she

told us that her expense of living here is only
five pauls a day.   She welcomed us, however,
with the greatest cordiality and ladylike simplicity, making no allusion to the humbleness
of her environment (and making us also lose
sight of it, by the absence of all apology) any
more than if she were receiving us in a palace.
There is not a better bred woman ; and yet one
does not think whether she has any breeding
or no.   Her little bit of a round table was already spread for us with her blue earthenware
teacups ; and after she had got through an interview with the Swedish Minister, and dismissed him with a hearty pressure of his hand
between both her own, she gave us our tea, and
some bread, and a mouthful of cake.   Meanwhile, as the day declined, there had been the
most beautiful view over the Campagna, out of
one of her windows ; and, from the other, looking towards St. Peter's, the broad gleam of a
mildly glorious sunset ; not so pompous and
magnificent as many that I have seen in America, but softer and sweeter in all its changes.
As its lovely hues died slowly away, the half-
moon shone out brighter and brighter ; for
there was not a cloud in the sky, and it seemed
like the moonlight of my younger days.   In the
garden, beneath her window, verging upon the
Tarpeian Rock, there was shrubbery and one
large tree, softening the brow of the famous

386

precipice, adown which the old Romans used to fling their traitors, or sometimes, indeed, their patriots.

Miss Bremer talked plentifully in her strange manner, — good English enough for a foreigner, but so oddly intonated and accented, that it is impossible to be sure of more than one word in ten. Being so little comprehensible, it is very singular how she contrives to make her auditors so perfectly certain, as they are, that she is talking the best sense, and in the kindliest spirit. There is no better heart than hers, and not many sounder heads; and a little touch of sentiment comes delightfully in, mixed up with a quick and delicate humor and the most perfect simplicity. There is also a very pleasant atmosphere of maidenhood about her; we are sensible of a freshness and odor of the morning still in this little withered rose, — its recompense for never having been gathered and worn, but only diffusing fragrance on its stem. I forget mainly what we talked about, — a good deal about art, of course, although that is a subject of which Miss Bremer evidently knows nothing. Once we spoke of fleas, — insects that, in Rome, come home to everybody's business and bosom, and are so common and inevitable, that no delicacy is felt about alluding to the sufferings they inflict. Poor little Miss Bremer was tormented with one while turning out our tea. . . . She talked, among other things, of the winters in Sweden, and said that she liked them, long and severe as they are; and this made me feel ashamed of dreading the winters of New England, as I did before coming from home, and do now still more, after five or six mild English Decembers.

By and by two young ladies came in, — Miss Bremer's neighbors, it seemed, — fresh from a long walk on the Campagna, fresh and weary at the same time. One apparently was German, and the other French, and they brought her an offering of flowers, and chattered to her with affectionate vivacity; and, as we were about taking leave, Miss Bremer asked them to accompany her and us on a visit to the edge of the Tarpeian Rock. Before we left the room, she took a bunch of roses that were in a vase, and gave them to Miss Shepard, who told her that she should make her six sisters happy by giving one to each. Then we went down the intricate stairs, and, emerging into the garden, walked round the brow of the hill, which plunges headlong with exceeding abruptness; but, so far as I could see in the moonlight, is no longer quite a precipice. Then we reëntered the house, and went upstairs and down again, through intricate passages, till we got into the street, which was still peopled with the ragamuffins who infest and burrow in that part

of Rome.   We returned through an archway,
and descended the broad flight of steps into the
piazza of the Capitol; and from the extremity
of it, just at the head of the long graded way,
where Castor and Pollux and the old milestones
stand, we turned to the left, and followed a
somewhat winding path, till we came into the
court of a palace.   This court is bordered by a
parapet, leaning over which we saw the sheer
precipice of the Tarpeian Rock, about the
height of a four-story house. . . .

On the edge of this, before we left the court,
Miss Bremer bade us farewell, kissing my wife
most affectionately on each cheek, . . . and
then turning towards myself, . . . she pressed
my hand, and we parted, probably never to meet
again.   God bless her good heart ! . . . She is
a most amiable little woman, worthy to be the
maiden aunt of the whole human race.   I suspect, by the bye, that she does not like me half
so well as I do her ; it is my impression that
she thinks me unamiable, or that there is something or other not quite right about me.   I am
sorry if it be so, because such a good, kindly,
clear-sighted, and delicate person is very apt to
have reason at the bottom of her harsh thoughts,
when, in rare cases, she allows them to harbor
with her.

To-day, and for some days past, we have
been in quest of lodgings for next winter ; a

weary search, up interminable staircases, which seduce us upward to no successful result. It is very disheartening not to be able to place the slightest reliance on the integrity of the people we are to deal with; not to believe in any connection between their words and their purposes; to know that they are certainly telling you falsehoods, while you are not in a position to catch hold of the lie, and hold it up in their faces.

This afternoon we called on Mr. and Mrs. —— at the Hôtel de l'Europe, but found only the former at home. We had a pleasant visit, but I made no observations of his character save such as I have already sufficiently recorded; and when we had been with him a little while, Mrs. Chapman, the artist's wife, Mr. Terry, and my friend, Mr. Thompson, came in. —— received them all with the same good degree of cordiality that he did ourselves, not cold, not very warm, not annoyed, not ecstatically delighted; a man, I should suppose, not likely to have ardent individual preferences, though perhaps capable of stern individual dislikes. But I take him, at all events, to be a very upright man, and pursuing a narrow track of integrity; he is a man whom I would never forgive (as I would a thousand other men) for the slightest moral delinquency. I would not be bound to say, however, that he has not the little sin of a

fretful and peevish habit ; and yet perhaps I am
a sinner myself for thinking so.

May 23. — This morning I breakfasted at
William Story's, and met there Mr. Bryant,
Mr. T——— (an English gentleman), Mr. and
Mrs. Apthorp, Miss Hosmer, and one or two
other ladies.   Bryant was very quiet, and made
no conversation audible to the general table.
Mr. T——— talked of English politics and public
men ; the Times and other newspapers, English clubs and social habits generally ; topics
in which I could well enough bear my part of
the discussion.   After breakfast, and aside from
the ladies, he mentioned an illustration of Lord
Ellenborough's lack of administrative ability,
— a proposal seriously made by his lordship in
reference to the refractory Sepoys. . . .

We had a very pleasant breakfast, and certainly a breakfast is much preferable to a dinner, not merely in the enjoyment while it is
passing, but afterwards.   I made a good suggestion to Miss Hosmer for the design of a
fountain, — a lady bursting into tears, water
gushing from a thousand pores, in literal translation of the phrase ; and to call the statue
Niobe, all Tears.   I doubt whether she adopts
the idea ; but Bernini would have been delighted
with it.   I should think the gush of water
might be so arranged as to form a beautiful

drapery about the figure, swaying and fluttering with every breath of wind, and rearranging itself in the calm; in which case, the lady might be said to have "a habit of weeping." . . . Apart, with William Story, he and I talked of the unluckiness of Friday, etc. I like him particularly well. . . .

We have been plagued to-day with our preparations for leaving Rome to-morrow, and especially with verifying the inventory of furniture, before giving up the house to our landlord. He and his daughter have been examining every separate article, down even to the kitchen skewers, I believe, and charging us to the amount of several scudi for cracks and breakages, which very probably existed when we came into possession. It is very uncomfortable to have dealings with such a mean people (though our landlord is German), — mean in their business transactions; mean even in their beggary; for the beggars seldom ask for more than a mezzo baiocco, though they sometimes grumble when you suit your gratuity exactly to their petition. It is pleasant to record that the Italians have great faith in the honor of the English and Americans, and never hesitate to trust entire strangers, to any reasonable extent, on the strength of their being of the honest Anglo-Saxon race.

This evening Una and I took a farewell walk in the Pincian Gardens to see the sunset; and found them crowded with people, promenading and listening to the music of the French band. It was the feast of Whitsunday, which probably brought a greater throng than usual abroad.

When the sun went down, we descended into the Piazza del Popolo, and thence into the Via Ripetta, and emerged through a gate to the shore of the Tiber, along which there is a pleasant walk beneath a grove of trees. We traversed it once and back again, looking at the rapid river, which still kept its mud-puddly aspect even in the clear twilight, and beneath the brightening moon. The great bell of St. Peter's tolled with a deep boom, a grand and solemn sound; the moon gleamed through the branches of the trees above us; and Una spoke with somewhat alarming fervor of her love for Rome and regret at leaving it. We shall have done the child no good office in bringing her here, if the rest of her life is to be a dream of this "city of the soul," and an unsatisfied yearning to come back to it. On the other hand, nothing elevating and refining can be really injurious, and so I hope she will always be the better for Rome, even if her life should be spent where there are no pictures, no statues, nothing but the dryness and meagreness of a New England village.

Città Castellana, May 24. — We left Rome this morning, after troubles of various kinds, and a dispute in the first place with Lalla, our female servant, and her mother. . . . Mother and daughter exploded into a livid rage, and cursed us plentifully, — wishing that we might never come to our journey's end, and that we might all break our necks or die of apoplexy, — the most awful curse that an Italian knows how to invoke upon his enemies, because it precludes the possibility of extreme unction. However, as we are heretics, and certain of damnation therefore, anyhow, it does not much matter to us; and also the anathemas may have been blown back upon those who invoked them, like the curses that were flung out from the balcony of St. Peter's during Holy Week and wafted by heaven's breezes right into the faces of some priests who stood near the pope. Next we had a disagreement with two men who brought down our luggage, and put it on the vetturo;
. . . and, lastly, we were infested with beggars, who hung round the carriages with doleful petitions, till we began to move away; but the previous warfare had put me into too stern a mood for almsgiving, so that they also were doubtless inclined to curse more than to bless,

and I am persuaded that we drove off under a
perfect shower of anathemas.

We passed through the Porta del Popolo at
about eight o'clock; and after a moment's de-
lay, while the passport was examined, began our
journey along the Flaminian Way, between two
such high and inhospitable walls of brick or
stone, as seem to shut in all the avenues to
Rome. We had not gone far before we heard
military music in advance of us, and saw the
road blocked up with people, and then the glit-
ter of muskets, and soon appeared the drummers, fifers, and trumpeters, and then the first
battalion of a French regiment, marching into
the city, with two mounted officers at their
head; then appeared a second and then a third
battalion, the whole seeming to make almost an
army, though the number on their caps showed
them all to belong to one regiment, — the 1st;
then came a battery of artillery, then a detachment of horse, — these last, by the crossed
keys on their helmets, being apparently papal
troops. All were young, fresh, good-looking
men, in excellent trim as to uniform and equip-
ments, and marched rather as if they were setting out on a campaign than returning from it;
the fact being, I believe, that they have been
encamped or in barracks within a few miles of
the city. Nevertheless, it reminded me of the
military processions of various kinds which so

often, two thousand years ago and more, have entered Rome over the Flaminian Way, and over all the roads that led to the famous city, — triumphs oftenest, but sometimes the downcast train of a defeated army, like those who retreated before Hannibal. On the whole, I was not sorry to see the Gauls still pouring into Rome; but yet I begin to find that I have a strange affection for it, and so did we all, — the rest of the family in a greater degree than myself even. It is very singular, the sad embrace with which Rome takes possession of the soul. Though we intend to return in a few months, and for a longer residence than this has been, yet we felt the city pulling at our heartstrings far more than London did, where we shall probably never spend much time again. It may be because the intellect finds a home there more than in any other spot in the world, and wins the heart to stay with it, in spite of a good many things strewn all about to disgust us.

The road in the earlier part of the way was not particularly picturesque, — the country undulated, but scarcely rose into hills, and was destitute of trees; there were a few shapeless ruins, too indistinct for us to make out whether they were Roman or mediæval. Nothing struck me so much, in the forenoon, as the spectacle of a peasant woman riding on horseback as if she were a man. The houses were few, and those of a dreary aspect, built of gray stone, and looking bare and desolate, with not the slightest promise of comfort within doors. We passed two or three locandas or inns, and finally came to the village (if village it were, for I remember no houses except our osteria) of Castel Nuovo di Porta, where we were to take a *déjeuner à la fourchette*, which was put upon the table between twelve and one. On this journey, according to the custom of travellers in Italy, we pay the vetturino a certain sum, and live at his expense; and this meal was the first specimen of his catering on our behalf. It consisted of a beefsteak, rather dry and hard, but not unpalatable, and a large omelette; and for beverage two quart bottles of red wine, which, being tasted, had an agreeable acid flavor. . . . The locanda was built of stone, and had what looked like an old Roman altar in the basement hall, and a shrine with a lamp before it on the staircase; and the large public saloon in which we ate had a brick floor, a ceiling with cross-beams, meagrely painted in fresco, and a scanty supply of chairs and settees.

After lunch we wandered out into a valley or ravine near the house, where we gathered some flowers, and Julian found a nest with the young birds in it, which, however, he put back into the bush whence he took it.

Our afternoon drive was more picturesque

and noteworthy.   Soracte rose before us, bulg-
ing up quite abruptly out of the plain, and
keeping itself entirely distinct from a whole
horizon of hills.   Byron well compares it to a
wave just on the bend, and about to break over
towards the spectator.   As we approached it
nearer and nearer, it looked like the barrenest
great rock that ever protruded out of the substance of earth, with scarcely a strip or a spot of
verdure upon its steep and gray declivities.   The
road kept trending towards the mountain, following the line of the old Flaminian Way, which
we could see, at frequent intervals, close beside
the modern track.   It is paved with large flagstones, laid so accurately together, that it is still,
in some places, as smooth and even as the floor
of a church ; and everywhere the tufts of grass
find it difficult to root themselves into the interstices.   Its course is straighter than that of
the road of to-day, which often turns aside to
avoid obstacles which the ancient one surmounted.   Much of it, probably, is covered
with the soil and overgrowth deposited in later
years ; and now and then we could see its flagstones partly protruding from the bank through
which our road has been cut, and thus showing
that the thickness of this massive pavement was
more than a foot of solid stone.   We lost it over
and over again ; but still it reappeared, now on
one side of us, now on the other ; perhaps from

beneath the roots of old trees, or the pasture land of a thousand years old, and leading on towards the base of Soracte. I forget where we finally lost it. Passing through a town called Rignano, we found it dressed out in festivity, with festoons of foliage along both sides of the street, which ran beneath a triumphal arch, bearing an inscription in honor of a ducal personage of the Massinii family. I know no occasion for the feast except that it is Whitsuntide. The town was thronged with peasants, in their best attire, and we met others on their way thither, particularly women and girls, with heads bare in the sunshine; but there was no tiptoe jollity, nor, indeed, any more show of festivity than I have seen in my own country at a cattle-show or muster. Really, I think, not half so much.

The road still grew more and more picturesque, and now lay along ridges, at the bases of which were deep ravines and hollow valleys. Woods were not wanting; wilder forest than I have seen since leaving America, of oak-trees chiefly; and, among the green foliage, grew golden tufts of broom, making a gay and lovely combination of hues. I must not forget to mention the poppies, which burned like live coals along the wayside, and lit up the landscape, even a single one of them, with wonderful effect. At other points we saw olive-trees, hiding their eccentricity of boughs under thick masses of foliage of a livid tint, which is caused, I believe, by their turning their reverse sides to the light and to the spectator. Vines were abundant, but were of little account in the scene. By and by we came in sight of the high, flat tableland, on which stands Città Castellana, and beheld, straight downward, between us and the town, a deep level valley, with a river winding through it; it was the valley of the Treja. A precipice, hundreds of feet in height, falls perpendicularly upon the valley, from the site of Città Castellana; there is an equally abrupt one, probably, on the side from which we saw it; and a modern road, skilfully constructed, goes winding down to the stream, crosses it by a narrow stone bridge, and winds upward into the town. After passing over the bridge, I alighted, with Julian and Rose, . . . and made the ascent on foot, along walls of natural rock, in which old Etruscan tombs were hollowed out. There are likewise antique remains of masonry, whether Roman, or of what earlier period, I cannot tell. At the summit of the acclivity, which brought us close to the town, our vetturino took us into the carriage again, and quickly brought us to what appears to be really a good hotel, where all of us are accommodated with sleeping chambers in a range, beneath an arcade, entirely secluded from the rest of the population of the hotel. After a splendid dinner (that is, splendid, considering that it was ordered by our hospitable vetturino), Una, Miss Shepard, Julian, and I walked out of the little town, in the opposite direction from our entrance, and crossed a bridge at the height of the tableland, instead of at its base. On either side we had a view down into a profound gulf, with sides of precipitous rock, and heaps of foliage in its lap, through which ran the snowy track of a stream; here snowy, there dark; here hidden among the foliage, there quite revealed in the broad depths of the gulf. This was wonderfully fine. Walking on a little farther, Soracte came fully into view, starting with bold abruptness out of the middle of the country; and before we got back the bright Italian moon was throwing a shower of silver over the scene, and making it so beautiful that is seemed miserable not to know how to put it into words; a foolish thought, however, for such scenes are an expression in themselves, and need not be translated into any feebler language. On our walk, we met parties of laborers, both men and women, returning from the fields, with rakes and wooden forks over their shoulders, singing in chorus. It is very customary for women to be laboring in the fields.

May 25. — We were aroused at four o'clock this morning; had some eggs and coffee, and were ready to start between five and six; being thus matutinary, in order to get to Terni in time to see the falls. The road was very striking and picturesque ; but I remember nothing particularly till we came to Borghetto, which stands on a bluff, with a broad valley sweeping round it, through the midst of which flows the Tiber. There is an old castle on a projecting point; and we saw other battlemented fortresses, of mediæval date, along our way, forming more beautiful ruins than any of the Roman remains to which we have become accustomed. This is partly, I suppose, owing to the fact that they have been neglected, and allowed to mantle their decay with ivy, instead of being cleaned, propped up, and restored. The antiquarian is apt to spoil the objects that interest him.

Sometimes we passed through wildernesses of various trees, each contributing a different hue of verdure to the scene ; the vine, also, marrying itself to the fig-tree, so that a man might sit in the shadow of both at once, and temper the luscious sweetness of the one fruit with the fresh flavor of the other. The wayside incidents were such as meeting a man and woman borne along as prisoners, handcuffed, and in a cart ; two men reclining across one another, asleep, and lazily lifting their heads to gaze at us as we passed by ; a woman spinning with a distaff as she walked along the road. An old tomb or tower stood in a lonely field, and several caves were hollowed in the rocks, which might have been either sepulchres or habitations. Soracte kept us company, sometimes a little on one side, sometimes behind, looming up again and again, when we thought that we had done with it, and so becoming rather tedious at last, like a person who presents himself for another and another leave-taking after the one which ought to have been final. Honeysuckles sweetened the hedges along the road.

After leaving Borghetto, we crossed the broad valley of the Tiber, and skirted along one of the ridges that border it, looking back upon the road that we had passed, lying white behind us. We saw a field covered with buttercups or some other yellow flower, and poppies burned along the roadside, as they did yesterday, and there were flowers of a delicious blue, as if the blue Italian sky had been broken into little bits, and scattered down upon the green earth. Otricoli by and by appeared, situated on a bold promontory above the valley, a village of a few gray houses and huts, with one edifice gaudily painted in white and pink. It looked more important at a distance than we found it on our nearer approach. As the road kept ascending, and as the hills grew to be mountains, we had taken two additional horses, making six in all, with a man and boy running beside them, to keep them in motion. The boy had two club feet, so inconveniently disposed that it seemed almost inevitable for him to stumble over them at every step; besides which, he seemed to tread upon his ankles, and moved with a disjointed gait, as if each of his legs and thighs had been twisted round together with his feet. Nevertheless, he had a bright, cheerful, intelligent face, and was exceedingly active, keeping up with the horses at their trot, and inciting them to better speed when they lagged. I conceived a great respect for this poor boy, who had what most Italian peasants would consider an enviable birthright in those two club feet, as giving him a sufficient excuse to live on charity, but yet took no advantage of them; on the contrary, putting his poor misshapen hoofs to such good use, as might have shamed many a better provided biped. When he quitted us, he asked no alms of the travellers, but merely applied to Gaetano for some slight recompense for his well-performed service. This behavior contrasted most favorably with that of some other boys and girls, who ran begging beside the carriage door, keeping up a low, miserable murmur, like that of a kennel stream, for a long, long way. Beggars, indeed, started up at every point, when we stopped for a moment, and whenever a hill imposed a slower pace upon us; each village had its deformity or its infirmity, offering his wretched petition at the step of the carriage;

and even a venerable, white-headed patriarch, the grandfather of all the beggars, seemed to grow up by the roadside, but was left behind from inability to join in the race with his light-footed juniors. No shame is attached to begging in Italy. In fact, I rather imagine it to be held an honorable profession, inheriting some of the odor of sanctity that used to be attached to a mendicant and idle life in the days of early Christianity, when every saint lived upon Providence, and deemed it meritorious to do nothing for his support.

Murray's guide-book is exceedingly vague and unsatisfactory along this route; and whenever we asked Gaetano the name of a village or a castle, he gave some one which we had never heard before, and could find nothing of in the book. We made out the river Nar, however, or what I supposed to be such, though he called it Nera. It flows through a most stupendous mountain-gorge; winding its narrow passage between high hills, the broad sides of which descend steeply upon it, covered with trees and shrubbery that mantle a host of rocky roughnesses, and make all look smooth. Here and there a precipice juts sternly forth. We saw an old castle on a hillside, frowning down into the gorge; and, farther on, the gray tower of Narni stands upon a height, imminent over the depths below, and with its battlemented castle above, now converted into a prison, and therefore kept in excellent repair. A long winding street passes through Narni, broadening at one point into a market-place, where an old cathedral showed its venerable front, and the great dial of its clock, the figures on which were numbered in two semicircles of twelve points each ; one, I suppose, for noon, and the other for midnight. The town has, so far as its principal street is concerned, a city-like aspect, with large, fair edifices, and shops as good as most of those at Rome, the smartness of which contrasts strikingly with the rude and lonely scenery of mountain and stream, through which we had come to reach it. We drove through Narni without stopping, and came out from it on the other side, where a broad, level valley opened before us, most unlike the wild, precipitous gorge which had brought us to the town. The road went winding down into the peaceful vale, through the midst of which flowed the same stream that cuts its way between the impending hills, as already described. We passed a monk and a soldier, — the two curses of Italy, each in his way, — walking sociably side by side ; and from Narni to Terni I remember nothing that need be recorded.

Terni, like so many other towns in the neighborhood, stands in a high and commanding position, chosen, doubtless, for its facilities of

defence, in days long before the mediæval war-
fares of Italy made such sites desirable. I suppose that, like Narni and Otricoli, it was a city
of the Umbrians. We reached it between
eleven and twelve o'clock, intending to employ
the afternoon on a visit to the famous falls of
Terni ; but, after lowering all day, it has begun
to rain, and we shall probably have to give
them up.

Half past eight o'clock. — It has rained in tor-
rents during the afternoon, and we have not
seen the cascade of Terni ; considerably to my
regret, for I think I felt the more interest in
seeing it, on account of its being artificial. Methinks nothing was more characteristic of the
energy and determination of the old Romans,
than thus to take a river, which they wished to
be rid of, and fling it over a giddy precipice,
breaking it into ten million pieces by the fall.
. . . We are in the Hôtel delle tre Colonne,
and find it reasonably good, though not, so far
as we are concerned, justifying the rapturous
commendations of previous tourists, who probably travelled at their own charges. However,
there is nothing really to be complained of
either in our accommodations or table, and the
only wonder is how Gaetano contrives to get
any profit out of our contract, since the hotel
bills would alone cost us more than we pay him

for the journey and all. It is worth while to record as history of vetturino commissary customs, that for breakfast this morning we had coffee, eggs, and bread and butter; for lunch an omelette, some stewed veal, and a dessert of figs and grapes, besides two decanters of a light-colored acid wine, tasting very like indifferent cider; for dinner, an excellent vermicelli soup, two young fowls, fricasseed, and a hind quarter of roast lamb, with fritters, oranges and figs, and two more decanters of the wine aforesaid.

This hotel is an edifice with a gloomy front upon a narrow street, and enterable through an arch, which admits you into an enclosed court; around the court, on each story, run the galleries, with which the parlors and sleeping apartments communicate. The whole house is dingy, probably old, and seems not very clean; but yet bears traces of former magnificence; for instance, in our bedroom, the door of which is ornamented with gilding, and the cornices with frescos, some of which appear to represent the cascade of Terni, the roof is crossed with carved beams, and is painted in the interstices; the floor has a carpet, but rough tiles underneath it, which show themselves at the margin. The windows admit the wind; the door shuts so loosely as to leave great cracks; and, during the rain to-day, there was a heavy shower through our ceiling, which made a flood upon the carpet. We see no chambermaids; nothing of the comfort and neatness of an English hotel, nor of the smart splendors of an American one; but still this dilapidated palace affords us a better shelter than I expected to find in the decayed country towns of Italy. In the album of the hotel I find the names of more English travellers than of any other nation except the Americans, who, I think, even exceed the former; and, the route being the favorite one for tourists between Rome and Florence, whatever merit the inns have is probably owing to the demands of the Anglo-Saxons. I doubt not, if we chose to pay for it, this hotel would supply us with any luxury we might ask for; and perhaps even a gorgeous saloon and state bedchamber.

After dinner, Julian and I walked out in the dusk to see what we could of Terni. We found it compact and gloomy (but the latter characteristic might well enough be attributed to the dismal sky), with narrow streets, paved from wall to wall of the houses, like those of all the towns in Italy; the blocks of paving-stone larger than the little square torments of Rome. The houses are covered with dingy stucco, and mostly low, compared with those of Rome, and inhospitable as regards their dismal aspects and uninviting doorways. The streets are intricate as well as narrow: insomuch that we quickly

endeavors to make his homestead an ornament to the place. We miss nothing in Italy more than the neat doorsteps and pleasant porches and thresholds and delightful lawns or grass-plots, which hospitably invite the imagination into a sweet domestic interior. Everything, however sunny and luxuriant may be the scene around, is especially dreary and disheartening in the immediate vicinity of an Italian home.

At Strettura (which, as the name indicates, is a very narrow part of the valley) we added two oxen to our horses, and began to ascend the Monte Somma, which, according to Murray, is nearly four thousand feet high, where we crossed it. When we came to the steepest part of the ascent, Gaetano, who exercises a pretty decided control over his passengers, allowed us to walk; and we all, with one exception, alighted, and began to climb the mountain on foot. I walked on briskly, and soon left the rest of the party behind, reaching the top of the pass in such a short time that I could not believe it, and kept onward, expecting still another height to climb. But the road began to descend, winding among the depths of the hills as heretofore; now beside the dry, gravelly bed of a departed stream, now crossing it by a bridge, and perhaps passing through some other gorge, that yet gave no decided promise of an outlet into the world beyond. A glimpse might occasionally be caught, through a gap between the hilltops, of a company of distant mountain peaks, pyramidal, as these hills are apt to be, and resembling the camp of an army of giants. The landscape was not altogether savage: sometimes a hillside was covered with a rich field of grain, or an orchard of olive-trees, looking not unlike puffs of smoke, from the peculiar hue of their foliage; but oftener there was a vast mantle of trees and shrubbery from top to bottom, the golden tufts of the broom shining out amid the verdure, and gladdening the whole. Nothing was dismal except the houses; those were always so, whether the compact, gray lines of village hovels, with a narrow street between, or the lonely farmhouse, standing far apart from the road, built of stone, with window gaps high in the walls, empty of glass; or the half castle, half dwelling, of which I saw a specimen or two, with what looked like a defensive rampart drawn around its court. I saw no look of comfort anywhere; and continually, in this wild and solitary region, I met beggars, just as if I were still in the streets of Rome. Boys and girls kept beside me, till they delivered me into the hands of others like themselves; hoary grandsires and grandmothers caught a glimpse of my approach, and tottered as fast as they could to intercept me; women came out of the cottages with rotten cherries on a plate, entreating me to buy them for a mezzo

baioccho; a man at work on the road left his
toil to beg, and was grateful for the value of a
cent; in short, I was never safe from impor-
tunity, as long as there was a house or a human
being in sight.

We arrived at Spoleto before noon, and while
our *déjeuner* was being prepared, looked down
from the window of the inn into the narrow
street beneath, which, from the throng of people
in it, I judged to be the principal one: priests,
papal soldiers, women with no bonnets on their
heads; peasants in breeches and mushroom hats;
maids and matrons, drawing water at a fountain;
idlers, smoking on a bench under the window;
a talk, a bustle, but no genuine activity. After lunch we walked out to see the lions of Spoleto, and found our way up a steep and narrow
street that led us to the city gate, at which, it
is traditionally said, Hannibal sought to force
an entrance, after the battle of Thrasymene,
and was repulsed. The gateway has a double
arch, on the inner one of which is a tablet, recording the above tradition as an unquestioned
historical fact. From the gateway we went in
search of the Duomo or Cathedral, and were
kindly directed thither by an officer, who was
descending into the town from the citadel, which
is an old castle, now converted into a prison.
The Cathedral seemed small, and did not much
interest us, either by the Gothic front or its mod-

ernized interior. We saw nothing else in Spoleto, but went back to the inn and resumed our journey, emerging from the city into the classic valley of the Clitumnus, which we did not view under the best of auspices, because it was overcast, and the wind as chill as if it had the east in it. The valley, though fertile, and smilingly picturesque, perhaps, is not such as I should wish to celebrate, either in prose or poetry. It is of such breadth and extent, that its frame of mountains and ridgy hills hardly serve to shut it in sufficiently, and the spectator thinks of a boundless plain rather than of a secluded vale. After passing Le Vene, we came to the little temple which Byron describes, and which has been supposed to be the one immortalized by Pliny. It is very small, and stands on a declivity that falls immediately from the road, right upon which rises the pediment of the temple, while the columns of the other front find sufficient height to develop themselves in the lower ground. A little farther down than the base of the edifice we saw the Clitumnus, so recently from its source in the marble rock, that it was still as pure as a child's heart, and as transparent as truth itself. It looked airier than nothing, because it had not substance enough to brighten, and it was clearer than the atmosphere. I remember nothing else of the valley of Clitumnus, except that the beggars in this region of proverbial fertility are wellnigh profane in the urgency of their petitions; they absolutely fall down on their knees as you approach, in the same attitude as if they were praying to their Maker, and beseech you for alms with a fervency which I am afraid they seldom use before an altar or shrine. Being denied, they ran hastily beside the carriage, but got nothing, and finally gave over.

I am so very tired and sleepy that I mean to mention nothing else to-night, except the city of Trevi, which, on the approach from Spoleto, seems completely to cover a high, peaked hill, from its pyramidal tip to its base. It was the strangest situation in which to build a town, where, I should suppose, no horse can climb, and whence no inhabitant would think of descending into the world, after the approach of age should begin to stiffen his joints. On looking back on this most picturesque of towns (which the road, of course, did not enter, as evidently no road could), I saw that the highest part of the hill was quite covered with a crown of edifices, terminating in a church tower; while a part of the northern side was apparently too steep for building; and a cataract of houses flowed down the western and southern slopes. There seemed to be palaces, churches, everything that a city should have; but my eyes are heavy, and I can write no more about them, only that I suppose the summit of the hill was artificially tenured, so as to prevent its crumbling down, and enable it to support the platform of edifices which crowns it.

May 27. — We reached Foligno in good season yesterday afternoon.   Our inn seemed ancient; and, under the same roof, on one side of the entrance, was the stable, and on the other the coach house.   The house is built round a narrow court, with a well of water at bottom, and an opening in the roof at top, whence the staircases are lighted that wind round the sides of the court, up to the highest story.   Our dining-room and bedrooms were in the latter region, and were all paved with brick, and without carpets ; and the characteristic of the whole was exceeding plainness and antique clumsiness of fitting up.   We found ourselves sufficiently comfortable, however ; and, as has been the case throughout our journey, had a very fair and well-cooked dinner.   It shows, as perhaps I have already remarked, that it is still possible to live well in Italy, at no great expense, and that the high prices charged to the forestieri at Rome and elsewhere are artificial, and ought to be abated. . . .

The day had darkened since morning, and was now ominous of rain ; but as soon as we were established, we sallied out to see whatever was worth looking at.   A beggar boy, with one leg, followed us, without asking for anything, apparently only for the pleasure of our company, though he kept at too great a distance for conversation, and indeed did not attempt to speak.

We went first to the Cathedral, which has a Gothic front, and a modernized interior, stuccoed and whitewashed, looking as neat as a New England meeting-house, and very mean, after our familiarity with the gorgeous churches in other cities.   There were some pictures in the chapels, but, I believe, all modern, and I do not remember a single one of them.   Next we went, without any guide, to a church attached to a convent of Dominican monks, with a Gothic exterior and two hideous pictures of Death, — the skeleton leaning on his scythe, one on each side of the door.   This church, likewise, was whitewashed, but we understood that it had been originally frescoed all over, and by famous hands; but these pictures, having become much injured, they were all obliterated, as we saw, — all, that is to say, except a few specimens of the best preserved, which were spared to show the world what the whole had been.   I thanked my stars that the obliteration of the rest had taken place before our visit; for if anything is dreary and calculated to make the beholder utterly miserable, it is a faded fresco, with spots of the white plaster dotted over it.

Our one-legged boy had followed us into the church, and stood near the door till he saw us ready to come out, when he hurried on before us, and waited a little way off to see whither we should go. We still went on at random, taking the first turn that offered itself, and soon came to another old church, — that of St. Mary within the Walls, — into which we entered, and found it whitewashed, like the other two. This was especially fortunate, for the doorkeeper informed us that, two years ago, the whole church, (except, I suppose, the roof, which is of timber) had been covered with frescos by Pinturicchio, all of which had been ruthlessly obliterated, except a very few fragments. These he proceeded to show us ; poor, dim ghosts of what may once have been beautiful, — now so far gone towards nothingness that I was hardly sure whether I saw a glimmering of the design or not. By the bye, it was not Pinturicchio, as I have written above, but Giotto, assisted, I believe, by Cimabue, who painted these frescos. Our one-legged attendant had followed us also into this church, and again hastened out of it before us ; and still we heard the dot of his crutch upon the pavement, as we passed from street to street. By and by a sickly-looking man met us, and begged for " qualche cosa " ; but the boy shouted to him " Niente ! " whether intimating that we would give him nothing, or that he himself had a prior claim to all our charity, I cannot tell. However, the beggar man turned round, and likewise followed our devious course. Once or twice we missed him ; but it was only because he could not walk so fast as we ; for he appeared again as we emerged from the door of another church. Our one-legged friend we never missed for a moment ; he kept pretty near us, — near enough to be amused by our indecision whither to go ; and he seemed much delighted when it began to rain, and he saw us at a loss how to find our way back to the hotel. Nevertheless, he did not offer to guide us ; but stumped on behind with a faster or slower dot of his crutch, according to our pace. I began to think that he must have been engaged as a spy upon our movements by the police, who had taken away my passport at the city gate. In this way he attended us to the door of the hotel, where the beggar had already arrived. The latter again put in his doleful petition ; the one-legged boy said not a word, nor seemed to expect anything, and both had to go away without so much as a mezzo baiocco out of our pockets. The multitude of beggars in Italy makes the heart as obdurate as a paving-stone.

We left Foligno this morning, and, all ready for us at the door of the hotel, as we got into the carriage, were our friends, the beggar man and the one-legged boy ; the latter holding out his ragged hat, and smiling with as confident an air as if he had done us some very particular service, and were certain of being paid for it, as from contract.   It was so very funny, so impudent, so utterly absurd, that I could not help giving him a trifle; but the man got nothing, — a fact that gives me a twinge or two, for he looked sickly and miserable. But where everybody begs, everybody, as a general rule, must be denied; and, besides, they act their misery so well, that you are never sure of the genuine article.

The Riverside Press

Electrotyped and printed by H. O. Houghton & Co.
Cambridge, Mass., U. S. A.

Hawthorne   5450

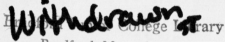
DATE DUE

GAYLORD			PRINTED IN U.S.A.